D1323499

Development,
Human Rights and
the Rule of Law

WITHDRAWAL

Development,
Human Rights and
the Rule of Law

Report of a Conference
held in The Hague
on 27 April—1 May 1981

convened by the

INTERNATIONAL COMMISSION OF JURISTS

PERGAMON PRESS

OXFORD · NEW YORK · TORONTO · SYDNEY · PARIS · FRANKFURT

K
3239.6
·D49
1981

U.K.   Pergamon Press Ltd., Headington Hill Hall,
                  Oxford OX3 0BW, England

U.S.A.   Pergamon Press Inc., Maxwell House, Fairview Park,
                  Elmsford, New York 10523, U.S.A.

CANADA   Pergamon Press Canada Ltd., Suite 104,
                  150 Consumers Road, Willowdale, Ontario M2J 1P9, Canada

AUSTRALIA   Pergamon Press (Aust.) Pty. Ltd., P.O. Box 544,
                  Potts Point, N.S.W. 2011, Australia

FRANCE   Pergamon Press SARL, 24 rue des Ecoles,
                  75240 Paris, Cedex 05, France

FEDERAL REPUBLIC Pergamon Press GmbH, 6242 Kronberg-Taunus,
OF GERMANY   Hammerweg 6, Federal Republic of Germany

Copyright © 1981 International Commission of Jurists

All Rights Reserved. No part of this publication may be reproduced, stored in a retrieval system or transmitted in any form or by any means: electronic, electrostatic, magnetic tape, mechanical, photocopying, recording or otherwise, without permission in writing from the copyright holders.

First edition 1981

British Library Cataloguing in Publication Data

Development, human rights and the rule of law.
1. Civil rights (International law)-Congresses
I. International Commission of Jurists
341.4′81   K3239.6

ISBN 0-08-028921-5 (Hardcover)
ISBN 0-08-028951-7 (Flexicover)

Printed in Great Britain by A. Wheaton & Co. Ltd., Exeter

CONTENTS

National Aspects

PREFACE

The International Commission of Jurists is a non-governmental organisation with consultative status with the United Nations, UNESCO and the Council of Europe. It was founded in 1952 to promote respect for the Rule of Law.

Its work is devoted to the legal promotion and protection of human rights and fundamental freedoms in all parts of the world. The Rule of Law is seen as a dynamic concept to be used to advance not only the classical civil and political rights of the individual, but also his economic, social and cultural rights, and to promote social and development policies under which members of the community in which he lives may realise their full potentiality.

The International Commission of Jurists held a Conference on Development and the Rule of Law in the Hague on 27 April—1 May 1981. Participants included Members and Honorary Members of the Commission, representatives of National Sections and a number of development experts, including economists and political scientists, as well as lawyers.

After the opening plenary session, held in the Peace Palace, the conference discussed the working papers in two Committees, one devoted to the international aspects of the subject and the other to the national aspects. The reports of these committees were considered in a closing plenary session. The summary of the discussions and conclusions, printed at the end of this report, was prepared later by the Secretariat of the ICJ in consultation with the participants.

The International Commission of Jurists considers that the relationship between the Rule of Law and development is of cardinal importance and deserves wider recognition and study. It hopes that the publication of the working papers and proceedings of this conference may contribute to this cause.

The International Commission of Jurists wishes to express its gratitude to the governments of the Netherlands, Denmark, Norway and Sweden and to the European Economic Community for their generous grants which made possible the holding of the Conference and the preparation of this report.

Niall MacDermot
Secretary-General

Geneva, August 1981

SPEECH OF WELCOME

Mr. De Ruiter

Minister of Justice, the Kingdom of the Netherlands

Ladies and Gentlemen,

It gives me great pleasure to welcome you all to this International Commission of Jurists conference. It is both an honour and a pleasure for me to see this illustrious assembly here today — and by this I mean both members of the Commission and other eminent experts.

Among the people of the Netherlands there is widespread interest in th development of the Third World and the promotion of human rights everywhere in the world, and both causes occupy a prominent place in Dutch foreign policy. The Government is aware of the close relationship between the two, as the following example shows.

A few years ago, Parliament asked the Minister for Foreign Affairs to prepare a comprehensive document on the promotion of human rights in the context of foreign policy. The Minister decided to set about this task jointly with the Minister for Development Cooperation, and so in May 1979 the result of their collaboration, the Memorandum entitled "Human Rights and Foreign Policy", was presented to Parliament. In its work to promote human rights the Dutch Government is conscious of the important part played by non-governmental organisations, and we regard the International Commission of Jurists as one of the outstanding organisations in this field; our appreciation is expressed through the financial assistance we provide.

The subject of your conference is undoubtedly of great topical importance. For a long time, perhaps too long, development has been considered almost entirely in economic terms, whereas in reality it is just as much a social problem as an economic one and one in which the law is vitally important. For example, many governments in the Third World make much use of laws and regulations in order to bring about economic and social change. In this sense it could be said that the role of law is already an important one in the development process. But is this also true for the rule of law?

4

Those bred in the western legal tradition generally mean more by the rule of law than just the formal use of legal instruments: it is also the rule of justice, of protection for all members of society against excessive government power, of reasonableness and good faith. If the concept of "law and order" is used purely as a means of controlling society effectively, it degenerates into an instrument for sharing out the benefits of forced economic development amongst privileged groups. In my view, the rule of law implies protecting the weaker members of society and helping them. This accords with the fundamental idea of human rights which the International Commission of Jurists has done so much to promote over a period of many years.

As the Dutch Government has already observed on a number of occasions, the fight for human rights is a fight not only against political repression but also against social deprivation and economic exploitation. This applies to countries as well as to people: in international relations the law of the jungle must be superseded by the rule of law, and the position of the weakest countries must be protected and promoted. It is in this context that the emerging concept of the right to development calls for special attention.

I am quite certain that your discussions during the coming week will make a valuable contribution towards our understanding of these matters.

Ladies and Gentlemen, thank you.

CHAIRMAN'S OPENING REMARKS

Monsieur Keba Mbaye

President of the International Commission of Jurists,
First President of the Supreme Court of Senegal, former President
of the United Nations' Commission on Human Rights

Mr Minister, Ladies and Gentlemen,

I would like, in my capacity as President of the International Commission of Jurists, to thank you, Mr Minister, and through you the Netherlands government.

In agreeing that the Conference organised by the International Commission of Jurists on Development and the Rule of Law be held in your beautiful town of The Hague, a town which was the first home of the Commission under the dynamic direction of Mr A.J.M. van Dal, your country has shown once again its attachment both to the principles of solidarity, which are the foundation of the Charter of San Francisco, and to a scrupulous respect for fundamental human rights, without which life in a society is not worth living.

The important part which your country plays in contributing to the improvement of the condition of life of disinherited peoples shows the extent to which the people of the Netherlands take to heart their sense of belonging to a universal society. Moreover, the very advanced positions taken by your various delegations to the Commission on Human Rights and to the General Assembly of the United Nations are an irrefutable proof of your unfailing attachment to the Charter of human rights.

Your personal support, Mr Minister, for this policy directed both to development aid and to respect for fundamental rights and freedoms is well known to us. We congratulate you upon it.

The International Commission of Jurists, as you know, is a non-governmental organisation which concerns itself with all matters relating to the rule of law. What characterises it is first its determination to be present whenever human rights need to be defended. Working in particular through its Secretary-General, Mr Niall MacDermot, whose competence, dynamism and generosity are well-known, it militates for a greater respect for rights and freedoms. It is active wherever it is necessary to mobilise against gross violations of human rights, to organise action to defend freedoms, or to implement decisions for an increasingly effective promotion or protection of fundamental rights and freedoms.

But our organisation's action is not only in the field. It complements this action with an unceasing activity of research with a view to enriching and developing the different components of human rights. For this purpose it has increased its efforts to organise throughout the world conferences and seminars, like this one, in which scholars from all regions, brought together around a theme which is of common concern, exchange their experiences and their ideas and produce conclusions and recommendations for the promotion of human rights.

The International Commission of Jurists has recently received a distinction from the international community. One of the most prestigious regional organisations for the protection of human rights, the Council of Europe, awarded it the first European Human Rights Prize. Thus the Commission is in the lead in the fields of action both for the defence of human rights and for scientific research, a persistent activity whose merits have been shown more than once by appreciable results achieved throughout the world.

This Hague Conference on development and the rule of law reflects the concern of the Commission to seek for all crucial problems of our time a solution based on reflection and realism.

The task which awaits us is not simple. The word 'development', which is used indiscriminately, has been devalued. It is often used but it is hardly easy to define. Robert Kapp has very rightly said that the incompatibility between development and respect for human rights, and thus for the rule of law, is conceivable only when development is defined solely in terms of growth.

This idea is right. Indeed, true development should meet the definition given by Malcolm Adiseshia for whom 'development is a form of humanism'. It is, he says, a "moral and spiritual fact as much as a material and practical one. It is an experience of the wholeness of man responding to his material needs (food, clothing and shelter) at the same time as his moral requirements (peace, compassion and charity). It is the expression of man in his greatness and in his weakness, ever striving forwards and further, but without ever ensuring definitively the redemption of his errors and his folly."

Understood thus, development implies the absence of repression as well as of gross violations of human rights. If one could establish the parameters of development on the one hand and of respect for civil and political rights on the other, one would see that the two curves appear the same.

It is this that has led us, among other ideas, to conceive of a human right called 'the right to development', which is already enscribed in filigree in the Charter of the United Nations as a normal consequence of the renunciation of the attributions of sovereignty and as an extension of the duty of solidarity.

This right to development I have defined as 'the recognised prerogative of every individual and every people to enjoy in just measure the goods and services produced thanks to the effort of solidarity of the members of the community'.

The States Parties to the Charter of the United Nations, in deciding to create a responsible international society to which they have assigned functions in the field of the international public economic order, have in so doing assumed responsibility, separately and in co-operation, for ensuring a solution to "international problems of an economic, social, cultural or humanitarian character..." (Article 1 of the Charter). Articles 55 and 56 of the Charter are even more explicit. They state that, based on the principle of equal rights of peoples, the United Nations are bound "to promote higher standards of living, full employment and conditions of economic and social progress and development, solutions of international economic, social, health, and related problems", as well as "cultural and educational cooperation".

Pearson expressed himself most justly when he said: "The concept of a moral community constitutes in itself a major reason for international cooperation for development." But we have said and many times repeated: for us there is no development without the rule of law.

Perhaps I am wrong to assert in this peremptory fashion a proposition which you will surely be called upon to discuss. You will pardon me, I hope, in ascribing my temerity to my conviction.

Development should integrate human rights and fundamental freedoms. It is a right of every man directly linked with the right to life, as Jean-Marie Domnach underlines when he says: "The right to life implies conditions which ensure the security and dignity of man and which give content to his power to be free as well as his capacity for happiness."

Mr Minister, Ladies and Gentlemen, the International Commission of Jurists is proud to have succeeded in bringing together today so many scholars, and to be ready to gather with care the fruits of their reflections, in order to bring them to the knowledge of researchers throughout the world who are similarly in search of a better future for mankind in a society of peace, freedom and prosperity.

KEY-NOTE ADDRESS

Shridath S. Ramphal

Commonwealth Secretary-General, Member of the International
Commission of Jurists and Member of the Brandt Commission

It is now almost thirty years since the International Commission of
Jurists was established with the objective of promoting throughout
the world understanding and observance of the rule of law and legal
protection of human rights. The Commission was born in the after-
math of a war whose horrors and barbarities had illustrated, starkly
and yet again, the depths of depravity to which human beings claim-
ing to be civilised can descend. Its scourge had swept through this
proud city — itself the symbol of man's efforts to bring the rule of
law to international life; and for the duration of the war the Netherlands endured the full weight of the tyranny which asserts itself from
the barrel of the gun. In the absence of the rule of law between nations, as within them, contempt for human rights is unconstrained.
Respect for the protection of human rights requires a global no less
than a national setting that is propitious. We meet now at another
time of threat to the rule of law world-wide — a time of danger when
the assertion of power could again assume primacy, and patriotism
begin to disdain the path of peace. There is something specially appropriate, therefore, about our meeting to talk of the rule of law
here in The Hague, which has within this century been so much at
the centre of man's hopes for its advancement in a global setting of
peace and justice in which fundamental human rights and the human
needs they mirror might find fulfilment.

Throughout history man has sought recognition of his own validity.
His perennial yearning found expression in the writings of our greatest philosophers and in all the world's major religions. Hinduism, rec-
ognising the dignity of the individual by identifying the human soul
with the Absolute; Islam with its emphasis on the brotherhood of
man; and Christianity with its enunciation of the Fatherhood of God.
Each reflects and in turn inspires the struggle for recognition of fundamental values. The same concern can be traced to the humanist
traditions of the Renaissance, and manifests itself in the struggle for
freedom and for social and economic justice that continues in many
parts of the world today. Each country, too, has its individual water-

sheds — England's Magna Carta (1215) and Habeas Corpus Act (1679); the Declaration of Independence by the 13 North American Colonies in 1776; the adoption of the Declaration of the Rights of Man and of the Citizen by the French National Assembly in 1789; and the publication of the Communist Manifesto in 1848, to mention but some.

Human rights are as old as human society itself, for they derive from every person's need to realise his essential humanity. They are not ephemeral, not alterable with time and place and circumstance. They are not the product of philosophical whim or political fashion. They have their origin in the fact of the human condition; and because they have, they are fundamental and inalienable. More specifically, they are not conferred by constitutions, conventions or governments. These are the instruments, the testaments, of their recognition; they are important, sometimes essential, elements of the machinery for their protection and enforcement; but they do not give rise to them. They were born not of man, but with man.

It is important to recall this; for upon it rests the validity, the legitimacy, of human concern with human rights — the inherent right, the essential duty, of the international community of states and our global society of people to be concerned with the human condition world-wide. Sovereignty may be a shield against officious external meddling; it was not fashioned to be a sword against a nation's own people. Nor must nationalism which sovereignty sustains become so moulded in an adversary system of international affairs that it provides cover for assaults upon the human condition beyond the national frontier. The world community must continue to assert its legitimate role in the advancement of human rights through the rule of law world-wide; and it must be in the vanguard of enlightened response to the insistent intimations of our common humanity that so characterise our time.

On the international plane much has been achieved at the not unimportant level of formulation: the Universal Declaration of Human Rights, the Human Rights Covenants, the Conventions on Genocide, on the Status of Refugees, on aspects of Slavery, on Racial Discrimination, on the Suppression and Punishment of the Crime of Apartheid. The list is long and impressive, and still keeps growing. By no measure can our international lawyers be labelled as idle in their creative and often imaginative work.

But between the avowal of the rule of law and its effective realisation, between the promotion of human rights and their actual enjoyment, there is an awkward, and often abysmal, gap. Formal recognition of human rights as an ideal, even as rights, is one matter: their observance in individual countries remains another. The horrors of Amin's Uganda took place against a Constitution that asserted the rule of law and inscribed the citizen's fundamental rights and freedoms in the traditional classic manner that most national constitutions do today; and there are many other countries — and not only among the newer nations — where the grandiose terms in which rights and freedoms are spelt out, and often boasted of, belie patterns of persistent infringement. It is an unhappy commentary that more than half the sovereign states in the world today have lacked the resolve and assurance to accede to or ratify the Human Rights Covenants, while more than five-sixths deny their citizens access to the Human Rights Committee established to oversee the implementation at the national level of civil and political rights and freedoms.

How do these derelictions persist? How are they squared with protestations of uprightness? In formal terms the answer lies in the formulations themselves; in the reality that at both national and international levels human rights are for the greater part aspired to and promised, not assured. In the main, they are expressed in the language of goals, of standards, of targets; where they have the status of guarantees they are nearly always qualified, avowedly in the public interest, — exceptions 'reasonably justifiable in a democratic society'.

But, in a sense more serious is the degree to which deprivations of human rights can become so subsumed in the national ethic espousing them that their very infringement takes on the colour of virtue and to protest their violation comes to be deemed subversive of the national interest. How long ago was it that one might have said of the United States' Constitution that its effect was testimony that "all men were created equal" — except in Alabama? The Soviet Constitution asserts the supremacy of the proletariat — but not of its right to dissent. South Africa reconciles apartheid with Christianity; its Prime Minister denies that its citizens have any right to a passport; it is, he asserts, a matter of 'privilege'; he might have added — a privilege reserved for those whom a ruling minority regime considers deserving. In all of these cases the state proceeds on the basis that there is no infringement, for there is no right to begin with. The denial is not a forfeiture; it doesn't even need to be excused. This is the most insidious condition of all when the vice of personal deprivation masquerades as national virtue.

Is it any wonder that one of the lessons of history is that resistance is inevitable to such attacks on man's essential humanity. Violence begets violence, and much of the violence of the present age derives from the violence inherent in overt denials of human rights; it is man's response to the violations of the human personality carried out in the name of authority, inflicted under the guise of the rule of law.

One does not need to look far to see how such violations have bred the violence that has marked the second half of the twentieth century. In this no continent has been spared: Uganda; Kampuchea; South Africa; Chile; Argentina; El Salvador! The contemporary human rights map has few regions free of major blemishes. Nor has the blight been confined to emergent countries, as events in Europe over the past fifty years have shown. But such is the human spirit that no matter how oppressive the government and no matter how dire the personal consequences, there will always be those who will assert their right to be human, at whatever the price. Yet where they seek to hold such governments to account — in circumstances in which the very oppression they resist denies them the means to organise peacefully and democratically to that end — they are now all too conveniently characterised as 'terrorists' or 'dissidents'. So aggressor and victim become confused; the 'good guys' become the 'bad', at least among those who know no better. But, of course, among those who do, there are many who suffer but persist. They are not confused; and in the end, because their cause is just, they succeed.

Four years ago, at Maputo, at the height of the struggle for Zimbabwe's freedom, I recall urging that:

> "The true 'patriots' are not always those who wear the conventional uniforms; the real 'terrorists' are not always those who come out of the darkness. The people of Southern Africa — of Zimbabwe, of Namibia and of South Africa itself — know that 'terrorism' has its headquarters in Salisbury and Pretoria, not in the forest sanctuaries of the Patriotic forces."

Today, with Zimbabwe's freedom won, it is easier to recognise that reality. Recently we have witnessed Robert Mugabe's abrupt translation in the Western media from the doctrinaire ogre he was alleged to be into the enlightened pragmatist those of us privileged to know him throughout have always believed him to be. The barbarities for which he and his embattled following had been condemned were in essence those of the regime he had been driven by his own essential humanity to counter; yet the regime could only have survived for as long as it did with world-wide connivance and support.

I have long been utterly convinced that if the people of the West were exposed to the full realities of Southern Africa — to the horrors of racism, of chronic poverty, of torture, of exploitation, of human degradation in all its ugly forms — they themselves would in revulsion demand their eradication. Yet how are they to know if, with notable and courageous exceptions, the world's media proceed on the premise that the evil that is commonplace is no longer news. And how much worse if they begin to project that evil as tolerable out of a distorted perception that those who resist it incline to the enemy in a new cold war stand-off. In the end, every semblance is lost of right and wrong, of moral purpose and immoral action.

We are beginning to enter this maze and to lose our way among its twists and turns. We need to breathe the fresh air of a more open internationalism, to acknowledge those issues that divide the world's nations, but to maximise the gains for consensus on those issues on which humanity can find common cause. Among these latter must be at least some major areas in which the world can advance the cause of the effective protection and realisation of human rights; and where more urgently appropriate than the area of development.

I hope you will not think it immodest to urge upon you the words of the Brandt Report as we tried to convey the true meaning of development. This is what we said:

"Statistical measurements of growth exclude the crucial elements of social welfare, of individual rights, of values not measurable by money. Development is more than the passage from poor to rich, from a traditional rural economy to a sophisticated urban one. It carries with it not only the idea of economic betterment, but also of greater human dignity, security, justice and equity.

Few people in the North have any detailed conception of the extent of poverty in the Third World or of the forms that it takes. Many hundreds of millions of people in the poorer countries are preoccupied solely with survival and elementary needs. For them work is frequently not available or, when it is, pay is very low and conditions often barely tolerable. Homes are constructed of impermanent materials and have neither piped water nor sanitation. Electricity is a luxury. Health services are thinly spread and in rural areas only rarely within walking distance. Primary schools, where they exist, may be free and not too far away, but children are needed for work and cannot easily be spared for schooling. Permanent insecurity is the condition of the poor. There are no public systems of social security in the event of unemployment, sickness or death of a wage-earner in the family. Flood, drought or disease affecting people or livestock can destroy livelihoods without hope of compensation. In the North, ordinary men and women face genuine economic problems — uncertainty, inflation, the fear if not the reality of unemployment. But they rarely face anything resembling the total deprivation found in the South.

The combination of malnutrition, illiteracy, disease, high birth rates, underemployment and low income closes off the avenues of escape; and while other groups are increasingly vocal, the poor and illiterate are usually and conveniently silent. It is a condition of life so limited as to be, in the words of the President of the World Bank, 'below any rational definition of human decency'. No concept of development can be accepted which continues to condemn hundreds of millions of people to starvation and despair."

I assume that it is about the eradication of these gross disparities between the world's people that we speak when we talk about 'development'. I assume that the theme of this meeting summons us, above all, to examine the relevance of the rule of law world-wide to the satisfaction of this most basic human need.

I have come to The Hague from Geneva and a meeting of the Independent Commission on Disarmament and Security Issues, chaired by Olof Palme, where it was manifest to us all that not only are the world's poor effectively required to subsidise the living standards of the world's rich, but that they must also now bear the brunt of the cost of the arms race in the coinage of human misery.

In terms of hunger, wretchedness, deprivation and death, intimations of the 'Third World War' have already claimed thousands of casualties; a toll that increases daily and which those who argue that the nuclear arms race has maintained a balance of peace conveniently ignore. The field of carnage may have been shifted from Europe; but the consequences to humanity remain the same.

Last year saw both the end of the First Disarmament Decade and the close of the Second Development Decade; two decades that in the result both wore false labels. Development faltered; disarmament remained a mirage. The facts are ugly and shameful and searing. It now seems that the number of people in absolute poverty — those who live and die without ever knowing why — at present estimated at 780 million, or nearly one in every five, may increase during the 1980s. And, says the World Bank, with clinical professionalism: "many developing countries will find it hard to maintain political stability". In other words, what lies ahead for many as the legacy of the Second Development Decade is human misery, social disintegration and an increased level of human rights denial.

The achievement of the much talked about 0.7 percent target for official development assistance requires an increase in aid equivalent to about 5 percent of military expenditure in developed countries both East and West. A freeze at the 1980 level of military expenditure could provide sufficient resources to reach that target in just one year. Development could be spectacularly advanced without lowering the world's expenditure on armaments but by simply not increasing it.

But the linkages between *détente*, disarmament, development, human rights and the rule of law are even closer. The decline from *détente* is dangerous for the world; but for the Third World it is calamitous. When East and West are each enlarging their arsenals of destruction and justifying it in terms of the other's offensive intent, we are indeed 'in a time of peril'. It is the kind of time when all else — including issues of development and human rights, both in their civil and political and their economic, social and cultural contexts — tend to be put aside, relegated to less troubled times; and when, of course, a massive supplement to military expenditure seems to signal confirmation that there may be not only a lack of will but even of means to go forward on development — a diversion, therefore, from progress toward a more orderly international economic environment. When these tensions subside it should occasion no surprise if the developing countries, and the cause of development and of human rights throughout the Third World, are found to be the principal victims.

The Brandt Commission has referred to the moral link between the vast spending on arms and the disgracefully low spending on measures to remove hunger and ill-health in the Third World. Its example of the eradication of malaria is typical of many others that could be cited. The World Health Organisation is short of funds. It estimates that it could control malaria world-wide at the cost of only $450 million. That is less than one thousandth of the world's military spending for one year. Eight hours of the arms race diverted from war to peace. One shift devoted to life not death. The examples could be multiplied. The central point is that a small reduction in military expenditure, a small step away from militarisation, can be a massive step in the fight against hunger and poverty and in the recognition of fundamental and inalienable human rights.

It was a distinguished statesman and soldier — Dwight D. Eisenhower — who reminded us: "Every gun that is made, every warship launched, every rocket fired, signifies in a final sense a theft from those who hunger and are not fed, from those who are cold and not clothed." If only those of East and West who see salvation mainly in the power to self-destroy would heed that wisest of counsels.

Meanwhile, total global expenditure on arms climbed from $180 billion in 1970 to $500 billion in 1980. Deepening global poverty; higher and higher expenditure on arms leading to greater and greater insecurity; mounting fear, mistrust and suspicion within the world community; in fact, after the two 'decades' that never were, the result is a world economic, social and security crisis.

But it is not only an international setting freed from war and crisis that development needs; it needs, in an acute degree, the application of the rule of law to international economic relations — an international legal order that upholds the objectives of economic and social justice world-wide. This, quintessentially, is what the New International Economic Order is about: bringing order and fairness to the market-place where nations do business to the account of their people. I should like to dwell a while on the fate of the dialogue between North and South designed to implement that new order. But let me try to make the point in relation to what might have been thought to be a less comprehensive, less controversial, less confrontationist, area.

For nine years now the international community has been engaged in attempting to draw up a treaty establishing a legal regime for the sea and the sea-bed. Here, where even in the heyday of empire the seas remained 'the high seas' above the reach of sovereign rights and where the sea-bed never passed into national domain; here, where

international lawyers could begin with a relatively clean title to regulate for the use and benefit of all people what they could truthfully
claim to be the heritage of mankind; here, after so great an effort, on
the very eve of what was believed to be the final session of the Conference on the Law of the Sea, a new administration in the United
States has in effect questioned global objectives in fundamental areas
of the negotiation.

The developing countries were among those who would be beneficiaries of a legal regime regulating the use of the sea and the sea-bed;
for, in these matters, they must look to the force of law; they cannot
look to the power of lawless action. Here were important new opportunities through which development might have been given a better
prospect and the international community might have matched its
assertions of commitment to development with a regime of international co-operation that involved no sacrifice of existing rights, but
merely a self-denying ordinance not to 'scramble' for new rights at
the expense of weaker and needier members of the international
community.

As I reflect on these developments, I recall article 11, paragraph 1,
of the International Covenant on Economic, Social and Cultural
Rights:

> "The States Parties to the present Covenant recognise the right of
> everyone to an adequate standard of living for himself and his fam-
> ily, including adequate food, clothing and housing, and to the con-
> tinuous improvement of living conditions. The States Parties will
> take appropriate steps to ensure the realisation of this right, recog-
> nising to this effect the essential importance of international co-
> operation based on free consent."

The 'States Parties to the Covenant' still have a chance to take appropriate steps to help to ensure a better standard of living for the
world's poor through an international treaty governing the sea and
sea-bed. But will they give their 'free consent' to international cooperation to this end? Will they, in this most propitious, almost sym-
bolic, area extend the rule of law and help to advance development?

But it is in the wider area of the North-South dialogue that the relationships between development and the rule of law are being most
actively canvassed. What are the prospects for results that will ensure
that the rule of law prevails between nations no less than within

them — that will advance social and economic justice for all the world's people?

This, of course, is what the 'development debate' is quintessentially about. Let me try to convey some of the contradictions that have discouraged and dismayed the Third World — and have done throughout the last eight years of dialogue — when they have urged the case for a new order of international economic relationships that would satisfy these basic human needs. The essential features of the new order for which the United Nations General Assembly in 1974 declared its support are not so different in kind from many of the measures already accepted within developed states. What is needed is not an act of invention but an act of will to carry perceptions of social and economic justice, of balanced growth, beyond the frontiers of the industrialised countries. We must understand, of course, that, in the present era of interdependence, issues like interests cannot remain in closed compartments. In the early years of the development debate — in the 50s and 60s — development was largely beyond the pale of East-West issues. It was touched here and there by cold war considerations; but, basically, the international effort for development was self-motivated and self-contined.

Today, the reality is very different. Failure in each area — North-South or East-West — tends to imperil progress in the other. A decline from *détente* means a steep drop for development. 'Afghanistan', in this sense, both in terms of action and reaction, represents one of the most damaging blows that development received in the 1980s. It may surprise the Soviets, in particular, to hear this; but these implications for development of the impairment of *détente* were wholly predictable.

And it would surprise the West to be told, but it is equally true, that the record of consistent failure to advance development through the North-South dialogue represents one of the most damaging blows struck against human rights in recent times. The implications of that failure for absolute poverty world-wide are as horrible as the depredations of any despot; and, again, they were wholly predictable. Indeed, as I have said elsewhere, and as Philip Alston was kind enough to notice in his excellent working paper on Development and the Rule of Law:

"All the dictators and all the aggressors throughout history, however ruthless, have not succeeded in creating as much misery and suffering as the disparities between the world's rich and poor sustain today."

Small wonder that human rights tend to be so differently perceived in rich countries and in poor! It is a difference of perception that the ICJ cannot afford to ignore. The industrialised countries, assured of material prosperity and, to a large degree, of civil liberties, tend to view human rights as an external issue, and to react with hostility to critics who suggest internal imperfections. The Third World, where hundreds of millions subsist at the very margin of existence, is concerned primordially with economic and social rights and are sometimes less than zealous in their protection of others. For the world's poorest, for whom survival is the basic human need, human rights can have no meaning unless they begin with the right to life itself at a tolerable level of existence.

To Third World countries it is a maddening contradiction that some developed states refuse to accept as legitimate at the international level mechanisms they have themselves employed, indeed devised, for advancing some of the most noble objectives within their own societies. Built into the ethos of Western democracies are the right of association, the legitimacy of collective bargaining. Yet when the poor of the world pursue similar approaches to redress economic injustices at the international level, some developed states dispute their reasonableness or even their legitimacy as an exercise in confrontation.

How else would the societies of Europe or North America have moved away from feudalism and privilege, have moved towards just economic societies, save through the collective effort of the deprived. How shall we ever move towards a just world community unless through organised effort of those now condemned to international poverty? How else, save by collective action, can they effectively challenge a system their experience compels them to reject as unjust?

The analogy with national conditions is valid, also, in relation to many of the equalising mechanisms actually employed at the national level. Within every major industrial country and regional economic community it is now accepted that the unrestricted operation of free market forces can lead to results out of tune with prevailing concepts of a just national or regional society. The operation of the market often fails to achieve an equitable distribution of income among peoples or of activities among regions. And the market is vulnerable to manipulation through the exercise of unequally distributed market power.

None of the modern industrial economies expose their citizens to the unmitigated effects of the forces unleashed by the market system. Farmers' incomes are stabilised through subsidies and levies; indeed, the whole system of price and income support policies is designed to secure for farmers in rich countries what the international programmes now under discussion could, if fully implemented, only partially secure for commodity producers in poor countries; yet objections are raised within the North. When jobs are lost in industrialised countries through technological or other change, unemployment relief is available; no obstacle is placed on the movement of factors of production; the retraining or relocation of labour is subsidised; and jobs are moved to the sources of labour through incentives, government contracts and other public measures. More systematically, monopolists are not allowed to exact their full toll on the public; restrictive business practice and anti-trust legislation keep them in check at the national level. In other words, the free play of market forces is curbed when it leads to results that work hardship upon unprotected elements of the national society. Yet these same countries insist that the people of the developing world be made subject to the unrestrained forces of the market which, partly because they are thus tempered in the industrial countries, operate with greater fury in the international field. One system is contrived for the industrialised countries, one which is humane. Quite another is ordained for the developing. For how long can a global society that espouses international co-operation allow the rule of law in these economic matters to halt at national frontiers?

The tragedy is that neither side of the political spectrum in the West acknowledges this. Those on the right, who propound the philosophy of free enterprise and the minimum degree of state intervention or control, freely admit the need to provide to entrepreneurs and producers within their national economies incentives and rewards which deviate from normal market forces. But when they turn to the international arena, and commend the path of free market forces to the developing world, what incentives do they see widely fluctuating and often depressed prices providing to the jute growers of Bangladesh, the tea planters of India, the sisal farmers of Tanzania? Those of the left, who argue the case for social justice and state intervention at home, and proclaim with such eloquence the universality of socialised brotherhood, appear only too ready to square this with giving market forces free rein abroad and being foremost among the protectionists at home.

In the Brandt Commission we recognised that "in the world as in nations, economic forces left entirely to themselves tend to produce growing inequality". We knew that "within nations public policy protects the weaker partners". We were satisfied that "the time has come to apply this precept to relations between nations within the world community". And we were convinced that "the mutual interests of North and South will be served, that the world will be a more secure and prosperous place", if mankind would but take this step towards creating a more just and a more equitable international economic system.

The North-South debate is often described as if the rich were being asked to make sacrifices in response to the demands of the poor. The Commission rejected this view. "The world", we said, "is now a fragile and interlocking system, whether for its people, its ecology or its resources. Many individual societies have settled their inner conflicts by accommodation, to protect the weak and to promote principles of justice, becoming stronger as a result. The world too can become stronger by becoming a just and humane society. If it fails in this, it will move towards its own destruction." And, we concluded in words particularly apposite to our theme here, "we are looking to a world based less on power and status, more on justice and contract; less discretionary, more governed by fair and open rules". We might have said — a world in which the rule of law will prevail in the domain of development, between states as well as within them, in our global community as well as within national societies.

It follows, of course, that a major responsibility rests upon developing countries themselves to generate through the rule of law at home an environment propitious to real development. The poor have no less right to the enjoyment of their civil and political rights than the rich. The condition of their poverty, it is true, diminishes their capacity to enjoy them effectively; that is why it is so hypocritical for rich countries to perpetuate poverty world-wide and preach to the Third World about what it chooses selectively to describe as 'human rights'. But this does not relieve the Third World of the need to establish the structures of a just society at home.

Respect for civil and political rights is an essential foundation for development strategies that are successful in lasting terms. Only if the people as a whole can participate in decision-making, be seen as partners in government rather than as recipients from it, can human resources be effectively mobilised for development. Only if criticism is seen as fundamental to a healthy society — rather than as being subversive of it — are decisions likely to be taken that are so sufficiently informed by the public will as to be supportive of the public interest. No one, no group, has a monopoly on a society's accumulated store of wisdom and experience. Development calls for all the enthusiasm, creativity and energy that can be harnessed; but these are hardly likely to be forthcoming in an environment hostile to the concept of freedom in its truest sense. It is not easy to advance simultaneously on all the fronts of nation-building (with all that the legacy of colonialism implies), of democracy, and of socially just development. But there is no alternative to trying.

Faced with monumental problems it will sometimes be tempting to believe that the exercise of civil and political rights and, in particular, regular submission to elections, poses a greater threat to a leader's ability to govern than does the temporary suppression of such rights. If there was a country where this might have been so, one would have expected it to be Iran: yet, even there, the oppression of the Shah led inexorably to his downfall, despite the riches and the technology at his disposal. A regime out of touch with the instinct of freedom of its people inevitably invites its own overthrow.

The therapy of free elections has no equal. I know of no better prescription for ensuring the health of the body politic, the denial to violence of its surest foothold, and the return of societies and their regions to vigour and confidence than an unquestioning and unquestioned commitment to the democratic process in word and deed. It is a process that brings its own strains to the fragile societies of the developing world; but all the experience of the post-war era of decolonisation and nation-building underscores the fact that there is no better or safer way.

Its counterpart, of course, is that the society itself must abjure violence; must acknowledge that the right of dissent does not imply the right of destruction; must insist that legitimate political action does not degenerate into illegality and the subversion of government. It is because these elements are mutually reinforcing — confidence in the democratic process and freedom from subversion of it — that their strengthening is the responsibility of the society as a whole — of government and people, of those in power and those who seek it. And it is not only a mutual responsibility but a mutual need; for just as these elements are mutually reinforcing so their erosion is mutually weakening — undermining, in the end, the very fabric of society itself.

Yet in judging the democratic record of the developing countries, the older nations must be careful to avoid easy but misleading comparisons. The two-party or multi-party systems enjoy no monopoly of democratic virtue. As the proceedings of the ICJ Seminar in Dar-es-Salaam clearly illustrated, participatory democracy is not incompatible with a one-party state — though the potential for abuse in such a system may be greater, and the need for safeguards more pressing. A country with scarce resources may well feel that it needs all its most able minds in government, and that an alternative government out of office is a luxury it cannot yet afford. It is the height of injustice for it then to be damned out of hand for doing no more than conserve its resources and mobilise for development. But it must then sedulously guard against abuse of the system.

The ICJ has made a signal contribution to the advancement of human rights throughout the world. It was accorded well-deserved recognition last year when the Council of Ministers of the Council of Europe, on the occasion of its award of the European Human Rights Prize, selected the Commission as the first recipient of the award. I make no apology as a member of the Commission for seeming immodesty; for the credit for this Award and for the achievements it acknowledges lies with Sean McBride and Niall MacDermot, names that have become so closely identified, as to be synonymous, with the upholding of the rule of law and respect for human rights. No organisation can ever have been better served by its chief executives than has ours. We applaud them proudly.

But, what of the future? If we face reality squarely even the most hopeful of us must concede that our world today stands in great danger — greater danger, perhaps, than at any time since 1945. The need to save the world from 'the scourge of war' is clearly more urgent now than it was when the Charter first promised to meet that need; the human condition which the crisis in development and in the global economy poses is more pressing now than it was then. For 'East-West' and 'North-South' it is a time of tension, uncertainty and agony, if not despair. That surely means, however, that it is a time when we stand in great need of wider visions, grander purposes, nobler pursuits, than those defined by our 'narrow domestic walls' and our shrinking international perspectives.

It is a time when the ICJ can surely, and must surely, help the international community by recalling it to its commitments to the rule of law world-wide; by emphasising that the rule of law is not the preserve of any one ideological paradigm, but must be an element of all; by counselling its relevance to the ending of the gross disparities that now exist in the quality of life of the world's people. The issue of development presents the Commission with a challenge that is as urgent as any it has faced in the past, with one that is relevant to the rule of law in its truest sense and is worthy of the Commission's vocation to promote and uphold it.

And if any should ask how are these social and economic issues the concern of lawyers, I would add that social and economic change is not a need confined to national societies and that the world's lawyers have as much to contribute, and as great a duty to make that contribution, to the inauguration of desirable change within our global community of states as they have always had, and sometimes discharged, within their own societies. It is a great challenge to lawyers world-wide, a challenge I do not hesitate to describe as the need for 'a new equity' to redress the wrongs that man now perceives in his global order. Nationalism and sovereignty, for too long a masquerade of jingoism and selfishness, must now give way to internationalism and interdependence — and not just for moral reasons related to human solidarity, but for practical reasons related to our planetary survival.

Lawyers must be in the forefront of a movement that will fashion a new, more relevant, world legal order for the 21st century; a new order that responds with boldness, with wisdom and with inventiveness to the old problems we are carrying over from our present century — like the problems of development and the rule of law.

OPENING OF THE PLENARY DISCUSSION

Niall MacDermot

Secretary-General of the International Commission of Jurists

By its statute the International Commission of Jurists is an organisation devoted to the promotion of the Rule of Law, that is to the legal protection of human rights.

I should like to trace briefly the history of the ICJ's interest in development, and explain how it comes about that we are holding this conference on Development and the Rule of Law.

At first our organisation saw the Rule of Law essentially in terms of the protection of the rights of the individual. However, at its first conference held in a developing country, the New Delhi Congress of Jurists in 1959, the Rule of Law was proclaimed as a "dynamic concept... which should be employed not only to safeguard and advance the civil and political rights of the individual in a free society, but also to establish social, economic, educational and cultural conditions under which his legitimate aspirations and dignity may be realised". The concept of the Rule of Law was thus expanded to include the legal protection of all fundamental rights and not merely those civil and political rights traditionally identified with the rights of the individual.

At subsequent conferences, and in particular at the Conference of Bangkok in 1965, lawyers in all countries were urged to exercise their skills to promote legislation and legal institutions and procedures to maintain and enforce economic, social and cultural standards.

During the period of this first series of ICJ conferences, 1955 to 1968, there was a general confidence among third world lawyers, many of whom had been trained in the west, that the independence movement would result in multi-party parliamentary democracies on the western pattern. Events soon proved otherwise, as the massive economic problems and social tensions inthe newly independent countries led to more authoritative forms of government.

This in turn resulted in a change of approach by the ICJ. It seemed more helpful in the new situation to seek to organise smaller meetings on a regional or sub-regional basis, with a mixture of lawyers and non-lawyers, to discuss what seemed to the people in the regions to be the most crucial issues for them in the field of human rights. These issues were discussed in private so as to enable freer communication on what were often very sensitive issues.

The turning point was an East and Central African seminar held in Dar-es-Salaam in 1976 on Human Rights in a One-Party State. Its very title was a challenge to hitherto accepted notions, and its conclusions and recommendations were the subject of a keen debate at the ICJ's Vienna Commission Meeting four years ago. The conclusions of the seminar were however endorsed and a decision was taken to organise further meetings of this kind. Accordingly, seminars were held in Barbados in 1977 on "Human Rights and their Promotion in the Caribbean", a francophone african seminar in Dakar in 1978 on "Le développement et les droits de l'homme", in Bogota in 1979 on "Human Rights in the Rural Areas of the Andean Region" and in Kuwait in 1980 on "Human Rights in Islam". Further seminars are in preparation in South East Asia later this year and in the Indian Sub-Continent next year.

The subjects for discussion at these seminars were chosen in consultation with the prospective participants. All of them dealt with issues of civil and political rights, but they included in varying degrees issues concerning economic, social and cultural rights, such as the right to participation in the decision making process (and the difficulties of giving effect to this right), trade union rights and other rights of association, rights of women and of young people, protection of family life, the right to education, adequate medical and health care and housing, the right to work, freedom from discrimination, the right to legal assistance, and so on.

I should like to refer in a little more detail to the Dakar seminar as this was the first to deal directly and explicitly with the relationship between development and human rights. It began with a masterful keynote address by our President, Mr. Kéba Mbaye, on the place and role of human rights in development and on the right to development, a concept of which he is the author and which has now been adopted by the UN Commission on Human Rights and the General Assembly.

The conclusions and recommendations of this seminar are so pertinent to our theme that I wish there were time to read them all. I must content myself with reading the section entitled 'the policy of development and its requirements in relation to human rights'. It reads as follows:

"3. The seminar examined this theme under two aspects, firstly, the place of human rights in development and the right to development, and secondly the relation between economic, social and cultural rights and civil and political rights. It stated that development should not be conceived of or understood simply in terms of economic growth, nor as an increase in the per capita income, but should necessarily include those qualitative elements which human rights constitute and which provide an essential dimension. It must be global.

4. The task of every government is to assure the development of its people. The fulfillment of this duty is a condition of the legitimacy of any government.

5. Consequently, violation of fundamental freedoms represents a serious failure in development policy and can in no way be justified by the demands of this policy. It follows that States should not invoke development or political stability as a pretext for rehabilitating practices which Africans unanimously condemned during the colonial period.

6. The application of a development policy responding to the needs of the population and respecting human rights does not depend on the model chosen. Every development policy should take into account the needs of the population and their right to choose freely the model of development.

7. In every case, whatever be the nature of the regime, development implies a free participation, active and real, of the whole population in the elaboration of the development policy and its implementation for the benefit of all. It follows that the development policy should be accompanied by effective measures to combat at all levels corruption and the waste of public resources.

8. A right to development exists. The essential content of this right lies in the need for justice, both at the national and international level. The right to development draws its force from the duty of solidarity, which entails international cooperation. It is at once collective and individual. It results clearly from the different organs of the United Nations and the specialised agencies.

9. In its international dimension, the right to development implies the rule of peace, the existence of a satisfactory environment and

the introduction of a more just economic order, so that each
people, each individual, profits from the common heritage of
mankind and the efforts of all strata of society are justly rewarded.

10. It is therefore essential that States respect the laws and apply the
international engagements to which they have subscribed."

The conclusions then go on to deal in some detail with the international aspects of the subject, with popular participation in development, non-discrimination and development, the citizen and the administration, and the role of the judiciary in development.

For the Bogota seminar in 1979, since some of the Andean governments had sought to justify their restrictions of civil and political
rights by the need to promote economic and social rights, it was decided to choose as the subjects for discussion a number of key economic and social rights, such as land reform, labour and trade union
legislation, the rights of the indigenous people, agricultural and economic policies, and legal services for the poor. The very forceful conclusions of this seminar are summarised on pages 59–62 below in
Mr. Alston's outstanding working paper. Suffice it to say that the
participants were unanimous in finding that the lack of progress in
these rights in the rural areas was due to the repression of their civil
and political rights, particularly freedom of association and freedom
of expression, the lack of peasant participation in formulating agricultural policies, and the adoption of development policies which
favour the minority urban sector, concentrate the ownership of land
in the rural areas, and place the emphasis on crops for export or industrial use.

Among the subjects dealt with at the Kuwait seminar on Human
Rights in Islam were 'Development, Property and Distribution of
Wealth' and 'the Right to Work' in Islam. On the first subject, it was
stressed that Islam views human life as an integrated whole and ad-
mits of no dichotomy between civil and political rights and economic
and social rights, and that man finds his freedom within the limits of
social responsibility which effectively integrate the individual with
his environment. It was the duty of Muslims to evolve and establish
a just and equitable economic order throughout the Muslim world in
accordance with the injunctions of the Quran and Sunnah, recognis-
ing that no such system, in a complete form, is to be found today.

In addition to organising these seminars, the staff of the ICJ have also tried to study some of the areas of real, as opposed to imagined, conflicts between different human rights. In particular, an american attorney, Robert Kapp, who worked with us for some time, produced an interesting document on the subject which is referred to in Philip Alston's working paper.

I hope this very brief outline of some our activities in the past five years shows how we have come to be increasingly involved with questions of development in our efforts to promote the Rule of Law, and why it is that we have convened this conference.

One of the problems in this field is the lack of contact between those who work in the field of development strategies and those concerned with promoting human rights. At first development economists regarded concepts of human rights as irrelevant and disruptive to their attempt to make development policies 'non-political'. This attempt was, of course, futile because no decision has such far-reaching political consequences for a country and, indeed, for the human rights of its people, as the choice of its development strategy. Nevertheless, this was the attitude in the era when the primary emphasis was on economic growth.

Now the pendulum has swung, and new development policies are being advocated with their stress on meeting basic needs, eliminating 'absolute poverty' and promoting 'self reliance'. There is still some reluctance to admit that this means that economic development has to concern itself with human rights. An exception is acceptance of the right of those concerned to participate in the decision making process, however little this right is realised in practice.

In these circumstances, we have been fortunate in persuading a number of distinguished experts in the field of development to assist us in grappling with some of the difficult questions which arise in the relationship between development and the Rule of Law, using this term in wide sense I have already indicated of the legal protection of human rights of all kinds.

May I conclude by posing some of these questions as they have confronted us in our work.

1. What is the concept of 'development'? Is it useful to distinguish three types of development:
   — development in terms of economic growth measured by GNP,

- development directed to meeting basic needs and enhancing the quality of life, and
- development as a global concept covering all human rights, economic, social, cultural, civil and political?

2. Should priority be given to development policies aimed at eradicating 'absolute poverty'?

3. When a repressive government says that it restricts civil and political rights in the interest of promoting development, is the explanation in many cases that it is pursuing a development policy which favours an urban industrial minority at the expense of the rural majority?

4. Is the western model of development appropriate for developing countries, or an illusion, or destructive of their societies and culture?

5. Is there a constructive role for lawyers in elaborating economic, social and cultural rights in specific terms in the context of their own societies?

6. Are legal practitioners equipped or motivated to assist in furthering the right of deprived sectors of the population? Or is there a need, in the words of the International Center for Law in Development, for 'a new breed of legal professionals... concerned with law as a community resource of self-reliant development'? If so, how is it to be created and organised?

7. What are the prospects for international solidarity? Can democratic governments in industrialised countries, persuade their electorates that they should accept sacrifices in the short term in order to create a New International Economic Order which will benefit them, or their descendants, in the long term?

8. If the industrialised countries are to make a real and substantial transfer of resources to less developed countries, should they be able to impose conditions about the development policies to be adopted by the recipients, e.g. to favour directly the poorest among their population? If not, why not? Is there a difference here between bi-lateral and multi-lateral aid?

9. Is the idea of an international development tax useful and realistic?

10. Above all, is it possible for this seminar to make a contribution to the proposed United Nations Declaration on the Right to Development? What is the scope of this right at both the national and international level? What is its legal basis? Who are the beneficiaries, the persons entitled to claim this right? What duties does it impose, and on whom, to give effect to this right? How can it be enforced?

THE BASIC WORKING PAPER

DEVELOPMENT AND THE RULE OF LAW:
PREVENTION VERSUS CURE
AS A HUMAN RIGHTS STRATEGY

Philip Alston

Consultant to the United Nations Division of Human Rights

CONTENTS

Introduction

Until very recently the pursuit of human rights objectives has been undertaken in relative isolation from the massive efforts which have been devoted to the elusive quest for development. The loss has been twofold. On the one hand human rights initiatives have foundered because they have sought to treat the symptoms of repression without paying adequate regard to the deeper structural problems which gave rise to the symptoms in the first place. In many instances these problems are rooted in underdevelopment or maldevelopment. On the other hand development programmes have made only very limited headway, due in large part to their overriding preoccupation with growth in macro-economic terms and their consequent neglect of the human factor. Even today the vast majority of economists and development planners look upon human rights issues as extraneous and largely irrelevant matters, the consideration of which can only hinder efficiency and provoke political controversy.

Since 1977, United Nations human rights organs have been engaged in a major effort to relate their specific concerns to a range of broader structural issues and to bring human rights endeavours closer to the mainstream of international social and economic concerns. Over the same period the International Commission of Jurists, in co-operation with other bodies, has organized a series of regional or subregional seminars around the broad theme of human rights and development. Seminars have been held in Dar-es-Salaam (1976), Barbados (1977), Dakar (1978), and Bogota (1979), and others are planned.

The present paper is designed to provide an overview of some of the main development issues with which the international human rights community has been attempting to grapple in recent years. While the treatment provided is by no means comprehensive, an effort has been made to describe as well as provide an objective assessment of progress to date in this field.

PART I

Redressing the Curative Imbalance
in the UN's Approach to Human Rights:
The Past and Future Role of Lawyers

Lawyers, with all their professional predilections, specialist experience and limitations, and disciplinary and other biases, have played a central role in determining the shape and parameters of the existing approach to human rights within the United Nations as well as in most of the major regional organizations. The role of philosophers, social scientists and exponents of other disciplines has been largely peripheral, although not entirely irrelevant, in the processes of drafting international instruments, shaping institutional policy approaches and supervising compliance with international standards. These processes have thus carried the strong imprint of the legal profession which, by virtue of its training and nature, has a tendency to be blind to the structures which support or even cause the problems with which they are dealing[1]. In some respects it may be argued that such structure blindness is appropriate and that it is simply a sociological way of describing the traditional mandate of lawyers to work on a case-by-case basis and to apply the law as it is rather than as they think it should be.

However, even at the national level, this narrow conception of the lawyer's role is becoming less and less in accord with reality as is illustrated by the increasingly important contribution of both permanent and *ad hoc* law reform commissions. Such bodies serve not only to expedite the process of translating social developments into legal form but also to provoke discussion and analysis within both the legal profession and the community at large of pressing social issues. At the international level such a conception is even less appropriate in view of the fact that law and politics are even more closely intermeshed than they are at the national level. Internationally, lawyers frequently exercise quasi-legislative and executive functions as well as their more traditional functions of advisers and legislative draftsmen. Thus, for example, the major characteristic which distinguishes the

---

1) See Johan Galtung, *Is the Legal Perspective Structure-Blind?* Oslo, Working Paper of Chair in Conflict and Peace Research, 1977.

Commission on Human Rights from other bodies such as the Commission on Social Development and even its parent body, the Economic and Social Council, is that its deliberations are to a very large extent based upon specific international legal standards. Its distinctive contribution is that it purports to approach different issues within a framework consecrated by international law. While in practice the political factor (as opposed to the legal or human one) all too often predominates, the overall work and the specific resolutions and decisions of the Commission on Human Rights are generally clothed in the garb of international law, although some of the garments used are clearly more transparent and fashion-conscious than is appropriate for such wardrobes.

The four phases of UN human rights action

The extent to which international lawyers in the human rights field have left their distinctive mark is best illustrated by a review of the four broad phases through which United Nations action (and inaction) in the field of human rights has passed. Writing in 1975, one scholar[2] discerned the first three of these to have been: (1) the phase of standard-setting (1945—55); (2) the phase of promotion (1955—65); and (3) the phase of protection (1965—75). Since 1977 a fourth phase, embodying a structural approach, has emerged.

The development of the first phase was a process in which international lawyers were instrumental. In a relatively short period of time the UN achieved a great deal, including the adoption of the Universal Declaration of Human Rights (1948), the completion of the major part of the drafting of the two Human Rights Covenants (1955), the adoption of Conventions on the Prevention and Punishment of the Crime of Genocide (1948), the Status of Refugees (1951), the Suppression of the Traffic in Persons and of the Exploitation of the Prostitution of Others (1949), the International Right of Correction (1952), the Political Rights of Women (1952), and the Status of Stateless Persons (1954), and the adoption of the Standard Minimum Rules for the Treatment of Prisoners (1955). Since 1955 this legal drafting work has continued at a sometimes impressive pace, with efforts currently being devoted to drafting conventions on the rights of the child, and the rights of minorities, and conventions against tor-

---

2) Jean-Bernard Marie, *La Commission des droits de l'homme de l'ONU* (Paris, Pédone, 1975).

ture, and religious and other forms of intolerance. In stark contrast
to this impressive feat of standard-setting the UN, during both its
first and second phases, was unable or unwilling to devise any procedure whatsoever for responding to the thousands of complaints
('communications') and pleas for help in human rights matters which
it acknowledged receiving every year.

In the second phase of UN action, involving an emphasis on the 'promotion' of human rights, some of the shortcomings of an unduly
legalistic approach were recognized and remedies were sought. During
this stage: a system of periodic reports on "developments and the
progress achieved... in the field of human rights, and measures taken
to safeguard human liberty" was instituted; a programme of advisory
services, consisting of the provision of expert advice, the holding of
seminars and training courses, and the awarding of fellowships, was
established; and a variety of studies was undertaken, mainly by rap-
porteurs, and particularly in the field of non-discrimination. According to one observer, "a great deal of time and energy was invested in
these promotional activities, but generally speaking they failed to
grasp the interest and the imagination of the UN membership and of
the public at large. Moreover, they were too far removed from the
main political currents in the world organization. The human rights
programme was functioning in isolation, and it seemed to lack the
political relevance and impetus which is needed for dynamic evolution"[3].

However, the response to these problems was only partially effective.
In its third phase the UN became concerned with international protection or, in effect, with responding to gross violations of human
rights. It was a natural transition for lawyers to move from law-mak-
ing to enforcement. They had been ill equipped to deal with 'promotion' in its broadest sense and were in any event constrained by the
reluctance of governments to tackle the complex and far-reaching
problems of promotion. By contrast, responding to violations involved legal and political issues of interpreting and applying the provisions of the UN Charter and relevant human rights instruments and
the devising of formal legal procedures all of which tasks lent themselves to a legalistic approach.

During this third phase, the Commission adopted more of a selective

3) T.C. van Boven, "The United Nations and Human Rights: A Critical Appraisal", *Bulletin
   of Peace Proposals*, Vol. 8, 1977, p. 201.

criminological approach and prescribed various measures which were alternately designed to punish, to deter of, less often, to reform. In an area characterized by enormous governmental sensitivity and wariness lest precedents be set, significant breakthroughs have been achieved in recent years both as regards general procedures for more prompt and effective action to combat specific violations and as regards individual 'problem' States. Nevertheless, the UN's response has been somewhat haphazard and there is some justification for criticism of the substantial discrepancies which exist in the type and extent of action taken in different but comparable cases. By contrast to the preference of many such critics, however, the need is not to soften (or abandon) the approach taken to date in particular instances but rather to work to make the overall level of response more comprehensive, balanced and, above all, effective. In this endeavour the central role to be played by the application of traditional legal skills is self-evident.

While the task of adequately responding to gross violations is a particularly important and pressing one, it constitutes only one facet of the overall challenge of promoting and protecting human rights. The third phase of UN action saw relatively few efforts to enhance the ability of potential victims, primarily the poor, to resist their oppressors, to promote economic, social and cultural rights as full-fledged human rights, or to create structural conditions which are simply less conducive to human rights violations. The transition from standard-setting to protection took the UN from one extreme to the other along the spectrum of approaches to human rights implementation. The second or promotional phase was one in which the actors were ill at ease and the efforts undertaken were accordingly weak and poorly defined and directed. Moreover, most of the 'promotional' measures taken were not of an essentially preventive nature. Above all, they did not, in general, address the wider economic and social issues that were of paramount concern to the Third World which was, by 1974, relentlessly pursuing in other fora its demands for a new international economic order.

The fourth, or 'structural' phase of UN action has its origins in a growing awareness that it is at least as important to identify and seek to remove structural obstacles that lie at the root of many an injustice as it is to deal with their symptoms in the form of particular violations. Thus the removal of inequities, such as those which deny the right of individuals and nations to participate in making decisions which affect them and which have in many instances become entrenched features of national and international society, holds out a better long-term prospect of enabling individuals and collectivities to ensure respect for their own rights. In many respects such an approach amounts to emphasizing a preventive rather than a curative strategy for improving enjoyment of human rights.

The seeds of this structural phase were sown at the International Conference on Human Rights held in Teheran in 1968. The harvest, however, was minuscule until 1977 when the Commission on Human Rights initiated its deliberations on the concept of the right to development and the General Assembly extended its NIEO work into the human rights field by adopting resolution 32/130. The right to development is dealt with later in this paper but it is important at this point to note the provisions of resolution 32/130 which has since served as the springboard for a variety of initiatives designed to change very substantially, for better or worse, the nature and direction of UN action in the human rights field.

General Assembly Resolution 32/130

The eight "concepts", which the first paragraph of the resolution provides should be taken into account in the approach to the future work within the United Nations system with respect to human rights questions, are delicately balanced propositions which represent much more than a mere consolidation of previously agreed principles. In some respects the list is as significant for the concepts that it excludes as for those which it includes. For these reasons it is inadvisable to try to condense or summarize the concepts, which are as follows:

(a) All human rights and fundamental freedoms are indivisible and interdependent; equal attention and urgent consideration should be given to the implementation, promotion and protection of both civil and political, and economic, social and cultural rights;

(b) The full realization of civil and political rights without the enjoyment of economic, social and cultural rights is impossible; the achievement of lasting progress in the implementation of human rights is dependent upon sound and effective national and international policies of economic and social development, as recognized by the Proclamation of Teheran of 1968;

(c)   All human rights and fundamental freedoms of the human person and of peoples are inalienable;

(d)   Consequently, human rights questions should be examined globally, taking into account both the over-all context of the various societies in which they present themselves, as well as the need for the promotion of the full dignity of the human person and the development and well-being of the society;

(e)   In approaching human rights questions within the United Nations system, the international community should accord, or continue to accord, priority to the search for solutions to the mass and flagrant violations of human rights of peoples and persons affected by situations such as those resulting from *apartheid*, from all forms of racial discrimination, from colonialism, from foreign domination and occupation, from aggression and threats against national sovereignty, national unity and territorial integrity, as well as from the refusal to recognize the fundamental rights of peoples to self-determination and of every nation to the exercise of full sovereignty over its wealth and natural resources;

(f)   The realization of the new international economic order is an essential element for the effective promotion of human rights and fundamental freedoms and should also be accorded priority;

(g)   It is of paramount importance for the promotion of human rights and fundamental freedoms that Member States undertake specific obligations through accession to or ratification of international instruments in this field; consequently, the standard-setting work within the United Nations system in the field of human rights and the universal acceptance and implementation of the relevant international instruments should be encouraged;

(h)   The experience and contribution of both developed and developing countries should be taken into account by all organs of the United Nations system in their work related to human rights and fundamental freedoms.

Other commentators have analysed these provisions from different perspectives and it is not proposed to add yet another interpretation of a resolution, the significance of which is still evolving in the practice of UN organs. Suffice it to say in the present context that:

(i)   the resolution reaffirmed the theoretical indivisibility of the two sets of rights while at the same time seeking to place substantially more emphasis than in the past on economic, social and cultural rights;

(ii)   while its omissions seem to play down the priority to be accorded to responding to situations which do not involve "mass and flagrant violations", its provisions clearly do respond more specifically than had previously been the case to the plight of the masses of humanity living in absolute poverty; and

(iii)   certain provisions (notably sub-paragraphs (d) and (h) go a long way towards countering suggestions that UN human rights standards are *per se* eurocentric and thus not appropriate for much of the world.

The Contribution of the International Commission of Jurists

The need to adopt a balanced preventive approach has long been acknowledged in the work of the ICJ in connexion with the development of the principle of the Rule of Law. Moreover, two ICJ-sponsored seminars, held in 1976 and 1977, contributed significantly to an understanding of some of the concerns which were subsequently to surface within the UN in the context of resolution 32/130. It is appropriate at this point to review briefly the broad thrust of these two seminars and to underline the preventive orientation to which they pointed. The results of two subsequent ICJ seminars on the theme of human rights and development, held in Dakar and Bogota, are considered later in this paper.

Seminar on Human Rights in a One-party State[4]

The first seminar, held in Dar-es-Salaam in September 1976, was devoted to the issue of "human rights in a one-party state". The participants came from Sudan, Tanzania and Zambia, all proclaimed one-party states, as well as from Botswana, Lesotho and Swaziland. At its April 1977 meeting the International Commission of Jurists reviewed

---

4) *Human Rights in a One-Party State*, International Seminar on Human Rights, their Protection and the Rule of Law in a One-Party State, convened by the ICJ (London, Search Press, 1978).

the findings of the seminar and adopted the following conclusions:

The Commission was of the view that there were dangers of abuse of power inherent in one-party systems which were less likely to arise if there existed an effective multi-party system. Human rights could, however, be endangered by ineffective attempts to duplicate multi-party systems without due regard to cultural traditions and the historical development of particular countries.

The Commission was pleased to note the real concern shown by all delegates at the seminar that the rule of law and human rights should be preserved in the countries from which they had come and agreed that the achievement of this goal would be facilitated if the following principles propounded at the seminar were actually observed:

1. Electoral freedom of choice is essential to any democratic form of society. The party should guarantee genuine popular choice among alternative candidates.
2. Everyone should be free to join the party or to abstain from party membership or membership in any other organization without penalty or deprivation of his or her civil rights.
3. The party must maintain effective channels of popular criticism, review, and consultation. The party must be responsive to the people and make it clear to them that this is party policy.
4. In a one-party state it is particularly important that
   (a) the policy-forming bodies of the party utilize all sources of information and advice, and
   (b) that within the party members should be completely free to discuss all aspects of party policy.
5. The independence of the judiciary in the exercise of its judicial functions and its security of tenure is essential to any society which has a respect for the rule of the law. Members of the judiciary at all levels should be free to dispense impartial justice, without fear, in conformity with the rule of law.
6. The independence of the legal profession being essential to the administration of justice, the duty of lawyers to be ready to represent fearlessly any client, however unpopular, should be understood guaranteed. They should enjoy complete immunity for actions taken within the law in defence of their clients.
7. Facilities for speedy legal redress of grievances against admin-

istrative action in both party and government should be readily available to the individual.

8. The absence of an opposition makes it essential to provide mechanisms for continuous, impartial, and independent review and investigation of administrative activities and procedures. In this respect such institutions as the ombudsman and *médiateur* with powers to initiate action can be usefully adopted.

9. In a one-party state, criticism and freedom of access to information should be permitted and encouraged.

10. The right to organize special interest associations such as trade unions, professional, social, religious or other organizations, should be encouraged and protected. Such organizations should be free to affiliate or not with established political parties.

11. All members of the society must be made aware of their human rights to ensure their effective exercise, and for that reason education in human rights at all levels should be a matter of high priority. In particular, officials of the party and government should be made to understand the limits on the exercise of power which derive from the recognition of fundamental human rights and the rule of law.

In a Preface to the report of the Dar-es-Salaam seminar the Commonwealth Secretary-General, Shridath Ramphal, emphasized the importance of appropriate structures for the promotion of human rights. He noted that "there must be a consciousness in the developing world of the need and capacity to accommodate these rights... in the new political structures. If not, it will become all too easy to acquiesce in their denial as an incident of valid structural change".

Seminar on Human Rights and Development[5]

The second seminar, organized together with the Organization of Commonwealth Caribbean Bar Associations, was held in Barbados in September 1977. In his introduction to the report of the seminar, entitled *Human Rights and Development*, the ICJ Secretary-General, Niall MacDermot, indicated that it was one of a proposed series of

---

5) *Human Rights and Development*, Report of a Seminar on Human Rights and their Promotion in the Caribbean, organized by the ICJ and the Organization of Commonwealth Caribbean Bar Associations (Bridgetown, The Cedar Press, 1978).

ICJ regional or sub-regional seminars designed to "study how best to promote human rights in the context of the current structures and problems of neighbouring countries having perhaps a similar background and history and common features in their societies". In its final conclusions and recommendations the Barbados seminar, *inter alia*, affirmed that all fundamental rights and freedoms are whole and inseparable and stressed that the effective realization of economic, social and cultural rights is necessary for the full attainment of civil and political rights. Perhaps more significant in the present context is the fact that the seminar virtually predicted the orientation to be adopted by the UN General Assembly in resolution 32/130 when it recognized in its conclusions "that the full realization of the economic and social rights of the peoples of the region, while primarily dependent on the action of individual governments, will also require radical transformation of international economic and social relations in accordance with the United Nations' Declaration and Programme of Action on the Establishment of the New International Economic Order and Charter of the Economic Rights and Duties of States".

Prospects and Pitfalls of Structuralism

The major advantages of a structural approach appear to be three-fold. First it offers the opportunity to tackle human rights problems on a far broader basis by emphasizing the relevance of human rights to a wide range of previously neglected issues and by facilitating the taking of preventive action before massive problems arise. Secondly, it reflects a number of the changes which have taken place in the international community since the adoption of the Universal Declaration in 1948 and makes possible, but does not ensure, a more effective response to the pressing problems facing the bulk of humanity. Thirdly, it offers the possibility of forging a more effective consensus among the various geopolitical and ideological blocs, thereby improving the prospects for a degree of genuine international cooperation in the pursuit of certain human rights goals. Thus a structural approach, if pursued hand-in-hand with a greater determination to respond effectively and promptly to human rights violations wherever they occur, can be viewed as a potentially major breakthrough. However, it is still too early yet to predict whether or not such a balanced approach will in fact prevail within the UN. Thus, for example, relatively little progress appears to have been made by the Commission on Human Rights under its confidential procedures (notably under Economic and Social Council resolution 1503 of 1970) for responding to "situations which appear to reveal a consistent pattern of gross and reliably attested violations of human rights". More rewarding, perhaps, have been the Commission's activities in connexion with its public consideration of human rights violations. In this regard its actions with respect to Equatorial Guinea, the Central African Empire and Uganda are of particular significance and are noted in Part IV of the present paper.

In addition to, if not always complementary to, these efforts to secure the protection of human rights, a number of important structurally-oriented initiatives have been taken in recent years, including: the initiation of steps towards the codification of the right to development; endorsement of the notion that there exists a right to peace or the right for societies to live in peace; discussion of the concept of a third generation of solidarity rights, and the preparation of studies on subjects such as: the new international economic order and the promotion of human rights; the impact of present international conditions on the realization of human rights; the adverse consequences for the enjoyment of human rights of political, military, economic and other forms of assistance given to colonial and racist regimes in Southern Africa; the impact of foreign economic aid and assistance on respect for human rights in Chile; and the human rights impact of the declaration of states of emergency.

Of the potential pitfalls of the structural approach, two in particular warrant attention. The first is the temptation to pursue it only in connexion with international or 'external' structures, thereby neglecting the equally important dimension of equitable domestic structures which are conducive to the realization of human rights. While the General Assembly has, on two occasions, affirmed that the right to development "is as much a prerogative of nations as of individuals within nations" the elaboration of the structural approach by UN human rights organs has yet to be linked specifically to domestic structural issues such as: the militarization of many societies; the pursuit of economic elitism as a purported remedy for inflation; repression of the participatory rights of individuals and economic and social interest groups; the forced assimilation or cultural destruction of indigenous populations and minority groups; and the maintenance of structures which effectively prevent the realization by large numbers of people of their rights to food, clothing, shelter and health care.

The second potential danger is that the structural approach will become identified with a sweepingly broad, non-legal, economically or sociologically-oriented approach. Its impact then would be to down-play the importance of other, specifically legal, approaches to human rights issues, to move the focus of UN human rights activities away from specifics towards global economic problems, and generally "to disappear into the clouds of a universality that leaves the larger world stranded far below". There is a touch of irony in the fact that, on the one hand an unduly legalistic approach gave rise to the need for a radical departure from existing approaches to the promotion of human rights, while on the other hand the adoption of a preventive approach to human rights serves to emphasize the need not to lose sight of the firm legal foundations of the modern concept of human rights. For without constant reference to the various legal standards that have been painstakingly negotiated, adopted and ratified, we are no further along the road to human dignity that were our ancestors when they theorized about different versions of natural law notions which often reflected little more than abstractions of specific community-bound moral standards.

Future Directions

The emergence of a structural approach to the promotion of respect for human rights has far-reaching implications for the nature and direction of the activities of many groups in the human rights field whether they be non-governmental, governmental or inter-governmental. For those whose primary role is to respond *ex post facto* to specific violations of human rights, the emergence of a structural approach is unlikely to make a great difference. The work of such groups is of enormous value in individual cases and provides an essential complement to the undertaking of initiatives of a structural nature.

However, it is to be regretted that in practice, work focused on specific violations is too often restricted to civil and political rights and even then is directed only at a limited number of those rights rather than at the broader structural rights of political participation. Until this focus is enlarged the experience of many groups is likely to be one of continuing frustration, interspersed by short-lived, even spectacular, successes, but with a limited impact on the overall human rights situation in the longer term. The pursuit of a structurally-oriented approach entails recognition of the reality that human rights problems do not arise in a vacuum and that lasting solutions must be sought through a variety of measures extending across the spectrum of societal activities. The fact is that most torturers are not psychopaths but, in addition to being victims of their own greed and weakness, are instruments of more powerful economic and political forces. Similarly, those whose actions contribute most to the perpetuation of starvation and malnutrition are rarely acting with the express intention of violating the rights of others to food but rather are acting in accordance with inequitable and exploitative social, economic and political structures.

It is of course useful for human rights groups to seek to combat such practices wherever possible but the achievement of more comprehensive, longer term, solutions also requires them to reach out and to seek to foster awareness of human rights issues among a wide range of groups which lie outside their more traditional spheres of influence and action. Until programmes of human rights education are promoted at all levels, until economists, planners and government officials become convinced of the inherent worth of promoting human rights objectives and until religious, development, and other specialist NGO groups are persuaded of the value of promoting respect for human rights in the context of their own activities, many of the efforts made to protect human rights will continue to touch only indirectly, if at all, the wellsprings from which flow the conditions conducive to human rights violations.

PART II

The Relationship Between the Two Sets of Rights:
Civil and Political Rights, and
Economic, Social and Cultural Rights

UN doctrine on this crucial issue is simple and straightforward: "all human rights and fundamental freedoms are indivisible and interdependent; equal attention and urgent consideration should be given to the implementation, promotion and protection of both civil and political, and economic, social and cultural rights". But the practical issues flowing from this doctrine are complex, and ambiguous and inevitably involve conflicting means and goals. Moreover the present practice of the vast majority of states is shewed strongly in favour of one set of rights at the expense of the other. For these reasons there are, as Richard Claude has written, "few problems as difficult to manage satisfactorily in philosophical discourse and legal analysis as that of rights in conflict with other rights".

These many issues of theory and practice warrant much more intensive consideration than they have so far been accorded either within or outside the UN system. In the present brief paper it is proposed only to deal with the historical origins of the dichotomy and the differences between the obligations assumed under each of the two International Covenants and then to offer a rather cryptic critique of the received wisdom on the relationship between the two sets of rights in the hope of stimulating further analysis based on a reconsideration of traditional approaches.

Origins of the dichotomy

Soon after the adoption of the Universal Declaration, in 1948, the question arose as to whether the proposed single Covenant on Human Rights should include economic, social and cultural rights, in addition to civil and political rights. The United States and the United Kingdom were opposed to the inclusion of the former category of rights on the basis that they were inappropriate for judicial enforcement and went beyond the rights contained in existing national constitutions. For entirely different reasons this approach was supported by the largest of the UN's specialized agencies, the International Labour Organisation (ILO). The latter's Governing Body originally expressed the view that economic and social rights should be excluded on the basis that responsibility for their implementation rested primarily with the agencies. The ILO was concerned that any more detailed elaboration, in a general Covenant, of the rights included in the Universal Declaration would inevitably involve overlapping with existing and proposed International Labour Conventions. Once this position became untenable the ILO changed its stance and it played a central role in the drafting of the economic rights provisions. After prolonged debate in the General Assembly it was finally decided, in 1952, to include both categories of rights but to draft two separate covenants. The Commission on Human Rights concluded its work on the drafting of the two covenants in 1954. However, it was not until 1966 that they were adopted by the General Assembly and opened for signature, accession and ratification by states[6].

Obligations assumed under each Covenant

Each of the Covenants imposes a different legal obligation on ratifying states. A state which becomes a party to the International Covenant on Civil and Political Rights (CPR) is under an immediate obligation to comply with its provisions. It undertakes "to respect and to ensure to all individuals within its territory and subject to its jurisdiction the rights recognized in the present Covenant..." By comparison, a state party to the International Covenant on Economic, Social and Cultural Rights (ESCR) "undertakes to take steps, individually and through international assistance and co-operation, especially economic and technical, to the maximum of its available resources, with a view to achieving progressively the full realization of the rights recognised in the present Covenant by all appropriate means, including particularly the adoption of legislative measures".

It is also relevant to note the extent to which limitations on human rights are permitted under the terms of each Covenant. The only limitations to which the rights included in the ESCR Covenant may be subjected are those which:

(i)   are determined by law;
(ii)   are compatible with the nature of these rights; and

---

6) For the drafting history see generally UN doc. A/2929 (1955).

(iii) are solely for the purpose of promoting the general welfare in a democratic society.

Under the CPR Covenant, States Parties may only take measures derogating from their obligations

(i)   in time of public emergency which threatens the life of the nation and the existence of which is officially proclaimed;
(ii)   provided that such measures are not inconsistent with their other obligations under international law;
(iii) do not involve discrimination based solely on the ground of race, colour, sex, language, religion or social origin. (art. 4(1))

It should be noted, however, that under article 4(2) this provision does not permit any derogation from articles 6 (right to life), 7 (right not to be subjected to torture or to cruel, inhuman or degrading treatment or punishment), 8(1) and (2) (right not to be held in slavery or servitude), 11 (right not to be imprisoned merely on the grounds of inability to fulfil a contractual obligation), 15 (right not to be convicted under a retrospective law), 16 (right to recognition everywhere as a person before the law) and 18 (right to freedom of thought, conscience and religion). In addition, the CPR Covenant permits restrictions to be placed on the exercise of certain rights in particular circumstances[7]. Thus, for example, no restrictions may be placed on the exercise of the right of peaceful assembly "other than those imposed in conformity with the law and which are necessary in a democratic society in the interests of national security or public safety, public order *(ordre public)*, the protection of public health or morals or the protection of the rights and freedoms of others" (art. 21).

A critique of the received wisdom

The received wisdom concerning the relationship between the two sets of rights goes something like this.

(1)   Historically, human rights norms emerged in two phases. The first, brought about as a result of the French and American revolutions of the late eighteenth century, produced the concept of civil and political rights. The second was a result of the Mexi-

---

7) See Articles 12, 14(1), 18(3), 19(3), 21 and 22(2).

can and Russian revolutions of the early twentieth century and introduced the notion of economic, social and cultural rights. The differences between the two sets of rights are enormous and are reflected in the following propositions.

(2) whereas ESCR requires positive state action for their realization, CPR require only abstention by the state;

(3) whereas CPR can therefore be fully implemented immediately, the promotion of ESCR depends entirely on the stage of economic development which a particular state has attained;

(4) whereas the context of CPR is clear, the content of the obligations assumed under the ESCR Covenant is vague and indeterminate;

(5) whereas CPR are readily enforceable through the courts ESCR are, with only very minor exceptions, not justiciable; and

(6) the completely different implementation procedures provided for under the two Covenants attest to the totally different nature of the obligations assumed by states.

(7) In general terms then it can be said that ESCR are in fact co-terminous with the broad aspiration to development itself.

(8) In an effort to give immediate effect to human rights guarantees in so far as they relate to the many millions living in absolute poverty it is therefore necessary to give priority to a small core of subsistence or welfare rights.

(9) The notion of the interdependence of rights, along with many of the actual rights formulated in UN instruments, are in fact eurocentric and both the notion and some of the rights are inappropriate to the conditions in many developing countries.

In seeking to refute the main thrust of each of the foregoing nine propositions in the space of a few paragraphs it is inevitable that full justice will not be done either to the arguments of their proponents or to the grounds for refutation. Thus the following analysis is designed to provoke thought rather than to present an authoritative revision of the accepted wisdom

(1) *Historical development*

Relating the two sets of rights to specific historical events is useful for purpose of illustrating some of the forces which supported the emergence of different rights. It is, however, totally inadequate in historical terms since it fails to take account of the philosophical development of natural law and rights concepts dating at least from

Aristotle and the influence of many other historical events, including for example the Magna Carta, the industrial revolution, and a diversity of socialist movements, and tends to observe the dynamic nature of rights theory which is much more in the nature of a continuum than an isolated number of dramatic leaps forward.

(2) *Abstention versus action*

This proposition reflects the historical approach to particular rights rather than present day realities. Thus, in today's world, ensuring the free exercise of civil and political rights will often involve significant State intervention and the incurring of considerable public expenditure in order to establish a system of courts, to train police and other public officials, and to establish a system of safeguards against potential abuses of rights by state officials themselves. Conversely, it is relatively easy to make the case that abstention by the state from certain activities would greatly enhance the prospects for realization of some ESCR such as the right to food and the right to cultural identity.

(3) *Immediate versus progressive*

The implementation of ESCR depends far more, in practice, on the type of development strategy adopted rather than on the stage of economic development achieved. While there is, of course, some validity in the general proposition it requires very careful qualification. For example, a country with a relatively high GNP per capita and thus at an advanced stage of economic development, but which persists in a growth-at-all-costs approach, will not satisfy the ESCR of the poorer segments of the community.

(4) *Precision versus vagueness*

First of all, some CPR are far from precise. Thus the right to participate can either be interpreted in a formalistic way which renders it devoid of all significance or it can be given an expansive interpretation which requires appropriate action on a broad range of fronts. Secondly, some ESCR can be given precision although it is true (and regrettable) that few efforts have yet been made in this regard. Moreover, in particular circumstances, it is often not difficult to give specific content to ESCR guarantees. As the President of the Inter-American Commission on Human Rights, Tom Farer has noted, "there is neither a moral nor practical difference between a government executing innocent people or one which tolerates their death by sickness or starvation when it has the means to obtain the food or health care that could save them".

(5) *Justiciability*

Contrary to the arguments of some commentators, it is submitted that justiciability, in the full traditional sense, is not an indispensable characteristic of human rights. Moreover, a number of ESCR have, in fact, already been made justiciable in certain legal systems.

(6) *Implementation procedures*

While the procedures for implementation are substantially different, this of itself does not diminish the nature of states' obligations to their citizens. It is, however, to be regretted that very little serious effort has been made by the international community to establish a meaningful framework for monitoring states' compliance with their obligations under the ESCR Covenant.

(7) *Development and ESCR are co-terminous*

"Development" is much more than having enough food to eat and water to drink. Any 'progressive' interpretation of the term must include CPR such as the right to association and to participation. Moreover, as noted in point 8 below, the right to food etc. is unlikely to be enjoyed on any sustained basis without political power, protected by respect for political rights.

(8) *Subsistence or welfare rights*

From time to time attempts are made to mobilize international and national action by emphasizing the urgency of at least satisfying 'subsistence', 'existence', 'welfare' or 'absolutely basic' rights. As a device for stimulating action in general terms such an approach has much to offer. As a specific policy it is dangerous and perhaps counter-productive. Even in the event of emergencies, food and other aid for those stricken is frequently siphoned off by powerful elites and used for their own purposes. Examples of such action abound. In times of calm and relative stability such aid is siphoned off or diverted even more readily unless it is accompanied by measures of a structural nature. Attempts to fight poverty by attacking the most obvious symptoms but not the underlying causes are in vain. An attack on poverty in its broadest sense thus requires more than the injection of funds which will bring all individuals up to subsistence level in terms of specific commodities. *Poverty reflects a relationship between people and between socio-economic groups.* Thus, the objective must be seen not merely in terms of feeding, clothing and sheltering each individual today and perhaps tomorrow, but in terms of an endeavour to enable all people to ensure their own well-being in the years to come.

(9) *Eurocentricity*

While this is a complex issue it is submitted that the argument has more validity in relation to the means of implementation which are sometimes proposed than to the rights themselves. The following views of a former Senator from the Philippines are of considerable relevance to the broader issue:

> "Two justifications for authoritarianism in Asian developing countries are currently fashionable.
>
> One is that Asian societies are authoritarian and paternalistic and so need governments that are also authoritarian and paternalistic; that Asia's hungry masses are too concerned with providing their families with food, clothing, and shelter, to concern themselves with civil liberties and political freedoms; that the Asian conception of freedom differs from that of the West; that, in short, Asians are not fit for democracy.
>
> Another is that developing countries must sacrifice freedom temporarily to achieve the rapid economic development that their exploding populations and rising expectations demand; that, in short, government must be authoritarian to promote development.
>
> The first justification is racist nonsense. The second is a lie: authoritarianism is not needed for developing; it is needed to perpe-

tuate the status quo.

Development is not just providing people with adequate food, clothing, and shelter; many prisons do as much. Development is also people deciding what food, clothing and shelter are adequate, and how they are to be provided."[8]

In conclusion three points may be noted. The first is that both in practice and in theory there is a degree of conflict between the two sets of rights[9]. The management of such conflict requires a careful balancing of interests in the light of all prevailing circumstances. Thus attempts to formulate universally applicable solutions to conflict situations are generally doomed to failure. The second is that the concept of ESCR and its implications is at present poorly understood and much work needs to be done if a better appreciation of that set of rights and its relationship to CPR is to emerge in the near future. The third is that many, if not most, of the hard and fast distinctions which are made between one set of rights and the other are of dubious validity or usefulness.

8) Jose W. Diokno, untitled lecture, International Council of Amnesty International, Cambridge, September 21, 1978, pp. 11–12, mimeo.

9) A useful survey of such conflicts is contained in Robert H. Kapp, "Some Preliminary views on the Relationship between Civil and Political Rights and Economic, Social and Cultural Rights in the Context of Development, and on the Right to Development", Geneva, International Commission of Jurists, 1978, mimeo, 21 p.

PART III

Participation in the Development Process

Few rights serve to demonstrate better the indivisibility and interdependence of economic and political rights than the right to participate. Popular participation in the context of economic and social development has been defined in a UN report as "active and meaningful involvement of the masses of people at the different levels in (a) the decision-making process for the determination of societal goals and the allocation of resources to achieve them; and (b) the voluntary execution of resulting programmes and projects"[10]. By way of illustration, participation as an essential element of a basic needs approach to development has been said to contribute in the following ways:

(i)   by playing a part in the definition of basic needs;
(ii) by enhancing the generation of resources to meet basic needs;
(iii) by improving the distribution of goods and services; and
(iv) by satisfying the psychological desire to participate in decisions which affect peoples lives[11].

In recent years a considerable amount of effort has been devoted to defining and elaborating concepts of participation, while rather less work has been done on the concrete issues that are involved in operationalizing the concept. It is a fact that traditional development strategies have either ignored the need for popular participation in decision-making or have heavily discounted it in practice. This is a function both of the inconvenience of involving local populations in the planning process and of the belief of many development planners and officials that their client populations are neither able to diagnose their own problems nor to formulate the corresponding needs.

The link between human rights and participation has long been recognized. As Fromm has written:

---

10) *Popular Participation in Decision-Making for Development* (UN Sales No. E.75.IV.10 (1975)), p. 4.

11) Donald Curtis *et al, Popular Participation in Decision-Making and the Basic Needs Approach to Development: Methods, Issues and Experiences*, WEP Working Paper (WEP 2-32/WP 12) (Geneva, ILO, 1978), p. 1.

"The only criterion for the realization of freedom is whether or not the individual actively participates in determining his life and that of society, and this not only by the formal act of voting but in his daily activity, in his work and in his relations to others."

This link was also given prominence in the report of the ILO Director General to the World Employment Conference:

"A basic-needs oriented policy implies the participation of the people in making the decisions which affect them... The satisfaction of an absolute level of basic needs as so defined should be placed within a broader framework — namely the fulfilment of basic human rights, which are not only ends in themselves but also contribute to the attainment of other goals."[12]

In the same vein, the Unesco General Conference in 1980 recognized that participation should be "regarded both as a human right and as a means for the exercise of human rights."[13]

These two dimensions are best illustrated by a brief review of the provisions of the International Human Rights Covenants. As a human right, *per se*, participation is acknowledged in the International Covenant on Civil and Political Rights in the form of guarantees of the rights to freedom of thought, conscience and religion (art. 18), to hold opinions (art. 19(1)), to freedom of expression (art. 19(2)), to peaceful assembly (art. 21), to freedom of association (art. 22) and, most significantly, "to take part in the conduct of public affairs, directly or through freely chosen representatives" and "to vote and to be elected at genuine periodic elections" which freely express the will of the electors (art. 25). In the International Covenant on Economic, Social and Cultural Rights the right to participate is included *per se* in the right to education (in art. 13(1) States "agree that education shall enable all persons to participate effectively in a free society") and in the rights to take part in cultural life and to enjoy the benefits of scientific progress (art. 15).

As a means for the exercise of human rights participation is of fundamental importance. It is possible to demonstrate a strong and direct link between participation and the enjoyment of almost any particu-

---

12) ILO, *Employment, Growth and Basic Needs: A One-World Problem* (Geneva, ILO, 1976), p. 32.
13) Resolution 3/01.3, para. (e) (1980).

lar right. For example, unless an individual in an agricultural society is able to participate effectively in the shaping of the structures which govern the production, processing and distribution of food within his local community he is unlikely to be assured of the realization of his right to food. Thus participation is an economic as much as a social and political right.

The relationship between the suppression of political participation and the non-realization of economic and social rights was recognized by the Inter-American Commission on Human Rights in its 1980 report. The approach adopted by the Commission is a significant departure from its previous practice and is worth quoting at length, particularly in view of the prevailing situation in many Latin American states, and the use which is made of the problem of terrorism.

"When examining the situation of human rights in the various countries, the Commission has had to establish the organic relationship between the violation of the rights to physical safety on the one hand, and neglect of economic and social rights and suppression of political participation, on the other. That relationship, as has been shown, is in large measure one of cause and effect. In other words, neglect of economic and social rights, especially when political participation has been suppressed, produces the kind of social polarization that then leads to acts of terrorism by and against the government.

The right to political participation leaves room for a wide variety of forms of government; there are many constitutional alternatives as regards the degree of centralization of the powers of the state or the election and attributes of the organs responsible for the exercise of those powers. However, a democratic framework is an essential element for establishment of a political society where human values can be fully realized. The right to political participation makes possible the right to organize parties and political associations, which through open discussion and ideological struggle, can improve the social level and economic circumstances of the masses and prevent a monopoly on power by any one group or individual. At the same time it can be said that democracy is a unifying link among the nations of this hemisphere."[14]

Since the present paper cannot even pretend to deal adequately with

---

14) OAS doc. OEA/Ser. G, CP/doc. 1110/80 (1980), p, 149.

the many issues of interpretation and application to which the concept of participation gives rise, it is proposed to develop two further points. The first relates to the superfluousness of participation under benign dictatorship and the second to participation and the rule of law.

Participation and benign dictators

In discussions about participation, reference is often made, explicitly or implicitly, to the possibility of having a truly benign dictator who acts constantly in the best interests of his people, but who brooks no opposition to his quest for equity. In such circumstances the right to participate, at least in its political dimension, is clearly the first right to suffer. Nevertheless, it is sometimes suggested that such a situation might not be "all that bad". But in practice the image of a benevolent dictator is a false one, for three major reasons. The first is illustrated by the application of Lord Acton's dictum that power corrupts and absolute power corrupts absolutely. Thus, even enlightened dictators soon become unenlightened. The second is that the right to participate cannot be suppressed in isolation — its effective suppression inevitably requires the violation of a range of other rights as well. The third is that even the most enlightened dictator cannot guarantee that the minimum subsistence rights of each individual are ensured.

Participation and the Rule of Law

There is a strong correlation between participation and effective enjoyment of the Rule of Law. In the absence of the right to participate in the formulation of laws and in the design and administration of structures to implement them, the Rule of Law becomes, at least in practice if not in terms of pure theory, a fraudulent concept. The classic example of this is the South African system in which the Rule of Law is vigorously promoted but is at the same time used to preserve and strengthen the structures which are directly responsible for the denial of the rights of the majority of the population, which plays no part either in the framing of the laws or in the choice of legal structures. While South Africa is an extreme example, the point deserves to be emphasized in general terms because of the potential dangers in any field in which the dominance of experts or professionals, be they lawyers, economists or others, reduces participatory mechanisms to the level of mere formalities. The challenge then for jurists is to devise means by which to ensure that laws and legal procedures reflect and facilitate full and effective participation by all those affected.

PART IV

Agrarian Reform, Labour Legislation and Legal Resources for the Rural and Urban Poor

In recent years the central importance of agrarian reform for the solution of problems of landlessness, poverty and unemployment has gained growing recognition. The present paper does not attempt to provide an outline of recent initiatives in this field. Rather the nature and scope of some of the issues is illustrated by reference to the principal conclusions and recommendations of the 1979 seminar on Human Rights in the Rural Areas of the Andes Region which was sponsored by the International Commission of Jurists and the Latin American Council for Law and Development.

The seminar addressed six major themes[15].

(1) Agrarian reform

Agrarian reform as a goal has been abandoned throughout the Andean region. Peasants and indians are being openly deprived of

---

15) *Derechos Humanos en las Zonas Rurales*, Bogota, Sociedad Ediciones Internacionales S.R.L., 1979, 306 p.

their lands, while their organisations and trade unions face a system of repression.

Agrarian reform should include not only a change in the pattern of land tenure, but also technical assistance, credit and basic services. It should be accompanied by freedom of association and allow for peasant participation in the discussion and implementation of land reform policies.

It was concluded that full observance of human rights in rural areas would be achieved only following the structural transformation of Andean societies.

(2) Labour legislation and trade union rights

The relatively progressive labour laws within the Andean region are not being implemented by governments. This is an effect of the restrictions imposed by the socio-economic system on popular peasant movements. Until the 1960's, any organising effort met with repression. Peasant movements were first recognized when an attempt at social reform was made in the 1960's. After a few years, increasingly authoritarian regimes — both civilian and military — reversed the reformist trend and crushed campesinos organisations. The goal of economic growth has replaced social policies. Land-owners and employers are using the armed forces to preserve the structures of social and political privilege.

If rural labour unions deviate from the apolitical, conformist line accepted by governments, they are accused of political subversion. Trade unions should defend the rights of all rural workers, including migrants, occasional and seasonal workers. ILO conventions on the right of association, the right to organise, on collective bargaining and rural workers organisations (conventions 11, 87, 98 and 141) are purposely not ratified or otherwise violated.

(3) Rights of indigenous populations

The right of indigenous populations to their ancestral lands is not protected. There is no freedom of association for indigenous groups. Indian leaders are victims of abuse and repression. Forced integration into "western" or "national" societies is destroying indigenous cultures. Education does not reflect the actual interests and needs of indigenous populations. The right to health is not guaranteed. Social security is insufficient and subject to political manipulation. Indigenous medicine is not recognized and sometimes it is even forcibly suppressed.

Religious institutions are having an increasingly negative influence on the way of life of indigenous groups, sometimes with the aid or support of governments. The exploitation of natural resources in tropical forests is destroying the environment where indigenous populations live and work. The respect for human rights depends on the capacity of indigenous peoples to fight for their rights and on their effective participation in the political process.

(4) Agricultural and economic policies

Agricultural policies are part of global development strategies that work against the interests of peasants. These strategies involve an increasing restriction of human rights in the region.

Current agricultural policies contain these elements:

— concentration of land ownership, with the result that the problem of access to the land for peasants has not been solved;
— absence of a food production policy, caused in part by the emphasis placed on crops for export or for industrial use;
— increasing presence of multinational corporations;
— unjust allocation of productive resources in the rural areas;
— lack of participation by peasants in agricultural policies;
— violent infringement of human rights in the rural areas.

The seminar recommended that:

— access to the land be guaranteed;
— priority be given to food crops;
— a fair prices policy for food crops should be adopted;
— freedom of association and other democratic rights should be enforced;
— peasant participation in making agricultural policy should be assured.

(5) Agrarian justice and access to legal services

The seminar stressed the importance of an autonomous system of agrarian courts to protect actively the rights of peasants in agrarian conflicts. The reversal of agrarian reform policies has resulted in limitations on the autonomy of agrarian judges and obstructive tactics in cases filed to protect peasants' rights.

The legal forum is not the only one where agrarian conflicts are discussed and resolved. Serious conflicts are also resolved through the use of force, political domination or deception. Consequently the creation of effective political and peasant organisations is by far the most urgent and important method of securing peasant rights. Lawyers can, however, make a useful contributionto their struggle by providing them with legal services.

A lawyer's training does not give him an understanding of social conflicts that affect the campesinos, thus making relations with lawyers difficult. Also, unethical and disloyal practices on the part of some lawyers have worsened these relations. Access to adequate defence services and the inviolability of defence rights should be supported by effective constitutional guarantees.

(6) Social services in the rural areas

Social security and social services for rural workers are incompatible with national security laws and capitalist economic systems established by force in some countries of the region.

Social services, including housing, health care and education, are generally lacking, or improvised, or subject to political and official manipulation.

PART V

Human Rights and the Formulation and Application of Development Policies Some Brief Observations on Human Rights and Development

The assumption that "development" is co-terminous with economic growth as measured in terms of an increase in the gross national product is now too discredited to warrant elaborate refutation. Thus the International Development Strategy adopted by the UN General Assembly in 1980 states that "the ultimate aim of development is the constant improvement of the well-being of the entire population on the basis of its full participation in the process of development and a fair distribution of the benefits therefrom". Nevertheless, it is instructive to review briefly the historical and institutional process by which the interpretation of "development" moved from macro-economic growth to human development. Within the setting of the UN, human rights and development issues began from the same starting point. Post-war economists were strongly aware of the broader social and cultural implications of their work and were concerned with a range of objectives which was considerably wider than growth *per se*. Similarly, the human rights activists of the UN manifested a breadth of scope which resulted in the incorporation, on a more or less equal footing, of economic, social, cultural, civil and political rights in the Universal Declaration of Human Rights of 1948. However, this auspicious debut was soon spoilt by the substantial narrowing of these two streams of endeavour, which by the mid-1950s were flowing in parallel courses with one isolated almost entirely from the other. Growth came to dominate development thinking, and concern with civil and political rights issues came to dominate human rights endeavours. It was not until the late 1970s that tributaries started to flow, albeit hesitantly, from one stream to the other. Today the process of reunification is only just beginning and all too often it is occurring with little appreciation of the communality of interest that should inform and motivate it.

The Trade-off Beween Equity and Growth

At the risk of unjustly offending a handful of enlightened economists, it can confidently be stated that the dominant strand of economic thought still assumes, either explicitly or implicitly, that in the short term it is impossible to reconcile the *need* for growth with the *aspiration* for equity. Thus the goal of growth is accorded precedence, with the proviso that "full account must be taken" of promoting equity "in the longer term". The problem is that the longer term never eventuates and, in the continuing short term, various elites move to consolidate their power and wealth. There are, nevertheless, encouraging signs that some economists are becoming more sensitive to issues of equity and justice both in terms of these objectives' specific economic impact and of their broader significance as the ultimate goals of development. (Ironically, these signs are now coming at a time when British, American and other national governments are moving rapidly to a position in which the revival of economic growth is an over-riding priority goal which must, in part, be achieved through large-scale transfers of funds from the poor to the rich).

Many volumes have already been written about the growth versus equity debate. In the present paper it is possible only to point to a few of the approaches that have been put forward. Thus, for example, in one recent attempt to fight economists on their own ground, the following arguments were singled out for refutation from a human rights perspective:[16]

1. Economic rights directly, and political rights indirectly, tend to shift resources from more to less well-off members of the community. The less well-off have a higher propensity to consume than do the more well-off individuals. Therefore, shifting resources from the more to the less well-off individuals reduces savings, investment, and aggregate capital accumulation generally in the community. Capital accumulation contributes importantly to economic growth. Therefore, economic and political rights hamper economic growth.
2. Certain social rights must be restricted in order to curb population growth, which is everywhere a great threat to economic development.
3. Electoral pressures force rulers to introduce periodic distorsions into the economy, heating it up for the election and cooling it off afterwards. Electoral competition, and political rights more

---

16) Robert E. Goodin, "The Development-Rights Trade-Off: Some Unwarranted Economic and Political Assumptions", *Universal Human Rights*. Vol. 1 (1979), pp. 31–42.

generally, must be curtailed to eliminate such distortions.

4. Resources are diverted from their most productive use in consequence of local pressures on politicians for public works projects in their home constituencies. By curtailing political rights these pressures and the consequent distortions could be eliminated.
5. Labour unrest significantly slows economic growth. Curtailing the freedom of workers to associate through trade unions can therefore reduce economically harmful union agitation.
6. The constant threat of criminal violence introduces uncertainties which discourage investors as well as demoralise workers, thereby reducing labour productivity. Limiting civil liberties can help reduce the crime rate and its economic costs.
7. Political instability discourages foreign investment, which is crucial to a developing economy. Instability can be reduced by curtailing political rights and the competitive democracy their free exercise produces.

A United Nations' report on "aspects of social development in the 1980s", after reviewing some of the data on income distribution and related issues, discerned the following "practical principles" which could guide policy in the present decade:[17] (1) Many social injustices, cumulatively oppressive, could be avoided without prejudice to economic efficiency; (2) Experience suggests that many ideals and measures that are consonant with the promotion of greater equity and social justice are also generally favourable to economic efficiency and expansion; (3) The production and distribution of public services remains an essential instrument to promote more equity, in spite of its as yet limited role in most developing countries; (4) Income inequality differs from country to country, and certainly among developing countries. Each country's circumstances are unique, and social justice, in income distribution as in other areas, can be pursued most effectively in the context of the country's over-all circumstances and priorities; but this is not to say that quite radical changes may not be possible; (5) A growing emphasis is to be expected in lower-income countries on policies seeking to promote equity through economic improvement for broad groups of the population, such as industrial workers and farmers, as opposed to a concern for individual welfare, especially in favour of the weak; (6) There is the ever present danger that economic setbacks can strain beyond breaking point the tensions already found in a society undergoing rapid growth and social change. Ingrained in rapid growth is a potential for undermining

---

17) UN doc. E/cN.5/585 (1981).

social consensus and social cohesion.

Finally, it is appropriate to note the importance of the approach advocated in the World Bank's *World Development Report 1980.*[18] The Report begins by acknowledging that human development is an end as well as a means of economic progress. While it goes on to state that the solution to poverty in poor countries is economic growth:

> "Whether absolute poverty is measured by low income, low life expectancy or illiteracy, there is a strong correlation between the extent of poverty in a country and its GNP per person."

However, the report offers the following qualifications to its growth advocacy. First it concedes that the correlation between the extent of absolute poverty and the level of GNP per person in different countries is far from perfect. Second, looking at changes over time within particular countries, the connection between growth and poverty reduction over periods of a decade or two appears inexact. Third, the report notes that "the connection between economic growth and poverty reduction goes both ways. Few would dispute that the health, education and well-being of the mass of people in industrialized countries are a cause, as well as a result, of national prosperity. Similarly, people who are unskilled and sick make little contribution to a country's economic growth. Development strategies that bypass large numbers of people may not be the most effective way for developing countries to raise their long-run growth rates." The relevant section of the Report concludes by stressing the contribution (over long periods) of social, political and cultural factors to the poverty of particular countries and groups.

The significance of this approach lies more in the source of its advocacy than in its novelty or insight. The World Bank has long been criticized for being oblivious to human rights concerns and has responded mainly by arguing that its Articles of Agreement prevent it from considering the human rights implications of its loan operations. It has, however, left the door open far enough to permit itself to take account of various issues insofar as they have direct economic consequences. The logical corollary of its human resource development approach is that policies of oppression should be considered to be clearly incompatible with development programmes. While it would be naive to expect the Bank to openly embrace this corollary,

---

18) Washington D.C., World Bank, 1980, pp. 32–82.

_ _ _ be hoped that its logic might come to receive stronger implicit acknowledgement. At the same time it must be said that the Bank's approach is not primarily, if at all, inspired by the ethical imperative to take account of the human factor or by the legal or normal weight of international human rights standards, but by the fact that its economists are now convinced that economic efficiency can be increased by doing so.

In general terms all that may be concluded from this brief survey is that attempts to produce clear-cut empirical evidence in favour of either a growth or an equity orientation are virtually assured of failure. There are no easy answers and in the last resort it is possible to say only that while each State is free to choose its own path of development, it must do so in full recognition of its human rights obligations.

Development and the Rule of Law

The present paper is primarily devoted to the promotion of human rights, and the role of lawyers therein, at the international level. Yet this emphasis must not be permitted to obscure the fact that in the vast majority of cases international efforts can do no more than complement national endeavours: (1) by helping to remove some of the external constraints which limit possibilities for, and the scope of, internal reforms; and (2) by presenting an external, and ideally objective, frame of reference against which internal efforts may be judged. The central role of the *Rule of Law* is noted in the Preamble to the Universal Declaration of Human Rights which states that "it is essential, if man is not to be compelled to have recourse, as a last resort, to rebellion against tyranny and oppression, that human rights should be protected by the Rule of Law". As Sir Hersch Lauterpacht wrote in 1950, only two years after the adoption of the Universal Declaration, "preoccupation with the enforcement of the Bill of Rights ought not to conceal the fact that the most effective way of giving reality to it is through the normal activity of national courts and other organs applying the law of the land."[19] While this prescription is primarily aimed at the enforcement of civil and political rights it can readily be expanded to encompass the implementation of economic, social and cultural rights through national and local institutions. Thus it must be emphasized that, just as true development can

---

19) *International Law and Human Rights* (London, Stevens and Son, 1950), p. 356.

only be achieved from within each society, so too can the realization of human rights. No amount of international pressure and no number of international development or other assistance programmes can serve to promote or protect human rights unless the community itself is convinced of their importance and is prepared to assert and defend them. As Julius Nyerere stated in 1962, "The ultimate safeguard of a people's rights, the people's freedom, and all those things which they value... is the ethic of the nation... The ultimate safeguard is the people's ability to say 'no' to the official, the ability to say to him: 'no you cannot do that, that is un-Tanganyikan and we cannot accept it from anybody'."[20]

Nevertheless, international efforts to promote awareness of human rights issues can play an important role in developing people's awareness of their rights and in mobilizing them for action. Thus, in his book on the social bases of obedience and revolt, Barrington Moore surveyed a variety of cases in which people have shown a degree of tolerance in situations of oppression and concluded that "people are evidently inclined to grant legitimacy to anything that is or seems inevitable no matter how painful it may be... The conquest of this sense of inevitability is essential to the development of politically effective moral outrage. For this to happen, people must perceive and define their situation as the consequence of human injustice: a situation that they need not, cannot and ought not to endure".[21] Yet the development and expression of this moral outrage is suppressed by constant national and international propagation of theories of economic development which take the view that "transitional" suffering is unavoidable if the goal of "development" is to be achieved. (There is usually a similar psychology involved in the declaration of states of siege or emergency.) Thus, international human rights standards, by presenting an objective frame of reference for defining justice versus injustice, can thus serve to stimulate a sense of injustice and the consequent outrage which can lead people to assert the obligation of others to respect their rights. This role for international standards is strengthened by the process of ratification of instruments by States and the subsequent widespread dissemination of the relevant texts.

In general terms, respect for the Rule of Law in accordance with international human rights standards can play an important role in har-

---

20) Quoted in *Human Rights in a One-Party State*, op.cit., pp. 28—29.

21) Barrington Moore, Jr., *Injustice: The Social Bases of Obedience and Revolt* (London, Macmillan, 1978), p. 459.

nessing the energy and turbulence which is inevitably generated both by emphasis on the need to respect human rights and by a range of development initiatives such as land reform, income redistribution schemes and the promotion of broader popular participation.

The work of the International Commission of Jurists since the early 1950s has recognized the value of this approach, first of all by seeking to define and develop an appreciation of the requirements of the Rule of Law, secondly by relating that concept to the provisions of the major international instruments which lay down the accepted standards for the application of the Rule of Law and the protection of human rights and thirdly, by emphasizing the role of lawyers in promoting respect for the Rule of Law. In this respect, it is appropriate to recall the following principles, relating to "the role of lawyers in a changing world", contained in *The Rule of Law and Human Rights: Principles and Definition*[22]:

"1. In a changing and interdependent world, lawyers should give guidance and leadership in the creation of new legal concepts, institutions and techniques to enable man to meet the challenge and the dangers of the times and to realize the aspirations of all people.
   The lawyer today should not content himself with the conduct of his practice and the administration of justice. He cannot remain a stranger to important developments in economic and social affairs if he is to fulfil his vocation as a lawyer: he should take an active part in the process of change. He will do this by inspiring and promoting economic development and social justice. The skill and knowledge of lawyers are not to be employed solely for the benefits of clients, but should be regarded as held in trust for society.
2. It is the duty of lawyers in every country, both in the conduct of their practice and in public life, to help ensure the existence of a responsible legislature elected by democratic process and an independent, adequately remunerated judiciary, and to be always vigilant in the protection of civil liberties and human rights.
3. Lawyers should refuse to collaborate with any authority in any action which violates the Rule of Law.
4. Lawyers should be anxiously concerned with the prevalance of poverty, ignorance and inequality in human society and should take a leading part in promoting measures which will help eradi-

---

22) Geneva, International Commission of Jurists, 1966, pp. 34—35.

cate those evils, for while they continue to exist, civil and political rights cannot of themselves ensure the full dignity of man.

5. Lawyers have a duty to be active in law reform. Especially where public understanding is slight and the knowledge of lawyers is of importance, they should review proposed legislation and present to the appropriate authorities programmes of reform.

6. Lawyers should endeavour to promote knowledge of and to inspire respect for the Rule of Law, and an appreciation by all people of their rights under the law.

. . . . . .

12. In an interdependent world, the lawyer's responsibilities extend beyond national boundaries. They require his deep concern for peace, and support for the principles of the United Nations and the strengthening and development of international law and organizations..."

Human Rights and National Development Plans

At the national as much as at the international level the most significant innovation in development planning in the late 1970s was the emphasis placed upon meeting basic needs.

In June 1976 the ILO World Employment Conference proclaimed as a fundamental principle that

"Strategies and national development plans should include explicitly as a priority objective the promotion of employment and the satisfaction of the basic needs of each country's population."

Basic needs were defined as including, first, certain minimum requirements of a family for private consumption: adequate food, shelter and clothing, as well as certain household equipment and furniture; and, second, essential services provided for and by the community at large, such as safe drinking water, sanitation, public transport and health, educationl and cultural facilities. "A basic needs-oriented strategy", the Conference emphasized, "implies the participation of the people in making the decisions which affect them through organizations of their own choice."[23]

---

23) ILO, *Meeting Basic Needs: Strategies for Eradicating Mass Poverty and Unemployment* (Geneva, ILO, 1977).

A number of the international agencies, including notably the World Bank, also endorsed this general concept. But while different versions of the basic needs approach were proliferating at a fast rate many developing countries began to express concern that the slogan of basic needs was being used: to distract attention from NIEO issues; to play down the importance of promoting economic growth in the Third World; and to facilitate unwarranted and unwelcome interference in the domestic affairs of developing countries. Since these allegations were far from being unfounded, one of the effects of Third World opposition to the concept was to give it a much lower profile internationally.

It is therefore somewhat paradoxical that the international suppression of debate on the basic needs concept was not paralleled at the national level. On the contrary, a survey of recently adopted national development plans indicates that basic needs and/or similar objectives have been accorded consistently high priority. The paradox is well-illustrated by the case of India. In 1978, India indicated to the UN General Assembly that it was "strongly against any attempt to direct the attention of the international community to alternative approaches to development cooperation, such as the basic needs approach".[24] Yet at the same time the Indian Planning Commission adopted a new Draft Five Year Plan for 1978—83 which listed three principal objectives: the removal of unemployment and underemployment; a rise in the standard of living of the poor; and action by the State to meet certain "basic needs" such as drinking water, literacy, elementary education, health care, rural roads, rural housing and minimum services in urban slums.[25]

However, the incorporation of basic needs goals into national development plans does not necessarily amount to the promotion of human rights. In the first place, it is clear that rhetoric embodied in development plans does not *per se* constitute a serious commitment, let alone ensure the implementation of the stated objectives. Secondly, and more importantly from the present perspective, most basic needs lists are confined in practice to 'material' needs such as food, clothing, shelter and health care. It is true that studies of the concept of basic needs undertaken by UN agencies usually include certain nonmaterial needs, notably participation, but in practice such aspects

---

24) UN doc. A/AC.191/21 (1978), p. 4.
25) Government of India, Planning Commission, *Draft Five Year Plan 1978—83*, Vol. 1, p. 8.

have been neglected if not entirely ignored.[26] Thus the espousal of a basic needs goal needs to be complemented by a commitment to the promotion of respect for human rights in the broad sense which extends well beyond the satisfaction of a minimum level of certain economic rights.

As noted in Part I of this paper, such a commitment must take account not only of the need to respond to specific rights violations but of the need to change those structures which give rise to and perpetuate such violations. This may be exemplified by reference to the right to food which is presently denied to hundreds of millions of people. It is clear that the problem of world hunger derives not from the inadequacy of world food supplies but from the existence of a grossly unequal distribution of purchasing power and control over productive assets, of massive rural and urban unemployment, of discrimination against various minority and indigenous groups, of the failure of land reform programmes, and of international factors which may introduce a variety of distortions and frustrate the achievement of local and national food self-reliance.

Human Rights and International Development Planning

This section is divided into four parts: (1) human rights and international development strategies; (2) human rights and development cooperation; (3) a structural approach to human rights in international relations and, (4) a case study of the preventive approach in action.

(1) *Human rights and international development strategies*

The major policy instrument in UN development planning has become the strategy for the UN Development Decade. To date three such strategies have been adopted by the UN General Assembly, the last two of which were preceded by prolonged and detailed negotiations. The strategy for the first development decade (DD1) was adopted in 1961, DD2 in 1970, and DD3 in December 1980.[27]

---

26) See Philip Alston, "Human Rights and Basic Needs: A Critical Assessment", *Revue des droits de l'homme*, Vol. XII, 1979, pp. 19–67.

27) DD1 was adopted by the General Assembly in resolution 1710 (XVI) (1961), DD2 in resolution 2626 (XXV) (1970) and DD3 in resolution 35/56 (1980).

Prior to the adoption of DD1, a comprehensive report on UN development activities, prepared by the Committee on Programme Apraisals, strongly emphasized the human rights and development link:

"One of the greatest dangers in development policy lies in the tendency to give to the more material aspects of growth an overriding and disproportionate emphasis. The end may be forgotten in preoccupation with the means. Human rights may be submerged, and human beings seen only as instruments of production rather than as free entities for whose welfare and cultural advance the increased production is intended. The recognition of this issue has a profound bearing upon the formulation of the objectives of economic development and the methods employed in attaining them. Even where there is recognition of the fact that the end of all economic development is a social objective, i.e. the growth and well-being of the individual in larger freedom, methods of development may be used which are a denial of basic human rights."[28]

Nevertheless, the strategy for DD1, adopted in the following year, was concerned only with increasing the rate of economic growth in order to expedite 'the economic and social development of the economically less-developed countries'. Apart from a passing preambular reference to the Charter's objective of promoting 'social progress and better standards of life in larger freedom' the strategy made no reference at all to general social objectives, let alone to the promotion of human rights in the development process. The latter concern was taken care of, symbolically at least, in 1965 when the General Assembly adopted a general resolution recognizing the need to devote special attention, on both the national and international levels, to the promotion of respect for human rights within the context of the Development Decade.

The adoption of the strategy for DD2 was preceded by the International Conference on Human Rights in Teheran in 1968 which, in a resolution of major significance, linked the realization of human rights to "economic development" at the national level and to the "collective responsibility of the international community".[29] In the following year: (a) the Commission on Human Rights adopted a resolution affirming that the universal enjoyment of human rights "depends to a very large degree on the rapid economic and social devel-

28) UN doc. E/3347/Rev. 1 (1960), para 90.
29) UN Sales No. E.68.XIV.2 (1968), resolution XVII.

opment of the developing countries"[30], (b) a Meeting of Experts on Social Policy and Planning, held in Stockholm, produced a lengthy report on the theme that "the economic approach to development analysis and planning had to be integrated with a social approach that was different in nature and would be more relevant to the problems of developing countries in the coming decade"[31], and (c) the General Assembly proclaimed the Declaration on Social Progress and Development which links human rights and development issues more explicitly and at greater length than any other UN instrument. Article 2 of the Declaration, for example, provides that "social progress and development shall be founded on respect for the dignity and value of the human person and shall ensure the promotion of human rights and social justice..."[32].

Despite this lead-up, the strategy for DD2 did not refer at any point to the concept of human rights although heed was paid to some social development issues by acknowledging the need to "bring about a more equitable distribution of income and wealth for promoting social justice and efficiency of production..." But such references to social justice and equity were interpreted narrowly to imply a more equitable distribution of goods and services to meet basic human needs. The vagueness of the DD2 strategy in human rights-related spheres stood in sharp contrast to the specific targets for economic growth and financial resource transfers and the statement of policy measures to be taken in the realm of international trade. Promotion of the enjoyment of civil and political human rights remained an extraneous element and, in some respects, the new approach amounted to little more than a grudging technocratic recognition of the effectiveness of broader-based development efforts unhampered by the discontent and non-productivity of the poverty-stricken masses.

During the 1970s, the General Assembly adopted a number of resolutions relating to DD2 in which note was taken of international obstacles to development including foreign aggression and occupation, *apartheid*, racial discrimination and colonial and neo-colonial domination. In 1979 a UN report suggested "that promotion of respect for human rights in general, including the human right to development, should be prominent among the states' objectives of a new

---

30) Resolution 15 (XXV) (1969).

31) UN, *International Social Development Review*, Vol 3, 1971, pp. 4—14.

32) Resolution 2542 (XXIV) (1969).

international development strategy".[33] In the following year, the Commission on Human Rights invited the Preparatory Committee for DD3 "to pay due attention to the integration of human rights in the development process".[34] The suggestion was reiterated by a UN human rights seminar in July 1980.[35]

In development terms, DD3 has been distinguished from DD2 on the grounds that it emphasizes the need for structural change at all levels, whereas DD2 had adopted only a mildly reformist approach. Nevertheless, among its nearly 20,000 words, DD3 does not number the two words "human rights". However, the final seven of the 117 paragraphs dealing with the specific policy measures to be taken, relate to social development.

Thus, neither DD1, nor DD2, nor DD3, contain any specific mention of the concept of human rights.

(2) *Human Rights and Development Cooperation*

The relationship between development cooperation and human rights has been considered by the principal specialist human rights organs of the UN — the Commission on Human Rights and its Sub-Commission — in three separate contexts. In two of these, relating to the provision of assistance to the white minority government in South Africa and to the present régime in Chile, the emphasis has been upon the consideration of trade and other economic sanctions. In the third context, the Commission, in the course of discussions on the right to development, placed on records its wariness of the concept of linking trade and human rights.

(i) *South Africa*

The racial policies of South Africa have been under discussion in the United Nations since 1946, when India complained that South Africa had enacted legislation against South Africans of Indian origin. The broader question of the system *apartheid* was first discussed by the General Assembly in 1952. Since that time the General Assembly has adopted a large number of resolutions,

---

33) UN Doc E/CN.4/1334 (1979), para 303.

34) Resolution 7 (XXXVI) (1980).

35) UN doc. ST/HR/SER.A/8 (1980).

many of which urge the cessation of all forms of economic collaboration, including trade.

The question of trade with South Africa has been subjected to more detailed scrutiny by the Human Rights Sub-Commission which, in 1974, appointed a Special Rapporteur to prepare a report on "the adverse consequences for the enjoyment of human rights of political, military, economic and other forms of assistance given to colonial and racist regimes in Southern Africa". The resulting report thoroughly documents the extent of foreign trade and assistance with South Africa, as well as with Namibia and Southern Rhodesia, and notes the network of repression by which the policy of *apartheid* is enforced. The report notes that "far from exerting leverage for changed policies, foreign funds are building up South Africa's economy so that it will be better able to resist any challenge to *apartheid* from the international community" and concludes that "a mandatory arms embargo, a complete withdrawal of economic interests and the severing of economic relationships are the minimum pressures required to bring about drastic change".[36]

(ii) *Chile*

In the overall context of UN action in response to the gross violations of human rights in Chile which followed the overthrow of the Allende government in 1973 no explicit reference was made by either the Commission on Human Rights or the General Assembly to the question of cutting off trade or other economic links with the Chilean government. However, the resolution adopted by the Assembly in 1976 left open the possibility of unilateral action of this nature. In 1977 in response to a suggestion by the General Assembly, the Sub-Commission appointed an Italian professor, Antonio Cassese, as its Rapporteur to prepare a "study of the impact of foreign economic aid and assistance on respect for human rights in Chile". In interpreting this mandate the Rapporteur concluded that it called for a comprehensive discussion of all foreign investments in Chile.

In his final report, the Rapporteur concluded that the gross violations of human rights were related to economic assistance in two

---

36) UN Sales No. E.79.XIV.3.

respects.[37] The first "is that the bulk of this assistance helps to strengthen and maintain in power a system which pursues a policy of large-scale violations of these rights". The second is that in order to obtain foreign assistance including investment "creditworthiness" must be achieved. This is achieved by a redistribution of income in favour of the rich and is helped by the availability of cheap labour encouraged to work by low levels of social welfare and widespread poverty. For a variety of reasons, the response to the report by governments and others concerned was highly unfavourable and very little action was taken on the basis of its recommendations.

(iii) *The Right to Development*

The relationship between realization of the right to development and the provision of official development assistance was analysed in the 1979 UN report on the right to development. The report noted that there was "widespread international interest" in the concept of foregoing closer links between human rights and aid and lamented the fact that no comprehensive analysis of the issues had yet been undertaken.[38] However, the proposal in the report that the Commission should "consider undertaking a more detailed study of the relevant issues with a view to formulating general principles and criteria which might guide future bilateral and multilateral assistance arrangements, insofar as they seek to promote human rights in general, and the human right to development in particular" met with significant opposition in the Commission. Proposals to link human rights and development assistance were termed a "distortion of the concept of cooperation". It was said that any attempt to devise generalized criteria in the matter must be made with caution, since it could be used to evade responsibility for the establishment of a New International Economic Order and could be used as a weapon in trade relations. In the event, the Commission adopted a resolution expressing its concern that "qualitative and human rights conditions are being imposed in bilateral and multilateral trade policies with the intention and effect of perpetuating the existing structure of world trade".[39]

---

37) UN doc. E/CN.4/Sub.2/412 (1978), paras 496—97.
38) UN doc. E/CN.4/1334 (1979), para 312.
39) Resolution 5 (XXXV) (1979).

Other Initiatives to Link Human Rights and Aid and Trade

Efforts by the United States and other Western States to link human rights considerations to their bilateral, and even on occasion multilateral, aid and trade relationships have been analysed extensively elsewhere. In the present context, however, it is useful to note a summing up of the present position of Western aid donors by the Chairman of the Development Assistance Committee of the Organization for Economic Cooperation and Development (OECD):

> "On the one hand, most donors, having been through their first baptism of reforming zeal, now are inclined to favour a sense of balance in this aspect of aid design. They note that basic human needs are not the only development needs that need addressing. They admit 'trickle-down' does sometimes work. The recognise there is little scope in sovereign-to-sovereign relations for imposing a donor's notions of what a recipient's distributional and political values should be on an unwilling partner. And where they encounter trade-offs between promoting economic human rights and withholding aid on political-rights grounds, most are inclined to favour the former.

> With such nuances in place, however, donors are disposed now to turn down or turn off aid to régimes that persist in severe and systematic repression. In their allocations of aid between countries most tend, other things being equal, to favour regimes demonstrating strong internal commitments to social justice, and to accord such recipients greater discretion in their uses of aid resources. Most DAC donors are interested in specifically targeting assistance on particular disadvantaged groups."[40]

Mention should also be made of an abortive proposal by the Commission of the European Communities to link trade liberalization concessions by the EEC to compliance with fair labour standards by the ACP States in the context of the second Lomé Convention. Regardless of the general merits or demerits of such a concept, the actual scheme proposed was so flawed and so open to manipulation for protectionist purposes that its exclusion was a foregone conclusion.[41]

---

40) *Development Cooperation, 1980 Review* (Paris, OECD, 1980, p. 61).

41) The proposal is analysed in detail in P. Alston, "Sinking Trade and Human Rights", *German Yearbook of International Law 1980*, vol. 23.

In conclusion, it is appropriate to list some of the *arguments* that may be made *for and against the linking of human rights and development cooperation* programmes. Arguments in favour include the following:

(a) Under the United Nations Charter all Member States have pledged to take joint and separate action to promote, *inter alia*, universal respect for, and observance of, human rights. Development cooperation activities should thus seek to promote these objectives.
(b) By virtue of having ratified the international human rights Covenants and of having subscribed to a range of ILO and Unesco sponsored human rights conventions and regional human rights charters, many States have undertaken specific obligations in international law with respect to the promotion of respect for human rights. Development assistance should be neither provided nor used in such a way as to facilitate violations of these human rights commitments.
(c) From a moral point of view, any form of complicity in human rights violations should be avoided.
(d) From an economic viewpoint, broad-based economic and social development cannot be achieved in an environment of repression and development assistance to repressive governments is therefore wasted.
(e) Development aid can be used to encourage or even make possible the development of more equitable and participatory structures.

But while all of these arguments are persuasive in varying degrees, the practical difficulties of designing and implementing an appropriate policy are not to be underestimated. A variety of criticisms is likely to be levelled against any such scheme both by its proponents in donor countries and by those in the recipient countries who might claim that it is inadequate, that it does not go to the root of the problem, that it is unlikely to be evenly and impartially applied, and that it adversely affects rather than improves the enjoyment of human rights in recipient countries. The latter might argue that criticism of specific human rights violations constitutes interference in the internal political affairs of a state, that withdrawal of funds committed under an international agreement would be an act of bad faith, that such withdrawal would amount to interference in the determination of domestic economic priorities, that there are so many human rights standards that the selective promotion of a handful of them violates the essential indivisibility of all rights, that economic, social and cultural rights formulations are so vague as to be unenforceable, and that it is hypocritical for countries with acknowledged human rights problems of their own to be 'penalizing' other States for their respective problems.

(3) A Structural Approach to Human Rights in International Relations

The ramifications at the international level, of a structural approach to the promotion of respect for human rights are immense. While many of the initiatives noted above have been of a primarily sanctionary nature, the pursuit of a structural approach requires a far greater emphasis on the removal of obstacles which stand in the way of societies seeking to achieve respect for human rights within their own boundaries. Thus at the international level, as much as at the national level, the human rights approach must go beyond providing a right of access to remedial institutions (e.g. food shipments, emergency medical services) and encompass the right not to be subject to structures which prevent the self-realization of human rights. All too often the remedial or curative approach serves to obscure the continuation of structural violations. In formulating many demands upon the international community in terms of positive assistance programmes (e.g. 0.7 % of GNP in development aid), it is easy to lose sight of a general demand that the international order should not create new impediments and should remove existing obstacles which hinder the realization of human rights objectives.

By way of example, reference may be made to the rights to food and health. The international obstacles which hinder food self-reliance have been analysed in depth elsewhere.[42] In the area of health, the provision of vast quantities of medical supplies will have far less impact on health in the longer term than the reduction of pollution, the control of exports of hazardous products and substances, and the cessation of inappropriate or misleading advertising practices. National and international action on issues such as these could do more to promote respect for human rights than many of the more spectacular sanctionary initiatives adopted in recent years.

---

42) See Lappé, Collins and Kinley, *Aid as Obstacle: Twenty Questions about our Foreign Aid and the Hungry* (San Francisco, Institute for Food and Development Policy, 1980).

(4) *A case study of the preventive approach in action*

The 1979 decision by the UN Human Rights Commission to transfer its consideration of human rights problems in Equatorial Guinea from the framework of its confidential procedure to its public sessions was hailed as a very significant procedural development.[43] Even more important however was the manner in which the Commission decided to tackle the issue from that point onwards. In 1979 it appointed a Special Rapporteur to study the situation in Equatorial Guinea thoroughly and to report to it the following year. Before that report was prepared President Macias was deposed[44] and the new government invited the Rapporteur to visit the country. In a detailed and constructive report the Rapporteur made a number of recommendations relating to the requirements for future action both at the national and international levels. Subsequently, the Commission, in response to a request by the Government of Equatorial Guinea, requested the Secretary-General to appoint an expert "with wide experience of the situation in Equatorial Guinea, in particular with a view to assisting the Government of that country in taking the action necessary for the full restoration of human rights and fundamental freedoms keeping in mind... the economic, political and social realities of that country".

In his report, the Expert, who was the same person as the Special Rapporteur, made a series of recommendations designed to establish equitable and participatory structures which would promote respect for human rights. Among his recommendations were the following: promote adoption of legislation to establish an appropriate legal system; an increase in the number of lawyers; full support for an existing programme of popular legal education; special measures to promote the legal equality of women; the provision of greater incentives for agricultural workers; the improvement of plantation working conditions and an increase in the number of labour inspectors; high priority for the training of teachers and for the training of citizens in the values of representative democracy; the adoption of a new Constitution with the adoption of the Universal Declaration of Human Rights as an interim national law; ratification of the International Human Rights Covenants; membership of the ILO and ratification of

---

43) Full details of the UN's handling of the situation in Equatorial Guinea are contained in UN docs. E/CN.4/1371 (1980) and E/CN.4/1439 (1980) and Add. (1981).

44) See generally Alejandro Artucio, *The Trial of Macias in Equatorial Guinea — The Story of a Dictatorship*, (Geneva, International Commission of Jurists, 1980).

its principal conventions; adoption of a law on associations and encouragement of the formation of co-operatives and other groups; and the restoration of a traditional system of popular election of town council members. The Expert also recommended that the UN should make expert services available in a variety of fields.

Thus the action taken by the UN in response to gross violations of human rights amounts to the adoption of a forward-looking structural approach and as such represents a very significant departure from previous practice. In confirming the value of such an approach the Commission on Human Rights in March 1981:

(a) recommended that the Economic and Social Council should extend the mandate of the Expert on *Equatorial Guinea* and request the Secretary-General to draw up a draft plan of action for implementing the Expert's recommendations (Res. 31 (XXXVII));

(b) requested "the Secretary-General to provide advisory services and other forms of appropriate assistance to help the Government of the *Central African Republic* to continue to guarantee the exercise of human rights and fundamental freedoms in that country" (Res. 15 (XXXVII)); and

(c) requested "the Secretary-General to provide advisory services and other forms of appropriate assistance to the Government of *Uganda* in its efforts to guarantee the enjoyment of human rights and fundamental freedoms" (Res. 30 (XXXVII)).

PART VI

Human Rights and
the New International Economic Order

"Everyone is entitled to a social and international order in which the rights and freedoms set forth in this Declaration can be fully realized."

Universal Declaration of Human
Rights (1948), article 28

"What is impossible in so heterogeneous an environment (as the United Nations) is to transform such economic human rights into rules of a living international economic order."

G. Schwarzenberger (1970)

"The realization of the New International Economic Order is an essential element for the effective promotion of human rights and fundamental freedoms."

General Assembly resolution
32/130 (1977)

In 1974 and 1975 the UN General Assembly adopted a series of resolutions which, in general terms, embodied a comprehensive strategy for the achievement of a new international economic order (NIEO). The Assembly called for the replacement of the existing order which, in its view, was characterized by inequality, domination, dependence, narrow self-interest and segmentation by a new order based on sovereign equality, interdependence, common interest and cooperation among States. The term human rights appears only once in the four seminal NIEO resolutions and the Assembly has not, in any subsequent resolution, specifically acknowledged that the promotion of respect for human rights is an important, let alone essential, ingredient of efforts to establish a NIEO. It has, however, affirmed this proposition in the reverse. In its landmark conceptual resolution in the area of human rights (res. 32/130 of 1977) the Assembly reaffirmed that "the realization of the New International Economic Order is an essential element for the effective promotion of human rights and fundamental freedoms and should be accorded priority". Comparable propositions have also been endorsed by UN conferences in fields closely linked to human rights such as the 1980 Copenhagen Conference on Women and the 1980 Caracas Congress on the Prevention of Crime and the Treatment of Offenders.

It is possible to discern three main areas of concern which must be addressed in the present context:

1. Is the debate on the relationship between human rights and the NIEO capable of producing any significant practical results by giving impetus to the attainment of the goals sought or is it doomed to remain forever at the level of abstraction? In this regard, does the linking of issues such as human rights, including women's rights, with the NIEO have the effect of emphasizing the fundamental importance of structural factors which underlie human rights violations or does it carry an undue risk of submerging the identity of specific rights problems and issues in an amorphous and ill-focussed debate on a wide range of technical economic and other questions?
2. Have UN organs in fact dealt with these two issues in a non-compartmentalized and integrated fashion or is the connexion mainly a rhetorical one which has been promoted for particular ideological purposes?
3. Is it possible to devise means by which the two issues can be effectively linked so that parallel progress can be achieved on both fronts without, on the one hand, interfering in matters which are essentially within the jurisdiction of any state or, on the other hand, providing an excuse for States which might wish to exploit the issue of domestic injustices and inequities in order to avoid the shared responsibility for the promotion of international equity?

Before considering the human rights-related origins of current NIEO demands and the link between human rights and the existing international economic order one preliminary point should be made. There is a temptation, particularly on the part of human rights specialists, first of all to assume that the NIEO relates largely to technical economic issues and then, as a consequence, to question how and why it can be of other than indirect relevance to human rights. This reasoning can be challenged at two levels. On the first, it is possible to demonstrate that in certain areas international economic factors have a direct and decisive impact on the enjoyment or otherwise of human rights. On the second level, it must be acknowledged that the NIEO is far and away the single most dominant issue on the agenda of the international community and that no other issue, including human rights, can be, or is being, discussed in isolation from the NIEO debate. Thus, for example, recent world conferences on issues as diverse as science and technology for development, the role of women and the prevention of crime have all placed their concerns squarely in the context of the need to achive a NIEO. The same trend is strongly apparent in the field of human rights. Given the strong trend in one direction, it is appropriate to question whether it is, or should be, a two-way process. In that regard, the question which arises is whether the mainstream of the NIEO debate is being conducted in isolation from the other issues to which it is so centrally important.

The Human Rights Origins of the NIEO Programme

Despite its lack of prominence in the NIEO debates in the 1970s and early 80s, the evolving concept of human rights played a strong, even catalytic, role in the post-war emergence of the demands for a NIEO. The seeds of the NIEO were clearly planted in the UN Charter provisions affirming the importance of "respect for the principle of equal rights and self-determination of peoples". Between 1945 and 1950 the developing countries (primarily the long-independent nations of Latin America) sought in various international fora to draw attention to their economic problems. However, the successes which they achieved were substantially outweighed by their disappointments. Of particular significance was their failure to secure the adoption by the General Assembly in the late 1940s of a "Declaration on Rights and Duties of States". Nevertheless, the result of such initiatives was that by the end of the 1940s many of the measures which were later to constitute the NIEO demands had already been proposed by the developing countries and discussed in international fora. Subsequently, starting in 1950, a number of these concerns were crystallized or subsumed under the rubric of the human right of self-determination, a principle which was steadily expanded in scope and significance.

Although the Universal Declaration of Human Rights of 1948 did not contain any explicit reference to self-determination it did include an Article to the effect that "everyone is entitled to a social and international order in which the rights and freedoms set forth in this Declaration can be fully realized" (Article 28). By 1950 the General Assembly had expressly recognized "the right of peoples and nations to self-determination" as a fundamental human right. While this coalescence of human rights and economic development issues was in many respects a natural and appropriate process it is also evident that the human rights approach offered a convenient and ready-made vehicle for the pursuit of demands which had generated little positive response elsewhere. In terms of the progressive development of international law including international human rights law, this approach proved to be immensely successful. In economic terms, however, progress was to be achieved rather more slowly.

Following its 1950 resolution, the General Assembly took only five years to finalize its formulation of the right to self-determination. By 1952 the Assembly had extended its interpretation of the right to include the concept of economic self-determination. In 1955 its Third Committee, after considerable debate as to the legal or political nature of the right, adopted a provision for inclusion in both the draft covenants on human rights which stated that:

"All peoples have the right of self-determination. By virtue of this right they freely determine their political status and freely pursue their economic, social and cultural development.

The people may, for their own ends, freely dispose of their natural wealth and resources without prejudice to any obligations arising out of international economic cooperation, based upon the principle of mutual benefit, and international law. In no case may a people be deprived of its own means of subsistence."[45]

Thenceforth, the progressive development of international law centred around the twin human rights principles of the right of self-determination and what was perhaps illusorily seen as its corollary, the right to permanent sovereignty over natural resources. The first of these principles was enshrined in the 1960 Declaration on the Granting of Independence to Colonial Countries and Peoples. By the following year the process of decolonization had been so successful that the balance of voting power in the General Assembly had shifted in favour of the Third World. Yet despite the fact that self-determination was recognized as a complex, multifaceted concept, its political aspects rapidly assumed an overriding importance during the struggles of the 1950s and 60s to achieve freedom from colonial rule. Although many newly-independent States subscribed to the conventional wisdom of the time relating to the need to achieve economic

---

45) W.W. Rostow, *The Stages of Economic Growth* (Cambridge, Cambridge University Press, 2nd ed., 1971), p. 12.

take-off, the economic, social and cultural dimensions of self-determination were largely neglected. Indeed, the concept of economic take-off, at least as interpreted by its principal proponent, Walt Rostow, was highly compatible with a large degree of economic dependence and was not at all associated with the broad notion of self-determination. Thus, for example, the first "stage of growth" as discerned by Rostow was "the transitional period when the preconditions for take-off are created *generally in response to the intrusion of a foreign power*, converging with certain domestic forces making for modernization". Thus although *de jure* political independence was achieved it was accompanied by continuing *de facto* economic, and often cultural, dependence.

Within the UN the right to permanent sovereignty over natural resources was the only element of economic self-determination which was pursued with any zeal. In 1958 the General Assembly established a Commission on Permanent Sovereignty over Natural Resources and charged it with the conduct of "a full survey of the status of this basic element of the right to self-determination". Thus while the human rights link was re-affirmed, responsibility for the further development of the right was given to a body other than the Commission on Human Rights and of equal status.

In 1962 the Assembly adopted the Declaration on Permanent Sovereignty over Natural Resources[46] in which it declared that

> "The rights of peoples and nations to permanent sovereignty over their natural wealth and resources must be exercised in the interest of their national development and of the well-being of the people of the State concerned"; that "The exploration, development and disposition of such resources", as well as the imported capital, "should be in conformity with the rules and conditions which the peoples and nations freely consider to be necessary or desirable..."; that "Nationalization, expropriation or requisitioning shall be based on grounds or reasons of public utility, security or the national interest..."; and that "International cooperation for the economic development of developing countries... shall be such as to further their independent national development and shall be based upon respect for their sovereignty over their natural wealth and resources".

---

46) GA Resolution 1803 (XVII) (1962).

But while the importance of the right of permanent sovereignty over natural resources is undisputed, despite the ability of publicists to agree on its precise implications, it can, at best, only be viewed as one of a number of elements which together constitute the right to economic self-determination. Thus, although, the immediate origins of the demands for a NIEO may be attributed to the 1973 oil embargo and its accompanying price rises, they are more appropriately seen in historical perspective as the logical, if belated, articulation of the various elements which inhere in the human rights principle of economic self-determination. The question remains, however, to what extent, if at all, the NIEO demands are still linked with or reflect their longer term origins in the progressive development of the international law of human rights.

The Impact of the Existing International Economic Order on Human Rights

It appears to be generally accepted that the existing international economic order is in a state of crisis which is more severe than any since the Great Depression and that all regions of the world are affected albeit to varying degress. The impact of a malfunctioning and inequitable international economic order on the enjoyment of human rights can be examined at two separate levels.

The first level is represented by statistics showing the dimensions of absolute poverty — defined by the World Bank as "a condition of life so characterized by malnutrition, illiteracy and disease as to be beneath any reasonable definition of human decency".[47] According to the *World Development Report, 1980*, the number of people in absolute poverty in developing countries (excluding China and other centrally planned economies) is estimated at around 780 million. In the low-income countries people on average live 24 years less than they do in the industrialized countries. Some 600 million adults in developing countries are illiterate, and one-third of the primary school-age children (including nearly half of the girls) are not going to school. In terms of economic and social human rights alone these figures represent massive and persistent violations.

---

47) World Bank, *World Development Report 1980* (Washington, D.C. 1980), p. 32. See also "Towards a NIEO Characterized by Equitable Structures at All Levels and the Absence of Absolute Poverty", Working Paper by P.J.I.M. de Waart, representing the International Commission of Jurists, UN doc HR/GENEVA/1980/WP4.

While the primary responsibility for alleviating these conditions rests with national governments, their prospects for success depend not only on equitable domestic policies but on major changes in the international order. Without the support provided by more equitable patterns of world production, trade, financial flows and resource transfers, and in the absence of efforts to reverse the worst features of maldevelopment including growing militarization, the pursuit of inappropriate lifestyles and the erosion of cultural identity in both the North and the South, the outlook for the improved enjoyment of human rights is, at best, bleak.

The second level at which the existing international economic order can be shown to be detrimental to the enjoyment of human rights involves a consideration of *specific policies and structures which impinge directly*, rather than indirectly, on *human rights*. It is not possible within the confines of this paper to give more than a couple of brief examples of such factors. One is the pursuit of *militarization*. According to certain currently fashionable perceptions, the protection of international peace and security, which must by definition include the reliable functioning of the international economic order, is dependent upon vastly increased arms expenditure and the further militarization, both from endogenous and exogenous sources, of national societies. Yet it requires neither detailed statistics nor any great insights to appreciate the magnitude of the adverse impact on human rights which will inevitably flow directly from the massive increases in proposed expenditures and in export goals announced by the developed countries alone since the beginning of 1981.

A second example is provided by the pursuit of *economic policies which rely primarily upon* the encouragement of dramatic increases in foreign capital inflows by *offering cheap and abundant supplies of labour*. The latter is assured by large-scale unemployment, the maintenance of low-wage levels, the repression of trade unions and other potentially "troublesome" groups, and the curbing of government welfare expenditure in order to reduce costs and increase the attractiveness of poorly paid jobs. While such policies arc pursued by national governments they are encouraged and facilitated by a number of the characteristics of the present international economic order.

A variety of other examples could be given of the way in which present international economic policics and structures often run contrary to the attainment of human rights objectives. It is clear therefore that efforts to establish a just and equitable international economic order must go hand in hand with endeavours to ensure the promotion of full respect for human rights. By the same token, it cannot be assumed that the achievement of a NIEO will be accompanied by full respect for human rights or even that it would *per se* significantly enhance the enjoyment of human rights. On the one hand, it is not difficult to conceive of the future existence of a NIEO characterized by automatic and greatly increased North-South resource transfers, higher and more stable prices for primary commodities, democratically run international financial institutions, more equitable arrangements for the transfer of technology, the location of a much higher proportion of the world's industrial capacity in the South, and the achievement of more effective control by host countries over the activities of transnational corporations, but which is nevertheless not accompanied by a significant improvement in the human rights situation. As Johan Galtung has written:

"In the NIEO there is a potential for more economic surplus to accumulate in the Third World countries. But the far more important question is whether it is used to meet the basic needs of those most in need. Economic surplus, it is well-known, can be used in several ways, depending on where in the society it is generated, who decides how it will be disposed of, and what kind of decision is made. To take it for granted that it will necessarily be used to meet basic needs is extremely naive. A more realistic understanding is that most people in control of the economy will tend to use it for what they see as the pressing needs — be they 'national needs', non-basic needs, or the needs of those less in need."[48]

In the most pessimistic outcome the major domestic impact of such international reforms as are envisaged in the NIEO programme would be the further enrichment of local elites and the reinforcement (and modernization) of repressive mechanisms for the control of the society. A much more optimistic outcome has been assumed in all the resolutions relating to the NIEO which have been adopted by UN human rights organs. The challenge remains, however, to devise policies which could conceivably facilitate the achievement of the optimistic scenario.

Before considering possible policy options it is proposed to consider the extent to which the major UN NIEO documents reflect a com-

---

48) J. Galtung, "The New International Economic Order and the Basic Needs Approach", *Alternatives*, Vol. IV, 1978—79, pp. 458—9.

mitment to the promotion of human rights. For this purpose, the Charter of Economic Rights and Duties of States is singled out for analysis on the grounds that it is reasonably representative of the major documents and that it is the only one of the relevant General Assembly NIEO resolutions which contains a specific reference to human rights.

The Charter of Economic Rights and Duties of States from a Human Rights Perspective

The Charter of Economic Rights and Duties of States was adopted by the General Assembly on December 12, 1974.[49] Unlike the Declaration and Programme of Action on the Establishment of a New International Economic Order, it was adopted not by consensus but by vote, with 120 States in favour, 6 against, and 10 abstaining. Also, unlike those two instruments, the Charter was conceived by its initiators as a means for the codification and progressive development of international law. It was, in the view of its proponents, an effort to "take economic cooperation out of the realms of goodwill and put it into the realm of law".[50] The extent to which it has succeeded in this endeavour is a matter for debate. Nevertheless, it remains, at the very least, a clear and important statement of the developing countries position and provides an overview of the general thrust of the demands for a NIEO. Thus the approach of the Charter to human rights issues is an important indicator in the context of the present inquiry.

When the drafting of such a Charter was first proposed, at the third session of UNCTAD in 1972 in Santiago, the representative of the Group of 77 stated that "it should be a counterpart in the economic field to the Universal Declaration of Human Rights and the International Covenants on Human Rights".[51] Subsequently, the link between the NIEO and human rights was expressly recognized by the Conference in its resolution establishing a Working Group to draw up the text of a draft charter. In the Preamble to the resolution the Conference recalled that the Universal Declaration and the Covenants "make the full exercise of those rights dependent on the existence of

---

49) GA Resolution 3281 (XXIX).
50) Mexican President Echeverria, quoted in UN Monthly Chronicle, Vol. XI, No. 9, May 1972, p. 4.
51) UNCTAD Proceedings, Third Session, UN doc TD/180 (1973), Vol. 1, para. 210.

a just international order and respect for the principle of self-determination of peoples and of the free disposition of their wealth and natural resources".[52] Nevertheless, in the four drafting sessions held by the Working Group between February 1973 and June 1974, the subject of human rights was conspicuous only by the paucity of discussion devoted to it.[53]

The final version of the Charter as adopted by the General Assembly contains only one reference to human rights *per se*. It appears in Chapter I which enumerates a list of 15 principles by which economic as well as political and other relations among States are to be governed. Principle (k) is "respect for human rights and fundamental freedoms". The other principles in this Chapter range from "non-intervention" and "non-aggression" to "no attempt to seek hegemony and spheres of influence" and "international cooperation for development". For the most part the list is a reiteration of generally accepted and oft-repeated principles taken from a variety of UN instruments. Yet this derivation raises the question of why no specific reference was made in the Charter to those instruments and especially to the elaborate Declaration on Principles of International Law concerning Friendly Relations and Cooperation among States in accordance with the Charter of the United Nations (General Assembly Resolution 2625 (XXV) of 1970). Such a reference would have provided a more scientific basis for the Charter's principles but by the same token would perhaps have made it more difficult to justify the inclusion of several 'coded' principles which were inserted to satisfy the demands of particular voting constituencies.

But even if we accept Bedjaoui's view that the Charter "is without doubt directly linked with Declaration 2625 (XXV) on the seven principles of international law, from which it draws the economic consequences"[54], the human rights foundations of the Charter are not thereby significantly strengthened. This is due to the fact that the two formal references contained in the Declaration are both set squarely in the context of international cooperation and respect for the principle of equal rights and self-determination of peoples. Both the vagueness and brevity of these references and their failure to spell out the individual as well as the collective dimensions of human

---

52) *Ibid.*, Resolution 45 III, 6th preambular para.
53) See UN docs TD/B/AC.12/1 and TD/B/AC.12/2 and Add.
54) Mohammed Bejaoui, *Towards a New International Economic Order* (Paris, Unesco, 1979), p. 185.

rights were subject to criticism at the time of the drafting of the Declaration.[55] An assessment of the validity of such criticisms requires an examination of the other facets of the Charter which are also of relevance to the present inquiry.

In general terms, the Charter addresses human rights-related issues in separate contexts. They are: (a) the specific reference to human rights in principle (k) of Chapter I; (b) in relation to the right to self-determination; (c) with respect to the concepts of equity and social justice; and (d) in affirming the responsibility of each State to promote the development of its people.

(a) *Principle (k)*
As noted above, this principle is not further developed either in the text of the Charter itself or by reference to other instruments such as the Universal Declaration, the International Covenants on Human Rights or even the Declaration on Principles of International Law. It thus stands on its own, adding little, if anything, to the qualitative aspects of the Charter and not going beyond a ritual reaffirmation of the vague and formal commitment contained in the United Nations Charter itself.

(b) *Self-determination*
In essence, the Charter is predicated upon the conviction that the establishment of a NIEO requires implementation of the right of peoples to self-determination and to permanent sovereignty over their natural wealth and resources. This is demonstrated by the inclusion in Chapter I entitled "Fundamentals of International Economic Relations" of the following principles, *inter alia*: "(a) sovereignty, territorial integrity and political independence of States; (b) sovereign equality of all States" and "(g) equal rights and self-determination of peoples". In Chapter II, on the Economic Rights and Duties of States, Article 1 and Article 2(1) are derived directly from the right of self-determination contained in the first Article of both the International Human Rights Covenants. In addition, Article 16 provides that it is the right and duty of all States, individually and collectively, to eliminate specified obstacles to the enjoyment of that right. Specifically, the article refers to "colonialism, *apartheid*, racial discrimination, neo-colonialism and all forms of foreign aggression, occupation and domination, and the economic and social consequences thereof".

---

55) E.g. UN doc A/AC/125/12 (1970).

Thus, the question arises, in view of the emphasis placed on the right to self-determination, as to whether we should conclude that the Charter attaches adequate importance to general human rights considerations. It is submitted that the answer must be in the negative since the individual dimensions of the human rights tradition, which are at least as important as its collective dimensions, are not referred to at all. While some commentators have viewed the right to self-determination as a bridge between those two dimensions and have posited an individual right of self-determination, even that right cannot be viewed as a substitute for the range of human rights oriented towards the individual and proclaimed in the Covenants. Moreover, in the context of the Charter, all references to the right of self-determination, perhaps not surprisingly, refer specifically and exclusively to the rights of States, not of peoples and certainly not of individuals. While endorsing the statement in a recent Unesco report that "the right of peoples to self-determination and to permanent sovereignty over natural resources is the very foundation upon which a new international economic order can be built"[56] it must also be said that the right to self-determination is not, in itself, sufficient to ensure that such an order will also encompass a new social or human order.

(c) *Equity and Social Justice*

In what has now become a long-standing tradition of UN resolutions in the economic domain, the provisions which come closest to expressing human rights-related sentiments are those which use such terms as equity and social justice. In this respect, the Charter is no exception. Its preamble declares that its fundamental purpose is to promote establishment of the new international economic order, based on equity, among other principles. While the Charter also uses formulations such as "equitable benefit" and "social progress" its most significant provision in this respect is contained in Chapter I which provides that among the principles which "shall" govern economic, political and other relations among States is the "promotion of international social justice". This provision was included in the draft at the request of Venezuela and its adoption was not preceded by any significant discussion.

The general significance in international law of terms such as

---

56) Unesco doc SS. 78/CONF.630/12 (1978) p. 41.

equity and social justice has been dealt with elsewhere and it must suffice in the present analysis to note that they are not adequate or effective surrogates for the term "human rights". Furthermore, in the context of the Charter, such terms invariably refer only to equity in relations *among* States and it would be exceedingly difficult to interpret "international social justice" as used in the Charter to include questions of social justice *within* States.

(d) *Promotion of Development by Each State*
Article 7 of the Charter is one of three provisions which provoked no controversy and was adopted unanimously. It is surprising then that it comes closer than any other provision to relating human rights concerns to the demands for a NIEO. It provides that:

> "Every State has the primary responsibility to promote the economic, social and cultural development of its people. To this end, each State has the right and the responsibility to choose its means and goals of development, fully to mobilize and use its resources, to implement progressive economic and social reforms and to ensure the full participation of its people in the process and benefits of development. All States have the duty, individually and collectively, to cooperate in eliminating obstacles that hinder such mobilization and use."

While none of this was in the least bit novel, especially when compared with the provisions of the Declaration on Social Progress and Development which was adopted five years earlier, it is nevertheless highly significant in the context of a Charter which otherwise deals almost exclusively with the rights and duties of States vis-à-vis the rest of the international community. It thus represents an important acknowledgement that the right of States to equitable treatment in NIEO-related matters cannot be considered in a vacuum, but must be related to the promotion of domestic equity. It is perhaps worthy of note that the use of the term 'responsibility' rather than 'duty' comports a slightly lesser degree of obligation on States but this would not seem to detract significantly from the importance of the provision. Once again, however, Article 7 avoids the use of specific human rights terminology. Nevertheless, by referring to participation in the process and benefits of development it does focus in a more balanced fashion than is often the case on the civil and political rights aspects of the human rights equation.

In conclusion, therefore, it can be said that while the Charter of Economic Rights and Duties of States contains several human rights-related provisions it does not accord adequate recognition to the fact that the enjoyment of the full range of human rights by all individuals must be seen as the ultimate rationale for the establishment of a NIEO. The Charter avoids specific references to human rights *per se* with the sole exception of the brief principle contained in the heterogeneous section on "fundamentals of economic relations", a principle which does not sit easily with either the overall scheme of the Charter or with its internal logic. Finally, it is appropriate to question the extent to which the reaffirmation and reinforcement of the dominant role of the nation State, which is probably the major accomplishment of the Charter, is conducive to the promotion of greater respect for the rights of individuals, a process which inevitably requires some degree of limitation upon the power of the State and some recognition of the State's accountability both to its inhabitants and to the international community.

Other NIEO Sources

Much of the foregoing analysis is directly applicable to the other major NIEO documents. The major exceptions are the programmes of action and specific resolutions adopted by subject-specific world conferences. Thus it can be argued that the NIEO does in fact have a distinctly human face by pointing to the linking of specific human rights issues with the NIEO in the context of conferences such as the Copenhagen World Conference of the United Nations Decade for Women: Equality, Development and Peace. Yet the reality is that the programme and resolutions of this and other such conferences, although giving their imprimatur to progressive policies in their respective fields, fall clearly outside the mainstream of NIEO negotiations and discussion. While they have played an important role in buttressing or reinforcing the case for a NIEO, they have not significantly affected the form which such an order will take. Moreover, the linkage is usually discerned to be a one-way rather than a two-way affair, in so far as the indispensability of a NIEO for the full realization of human rights is emphasized, but the reverse of that proposition is rarely endorsed. Yet the corollary is important, since without improved respect for both the concept of human rights and for the rights themselves in practice, in both North and South the achievement of a NIEO is unlikely.

Conclusion

The linking of human rights and NIEO objectives has much to recommend it. In general terms it is clear that the real bargaining power of the developing countries is primarily political rather than economic. By framing their economic demands in terms of human rights issues their political power assumes an added ethical dimension, which, as the Brandt report has pointed out, is an indispensable element in the mobilization of widespread support for an NIEO programme. Thus, extension of the NIEO debate to the UN's human rights fora serves to highlight its ethical content. Moreover, the juxtaposition of human rights and NIEO issues also provides a means by which to highlight the many inconsistencies which characterize state policies in these areas. Thus, to give just one example, calls for developing countries to desist from particular practices which are detrimental to the enjoyment of human rights are rarely accompanied by efforts on the part of the appellants to change those of their own international policies and activities which encourage or facilitate such practices. As Shridath Ramphal has noted:

> "For a rich industrialized society to confirm its vested interest in the world's present disparities, is to acquiesce in, indeed even to promote, denial of the most basic of human rights — the right to life itself at a tolerable level of existence. It does the cause of human rights no good to inveigh against civil and political rights deviations while helping to perpetuate illiteracy, malnutrition, disease, infant mortality, and a low life expectancy among millions of human beings. All the dictators and all the aggressors throughout history, however ruthless, have not succeeded in creating as much misery and suffering as the disparities between the world's rich and poor sustain today."[57]

To those who seek watertight guarantees that the benefits of the NIEO will be directly reaped by those most in need the only response is that no such guarantees can ever be devised. The simple reality is that in the South, as much as in the North, a sense of equity and justice can never really be imposed from outside but must develop from within. The promotion of human rights standards by the international community can serve to strengthen and encourage the resolve of internal elements, be they leaders, the masses or both, to work to-

---

57) "Banners that Buy No Bread: The Legal Profession into the Eighties", *Commonwealth Law Bulletin*, Vol. 6, No. 4, 1980, p. 1459.

wards the achievement of social justice. In this sense the content of human rights standards is potentially revolutionary. At the same time international measures can go a long way towards the creation of conditions which are conducive to the success of domestic endeavours to promote the realization of human rights. The key is that both national and international efforts must go hand in hand and lack of progress at either level should not be invoked as an excuse for doing nothing at the other level.

Finally, those who genuinely wish to see concurrent progress achieved at both levels are inevitably tempted to try to formulate hard and fast linkages whereby concessions made at one level are matched by concessions at the other. For example: more development assistance in return for more resources being devoted to the meeting of basic needs; or, trade concessions in return for undertakings to improve domestic labour conditions. As noted in Part V (b) above, such proposals are usually unacceptable either because they are in fact designed to achieve other than their stated objective; because they are so specific as to amount to interference in domestic affairs; because, in reality, their benefits are illusory; or simply because they smack of paternalism and double standards. That is not to say that linkages should never be sought, but that any such proposals must be of a positive (e.g. increased trade or aid) rather than negative (sanctions) nature and should be openly and freely negotiated by all sides concerned.

PART VII

The Right to Development

The single most important element in the launching of a structural approach to human rights at the international level has been the concept of the right to development. The notion that "equality of opportunity for development is as much a prerogative of nations as of individuals within nations" and that there exists a human right to development is now firmly entrenched in United Nations human rights doctrine. The UN General Assembly has twice confirmed the existence of the right and the Commission on Human Rights has done so regularly since 1977. In March 1981 the latter body agreed by consensus to establish a Working Group of 15 governmental experts charged primarily with the task of submitting concrete proposals for a draft international instrument on the right to development. The Group has been requested to present its report in February 1982. A number of the sponsors of the Commission's resolution indicated that the eventual outcome of the Group's work is expected to be the adoption of a Charter or a Declaration on the right to development. It is worth recalling in this context that, in United Nations practice, a Declaration, which is lower in the hierarchy than a Charter, has been described as "a solemn instrument resorted to only in very rare cases relating to matters of major and lasting importance where maximum compliance is expected".[58]

Mention must also be made of two further sources of multilateral endorsement of the right to development. The first is the Conference of Heads of State and Government of Non-Aligned Countries at its Sixth Conference in Havana in 1979[59]. The second source is the Organization of African Unity. In addition to a 1979 decision of the Assembly of Heads of State and Government of the OAU endorsing the concept[60], the OAU Ministers of Justice, meeting in January 1981, approved a draft Charter of Human and Peoples' Rights which gives formal recognition to the right to development as a right of peoples. The Charter, which has since been adopted in July 1981 by the Conference of Heads of State and Government of the OAU, states in

---

58) *United Nations Action in the Field of Human Rights* (New York, UN, 1980), p. 310.

59) UN doc A/34/542 (1979), Annex, para. 266.

60) UN doc A/34/552 (1979), Annex II, pp. 92–93, Preamble and para. 1 of Decision 115 (XVI).

the preamble that: "it is henceforth essential to pay a particular attention to the right to development, and that the promotion of this right implies respect for other fundamental human rights recognized and guaranteed by conventions, laws, regulations and customs in force in States".[61] Accordingly, Article 22 of the draft Charter provides that:

"1. All peoples shall have the right to their economic social and cultural development in strict respect of their freedom and identity and in the equal enjoyment of the common heritage of mankind.
2. States shall have the duty, separately or in cooperation with others to ensure the exercise of the right to development."

But either despite or because of the rapidity with which it has acquired its now almost impeccable pedigree, the right to development is distinguished from other human rights not only by its novelty but by the vagueness and imprecision with which it has been formulated, by the lack of clarity as to its content or implications, by significant doubts as to its usefulness, and by uncertainty as to whether it will prove acceptable to a significant number of Member States of the UN. Before turning to these issues it is appropriate to note briefly the origins of the right to development and to consider the broader categorization of third generation human rights, or solidarity rights, among which the right to development has been placed.

Origins of the Right to Development

The concept implicit in the notion of a right to development was clearly stated in the Declaration of Philadelphia, adopted by the General Conference of the International Labour Organization in May 1944. In the Declaration, the Conference affirmed that:

"all human beings, irrespective of race, creed or sex, have the right to pursue both their material well-being and their spiritual freedom and dignity, in conditions of economic security and equal opportunity."

However, it was not until 1972 that the right to development surfaced at the international level in its present form. In that year the Chief Justice of Senegal (and present President of the International Commission of Jurists), Kéba Mbaye, entitled his inaugural lecture to the

---

61) OAU doc CAB/LEG/67/3/Rev. 1 (1979).

study session of the International Institute of Human Rights in Strasbourg "the right to development as a human right"[62]. At about the same time, the Institute's Director, Karel Vasak, launched his theory that a third generation of human rights had evolved. Both Mbaye and Vasak subsequently played important roles in securing the adoption of a resolution by the Commission on Human Rights in 1977 calling for a study on the international dimensions of the right to development. The study was not to consider whether the right actually existed, as its existence was implicit in the resolution. Two years later, having considered the Secretary-General's study, the Commission reaffirmed the existence of the right. In the intervening period, the Declaration on Race and Racial Prejudice adopted in 1978 by Unesco's General Conference made reference to "the right of every human being and group to full development". According to the Declaration the right to full development implies "equal access to the means of personal and collective advancement and fulfilment in a climate of respect for the values of civilizations and culture, both national and worldwide". Also in 1978 the General Assembly in the context of its "Declaration on the Preparation of Societies for Life in Peace" stated that all peoples have the right "to determine the road of their development"[63]. This process was 'consummated' by the General Assembly in 1979 in its resolution 34/46 in which it emphasized "that the right to development is a human right and that equality of opportunity for development is as much a prerogative of nations as of individuals within nations".

The Content of the Right to Development

It must be stated at the outset that no precise formulation or definition of the right to development exists. The closest approximation is the very general formulation adopted by the Commission on Human Rights and the General Assembly which, as noted above, provides that *"equality of opportunity for development* is as much a prerogative of nations as of individuals within nations".

The only vaguely comprehensive study of the right to development which has been undertaken to date is a 1979 report by the UN Secretary-General, prepared at the request of the Commission on Human

---

62) K. Mbaye, "Le droit au développement comme un droit de l'homme", *Revue des droits de l'homme/Human Rights Journal*, Vol. V, No. 2-3, 1972, pp. 5-3—534.

63) GA Resolution 33/73 (1978).

Rights[64]. Its cumbersome title gives some indication of the political currents which were prominent in 1977 when the study was requested. It is: "the international dimensions of the right to development as a human right in relation with other human rights based on international cooperation, including the right to peace, taking into account the requirements of the new international economic order and the fundamental human needs".

Having noted the diversity of interpretations which over the years have been applied to the concept of 'development', the UN report begins by noting "the existence of a general consensus" that the following elements are part of the concept: the central purpose of development is the realization of the potentialities of the human person in harmony with the community; the human person is the subject and not the object of development; both material and non-material needs must be satisfied; respect for human rights is fundamental; the opportunity for full participation must be accorded; the principles of equality and non-discrimination must be respected; and a degree of individual and collective self-reliance must be achieved.

In seeking to establish the foundations of the right to development the report places ethical considerations before relevant legal norms although it fails to elaborate upon the link between the two themes. The six separate ethical arguments outlined in the report reflect a mixed bag of ideas ranging from a general notion of justice and fairness, through solidarity, interdependence and the maintenance of peace to reparation for past exploitation. The report's analysis of legal norms relevant to the right to development is eclectic and catholic but lacks a degree of legal rigour. Considerable reliance is placed upon the right of peoples to self-deterination. Reference is also made, *inter alia*, to the right to life and the right to an adequate standard of living. The United Nations study also emphasizes the importance of General Assembly resolutions relating to the need to establish a New International Economic Order, the constituent instruments of certain United Nations specialized agencies and relevant instruments of regional organizations such as the Charter of the Organization of American States and the European Social Charter. The report concludes that: "there is a very substantial body of principles based on the Charter of the United Nations and the International Bill of Human Rights and reinforced by a range of conventions, declarations and resolutions which demonstrate the existence of a human right to de-

---

64) UN doc E/CN.4/1334 (1979). See also E/CN.4/1421 (1980).

velopment in international law". The report does not attempt to undertake a synthesis of the various norms to which it refers and nor does it differentiate between the different legal weighting which is appropriately accorded to the different instruments relied upon. The same, relatively haphazard, approach has been reflected in the subsequent debates in the Commission on Human Rights between 1979 and 1981.

On the basis of its analysis of the ethical and legal foundations of the right to development the report then proceeds to list a number of subjects and beneficiaries of the right on one hand, and those for whom the right implies duties on the other hand. Amongst the former are states, peoples, minorities and individuals, while the duty-bearers include the international community, international organizations, states, industrialized states and former colonial powers, regional and sub-regional state groupings, other transnational entities such as transnational corporations, producers' associations and unions and individuals. The report plays down the potentially divisive ideological debate over whether the right to development is an individual right or a collective right by suggesting that it is both. It notes, however, that the enjoyment of the right "necessarily involves a careful balancing between the interests of the collectivity on one hand, and those of the individual on the other". While some academic commentators have argued that the right to development makes sense only as a collective right, the formulation adopted by the General Assembly would appear to imply endorsement of the analysis contained in the Secretary-General's report.

The remainder of the report is devoted to the consideration of the relationship between the right to development and a number of specific issues such as the right to peace, the new international economic order and the basic needs approach to development. Considerable emphasis is also attached to the need to ensure that the promotion of respect for human rights is an integral element in all development-related activities. In his concluding observations the Secretary-General makes it clear that his analysis does not purport to be exhaustive and predicts that "a more detailed appreciation of the implications of the right... can be expected to emerge in the course of the next few years". He also emphasizes that the right to development is an evolving rather than a static concept.

The major response of the Commission on Human Rights was to request the preparation of a follow-up study on "the regional and national dimensions of the right to development". However, a number of the guidelines proposed in 1980 by the Commission to assist the Secretary-General in the preparation of that report again related to international issues. In general terms it may be said that the debates on the right to development in the Third Committee of the General Assembly and in the Human Rights Commission have been inconclusive and have not served to shed much light on the precise content and implications of the right.

Nevertheless, despite the vagueness and uncertainty which continue to characterize discussions of the right, and despite some not entirely unwarranted fears that the right may be misused so as to distract attention from specific human rights issues, it is important to acknowledge the *potential usefulness of the concept*. In this regard it is relevant to note one of the major criticisms which has been levelled at the right to development as a concept. It has been argued that the demonstration of a "synthesis" right adds nothing to that which is already contained in existing human rights instruments. However, this objection overlooks three factors. The first is that a synthetic approach helps to emphasize the dynamism of existing rights. The second is that the process of interpretation involves reference not only to the text of the International Bill of Human Rights but also to a variety of other sources which authoritatively express the relevant values and goals of the international community. Thus, by taking account of the development objectives expressed in documents such as the international development strategy or the resolutions relating to the establishment of a New International Economic Order, the "aggregate" of rights assumes an added dimension. The third factor is that a synthesis of rights, such as the right to development, assumes dimensions which are greater than the mere sum of its constituent parts. Through a process of cross-fertilization the sum of the various component norms forms a holistic entity. However, it must be conceded that in the final analysis, the question of whether solidarity rights are "new" or "synthetic" is unlikely to be of much practical significance since the outcome will be much the same regardless of the preferred methodology adopted by the international community.

The Dakar Colloquium on Human Rights and Development

Before looking at what the future might hold for the right to development it is appropriate to note that several major international meetings in recent years have considered the concept of the right in some depth. They include: (1) a Unesco "expert meeting on human rights, human needs and the establishment of a new international economic order" held in Paris in June 1978[65] ; (2) a Colloquium organised by the Hague Academy of International Law in conjunction with the United Nations University on the subject of "the right to development at the international level"[66] ; (3) a United Nations seminar on "the effects of the existing unjust international economic order on the economies of the developing countries and the obstacle that this represents for the implementation of human rights and fundamental freedoms" held in Geneva in 1980[67]; and (4) the Dakar Colloquium on Human Rights and Development, organized in September 1978 by the International Commission of Jurists and the Association Sénégalaise d'Etudes et de Recherches Juridiques[68].

The Dakar colloquium concluded, *inter alia*, that human rights are an essential component of development, and that the requirements of development and political stability cannot be taken as a pretext either to violate them or, in an area such as Africa, to rehabilitate practices which have been unanimously condemned during the colonial period. Furthermore, every development policy must take into account the needs of the population and its right freely to choose its model of development. Whatever the regime, the free, active and genuine participation of everyone in preparing and implementing a development policy for the general good is essential. The basic content of the right to development is the need for justice, both nationally and internationally. It is a right which derives its strength from solidarity and international cooperation and is both collective and individual. On the international level, it means peace, a satisfactory environment and the establishment of a more just economic order so that all can profit from the common heritage of mankind and so that the efforts of all strata of the population can be justly rewarded.

With respect to regional organizations, the seminar pointed out that human rights violations in Africa have been passed over in silence and requested the Organization of African Unity and all African States to ensure the implementation of human rights there through the conclusion of a regional human rights convention and the establishment of

---

65) Unesco doc SS.78/CONF.630/12 61978).

66) Papers and proceedings published by the Hague Academy of International Law (Alphen aan den Rijn, Sijthoff and Noordhoff, 1981).

67) UN doc ST/HR/SER.A/8 (1980).

68) *Revue Sénégalaise de droit*, No. 22, December 1977.

subregional institutes to promote human rights through information, research and education, inter-African commissions to hear complaints regarding human rights violations and mass organizations to defend human rights.

As to participation of the people, the seminar found that the primary task of development is to satisfy fundamental human needs, and that should any individuals impede that task the people could authorize their leaders to exert reasonable restrictions under carefully defined conditions; moreover, the people should make their leaders accountable for their actions and monitor them so that those leaders could enjoy the confidence and respect traditionally due to them.

It was also suggested that the African States should adopt a statute for migrant workers, non-national minorities and refugees and introduce an institution of the ombudsman type to make useful recommendations to the competent authorities.

In connexion with the judiciary, the seminar noted the existence of a number of obstacles to the effectiveness of judicial action in Africa and recommended: the establishment of a genuinely independent judiciary; the adoption of laws and regulations in conformity with the Constitution; the provision of guarantees to protect defendants and ensure execution of court decisions, especially those directed against the administration; the suppression of emergency courts; and the establishment of an association of African magistrates under the aegis of the OAU.

Future Action on the Right to Development

It is appropriate to acknowledge that, as a general proposition in terms of international human rights law, the existence of the right to development is a *fait accompli*. Whatever reservations different groups may have as to its legitimacy, viability or usefulness, such doubts are now better left behind and replaced by efforts to ensure that the formal process of elaborating the content of the right is a productive and constructive exercise.

The procedure to be employed in this undertaking was outlined by the Commission on Human Rights in a resolution adopted in March 1981. The Commission decided "to establish a working group of 15 governmental experts appointed by the Chairman of the Commission, taking into account the need for equitable geographic distribution, to study the scope and content of the right to development and the most effective means to ensure the realization, in all countries, of the economic, social and cultural rights enshrined in various international instruments, paying particular attention to the obstacles encountered by developing countries in their efforts to secure the enjoyment of human rights." The working group is to meet three times for a total of five weeks before the beginning of the thirty-eighth session of the Commission (February 1982). At that session the group is to submit to the Commission a report based on its work "with concrete proposals for implementation of the right to development and for a draft international instrument on this subject". At the same session the Commission is to accord high priority to its consideration of the question "with a view to adopting concrete measures on the basis of the recommendations of the working group". The emphasis therefore is on rapid progress and concrete measures. In many respects the work of the group will bring a time of reckoning for a concept which to date has been characterized by a concreteness akin to that of the right to happiness.

The challenges which will confront the drafters of an instrument on the right to development are two-fold. The first is to produce a text which will be acceptable to a substantial majority of UN members and which is capable of drawing strong support from within all ideological and geopolitical blocs. At the same time they must achieve a delicately balanced package of principles which gives equal weight to the national and international dimensions of the right, and which acknowledges the indivisibility and interdependence of all the rights contained in the International Bill of Human Rights. Unless these challenges are met the final product is unlikely to achieve any degree of consensus or to have any significant impact either on the promotion of respect for human rights or on the goal of establishing a new international order.

If the working group is to succeed in its task it will have to address itself to the following goals *inter alia*:

(1) achieving agreement upon a general, humanistically-oriented definition of development;
(2) emphasizing the importance of respect for human rights as an essential ingredient in the development process;
(3) reiterating that all human rights, including the right to development, are interdependent and indivisible;

(4) framing a broad definition of the right to development which makes clear that it is:
   - a dynamic and not a static concept;
   - a synthesis of existing rights given an extra dimension by refence to a number of interrelated goals;
   - a balanced package consisting of equally important national and international dimensions; and
   - a right which is as much a prerogative of nations as of individuals within nations;
(5) affirming that a development strategy based on repression and the denial of either civil and political rights or economic, social and cultural rights or both not only violates international human rights standards but is a negation of the concept of development;
(6) emphasizing the fundamental links between disarmament, demilitarization, peace, security and development;
(7) reflecting the concepts contained in General Assembly Resolu- 32/130;
(8) encouraging Member States to give substance, through increased international cooperation for development, to their pledge "to achieve, in cooperation with the United Nations, the promotion of universal respect for and observance of human rights and fundamental freedoms";
(9) ensuring that negotiations for the establishment of a new international economic order pay appropriate regard to their ultimate objective of enhancing respect for and the realization of human rights; and
(10) relating promotion of the right to development to the implementation procedures provided for under the two International Human Rights Covenants.

Note: The views expressed herein are solely the responsibility of the author. Some of the analysis reflected in this paper has been undertaken in connexion with a research project on the right to development, funded within the framework of the United Nations by a grant from the Dutch Government.

THE DECLARATION ON HUMAN RIGHTS AND THE RIGHT TO DEVELOPMENT: THE GAP BETWEEN PROPOSALS AND REALITY

Jacques Chonchol

Former Minister of Agriculture, Chile; Professor at the Institut des Hautes Etudes pour l'Amérique Latine, Paris

The Universal Declaration of Human Rights adopted and proclaimed by the General Assembly of the United Nations in 1948 imposes an obligation on State members of the international community to ensure a collection of rights to all people.

These rights should not only guarantee to each individual as against his own state certain civil and political freedoms considered as fundamental, but should also ensure for him a series of socio-economic and cultural conditions which will make possible the full realisation of his life and dignity as a human being. Among these conditions may be noted in particular the right to work, to education, to a sufficient standard of living, in particular as to food, clothing, housing and medical care and social services necessary for his health and well-being.

Thirty-two years have passed since this Declaration and during this historic period, rich in the most varied events, it seems right to draw attention to two major factors which seem important for our thesis. On the one hand, there has been a world-wide economic growth without parallel in any other period of universal history, which has seen world-wide production triple in value between 1950 and 1970 and double in value per inhabitant. On the other hand, there has been a constant emphasis becoming more and more widespread on the need to translate into reality the guarantees of human rights. This is shown by a considerable number of conferences, meetings, declarations and conventions with the participation of an increasing number of states which today include the greater part of the population of the world.

All this has been recognised by international public opinion through numerous "Years" aimed at drawing attention to the problems of particular persons and groups (the World Year of the Refugee, the

International Year of the Struggle against Racism and Racial Discrimination, the International Women's Year, the International Year of the Child), while we are awaiting in the 1980s the Year of the Handicapped, the Year of Youth and the Year of Old Age.

Nevertheless, today at the beginning of the 1980s, without taking into consideration (as being outside the scope of this paper) the millions of refugees and victims of political persecution who are compelled to live against their will outside their own country, and the millions of citizens and political prisoners living at home but subjected to a lack of essential freedoms as well as to the arbitrary rule of those who control their government, the situation of elementary economic and social rights is no better.

Economic and Social Rights

In a world in which, even with the recent economic crisis, growth has slowed up but has not ceased, and in which the governments of the planet swallow up every minute a million dollars in the frenzied armament race, the gap between rich and poor becomes greater each year. And this occurs not only at the international level as between the so-called "developed" and so-called "developing" nations, but also at the national level within these latter countries.

At the international level, according to the statistics collected by the United Nations on 130 countries, the 25 industrialised countries with a capitalist economy, in which live nearly 800 million people (20 % of the world population), disposed in 1976 of 66 % of the world GNP. At the opposite extreme, the 45 poorest developing countries, in which live 1,408 million people (35 % of the world population) disposed in the same year of 4 % of the world GNP. In individual terms the difference in average incomes was in the proportion of 30 to 1 ($5,716 per inhabitant against $191).[1] In the countries called by the United Nations "low income developing countries", the immense majority of the population lives in great poverty and has access only with difficulty to the most basic essentials, such as food, housing, clothing, water, health care and education.

It must be added that the 2,000 million people living in the other 40

---

1) See "Un Seul Monde: Supplément mondial pour un Nouvel ordre économique international", *Le Monde*, Paris, 24—25 June 1979.

countries, called "average income developing countries", disposed in 1976 of less than 13 % of the world income with an average annual income per inhabitant of $457; a large proportion of this population also lives in very difficult material conditions. This is due to the unequal distribution of income which characterises most of these countries and which favours above all the upper and middle urban classes and the big rural landowners.

But average incomes often hide the dramatic reality of the situation of the poorest population. This is seen more clearly when the analysis is focussed on the social groups which the terminology of international organisations now calls "the absolutely poor" or the "deprived" who are estimated today by the World Bank at nearly 800 million men, women and children without counting China and the other socialist countries.

These poorest and deprived people live in conditions of permanent under-nourishment; they have no certain access to water and what there is is often not drinkable; they are subject to all sorts of endemic illnesses such as schistosomiasis, malaria, cholera and parasitic worms; they do not have regular access to the most elementary education; the women have to work 15 to 16 hours a day to look after their homes and families and their productive work is often extremely arduous; and the expectation of life is less than 50 years and infant mortality above 150 deaths per 1,000 births. Of these 800 million people over 300 million are children. In this group of deprived people, three quarters of whom live in rural areas, unemployment and under-employment in remunerated work affects the majority of workers.

The greatest concentration of these absolute poor is in South-East Asia. Half the population of the world suffering from hunger are to be found in these countries; in this region 8 million children aged under five died during 1980, and 77 million children between the ages of 6 and 11 could not go to school.

In percentages, it is in Sub-Sahara Africa that the problems of destitution are most acute. Here one child in two is not properly nourished and one child in five dies before reaching its fifth year.[2]

---

2) "The State of Children in the World in 1980", James P. Grant, Director of UNICEF, Geneva.

Why such Great Contrasts?

How are such great contrasts to be explained between the enormous growth in production and productivity in the world in the last 30 years, the real possibilities which this growth provides for solving the essential problems of living of all mankind, the constant undertaking repeated during these 30 years by states saying they want to guarantee fundamental social rights, and the reality of the destitution which continues for so many people?

Moreover, it does not seem that this destitution will be reabsorbed in the two decades to come, since the World Bank tells us that if economic growth starts again at a good rhythm during the coming years — a hypothesis which it considers likely — 700 million people would be living in absolute poverty at the end of the century.[3]

How is the gap to be explained between what is said, and what happens, and what, it seems, will continue to happen?

At first sight one might think that it was a case of evident hypocrisy, of a flagrant contradiction between the assertions of state representatives who affirm the importance of international interdependence and solidarity, and their actual behaviour serving their national interests and the interests of those privileged groups which they represent. No doubt there is a substantial element of this kind of hypocrisy. But this alone is not sufficient to explain the results obtained. There is also something else. This something else is the manifest inability up to now of those who direct and influence the affairs of the international community to accept the fundamental falsity of certain myths which have governed the policies of development and the relations between states and peoples.

It seems to us important to analyse certain of these myths since it is they which largely make it impossible to equate the declarations on economic, social and cultural human rights with the policies which are followed.

The Myth of Growth as the Solution to the Problem of Poverty

Growth is a necessary condition, but is not sufficient in itself, to

3) World Bank "Report on Development", 1979.

bring an end to poverty. The experience of the last 30 years shows that a high rate of growth (as in the case of Brazil) can often be accompanied by an increase in the relative and even absolute poverty of large social groups, and that a considerable increase in the standard of living of the majority of the population can be obtained with a lower rate of growth in the GNP if, instead of focussing the main effort on growth, it is focussed on the way to resolve the problem of poverty.

The report of the Director of UNICEF which we have quoted above contains some very interesting examples to this effect like those of China, Sri Lanka and the State of Kerala in India.

In China in 1950 the average expectation of life was less than 45 years. Today it exceeds 70 years. During this period the numbers attending primary school has risen from 25 % to 94 % and the infant mortality rate which was among the highest in the world today is among the lowest of the developing countries. Nevertheless the present GNP in China is less than $300 per inhabitant.

In Sri Lanka, where the GNP is less than $200 per inhabitant, the literacy rate is 80 %, the infant mortality rate is less than 50 per 1,000 and the expectation of life is 68 years.

Kerala, with a population of 25 million inhabitants is one of the poorest states in India. Its GNP is $135 per inhabitant, lower than the $180 average for the whole of India. With this economic level and a rate of growth only a little above 1 % per person per year, Kerala has succeeded in providing primary school education for the majority of its children, three quarters of its adults know how to read and write, its infant mortality rate is 50 per 1,000 and the average expectation of life is 61 years.

These three countries are from the point of view of guarantees of economic, social and cultural rights well above many other countries whose GNP is two or three times greater and which have a very rapid rate of economic growth.

This shows the failure, from the point of view of human rights, of the development strategies which are focussed fundamentally on GNP growth, whereas the emphasis ought to be put above all on the means of solving the problems of poverty. The growth of GNP ought to be a complement and not an essential goal of an economy aimed at satisfying fundamental human rights.

This is the first of the myths which must be abandoned for it constitutes a fundamental obstacle to the realisation of these rights for most people.

The Myth of Western-Style Modernisation

The second myth is the express or implied belief that the forms of modernisation and of social organisation which developing societies should adopt is the model and cultural values of western industrial societies. The mode of development of these societies (and the differences between the capitalist and socialist industrialised countries on this subject is much less than is usually thought[4]) is based on a high accumulation of capital, on the most up-to-date technologies seeking to utilise less and less labour, on more and more sophisticated consumer goods, on a considerable use of fossil fuels per unit of production, on a highly developed urbanisation which absorbs the majority of the population and on a close link between industrialisation and urbanisation.

The spread of this model to third world countries only increases the gap within these countries between the minorities which the model can incorporate as modern producers and consumers and the majorities largely marginalised by their ever increasing number as well as by their poverty.

The extension of the western model of modern society to all peoples is impossible not only having regard to the limitations of certain resources essential for its functioning, but also by the ever-increasing costs. This is true even when applied to sectorial levels.

As Aurelio Peccei, President of the Club of Rome, said recently: "American agriculture devours a considerable energy. It is based on the absurd idea that petrol like water or air is inexhaustible... Today to produce a calory of food, an American farmer consumes a hundred times more calories of petroleum than an Indian."[5]

---

4) Except with reference to which social class controls the means of production and which class benefits primarily from the economic and social advantages of the system.

5) Aurelio Peccei, "L'humanité va vers un déclin progressif à moins que...", *Le Monde*, Paris, 2 June 1979.

Moreover, if one considers that in the developiing countries with a capitalist economy there were in 1975 700 million workers whose rate of unemployment and under-employment was 40 % and that this number will double by the year 2000,[6] it is difficult to see how the spread of the present western economic model can solve the problem of employment which is the essential basis for improving the income and satisfying the essential needs of the poorer populations.

It may be added that this model is in crisis today even in the industrialised countries and its continuance seems doubtful without fundamental changes which in effect imply the construction of a new model. This is by reason of the high cost of energy which, after declining in real terms over a period of 70 years, has since the 1970s increased in an explosive fashion.[7]

This is going to compel the western countries to review substantially the problem of its technologies, of its means and systems of transport, its means of housing, its way of life and its consumption, and at the same time this is going to modify considerably the comparative advantages of the different regions of the world from the point of view of international trade.

The myth of the western industrialised model as a universal model of development is also a fundamental obstacle to the guarantee of social, economic and cultural rights for the deprived populations of the third world.

The Myth of International Solidarity between States

A third myth to overcome is that of international solidarity between states. This can exist as between particular persons and social groups, and it may even exist between peoples in special circumstances. It is less evident between states, except between states which have common interests at stake. In the relations between states, the egoism of national interest predominates. Moreover, in the unequal relations

---

6) ILO, "Employment, Growth and Essential Needs", Geneva 1976.

7) In 1920 the price per barrel of petroleum was $1.20, when America entered the war after Pearl Harbour it was $1.14, at the time of the Marshall Plan $1.20, during the cold war of the 1950s $1.70 and in 1970 $1.80. In 1980 it exceeded $32 per barrel. "Le Défi mondial", Jean-Jacques Servan-Schreiber, Paris 1980.

between powerful and weak states what one sees is the desire to dominate and to influence in order to further the interests of the powerful states. In the latter case the "solidarity" may be manifested by keeping under control a "friendly" government or by trying to release a weak state from its dependence upon another strong state which is considered as an enemy.

If the government of a weak state wants to assert its independence as against the state which dominates it, the "solidarity" disappears and the state is transformed into an enemy, independently of the consequences this can have for its people.

On the other hand, most of the leaders of states who are subject to an electoral sanction think only in terms of their short-term interests and would be looked upon as mad if they applied policies which could have negative short-term consequences for their population, even if these policies would better their conditions in the long term. This is particularly true in times of crisis.

This shows the difficulties of making progress in negotiations to harmonise in the long term the interests of peoples living in conditions of profound inequality. This is the spectacle we have seen since 1974 when the General Assembly of the United Nations demanded the introduction of a "New International Economic Order".

More equitable relations between unequal states is thus a difficult and complex problem and without doubt there will not be significant progress by negotiation unless the majority of national leaders and public opinion formers in the industrialised countries are firmly convinced that:

— profound changes in the international economic system are in any event inevitable owing to the increasing weight (demographic, economic and political) of third world countries on the international scene, as well as by the new circumstances in their own system (energy costs, unemployment, inflation, need to find new and enlarged markets for their products, etc.);
— if profound changes are not undertaken by means of negotiation and joint long term planning, they will in any event be produced by successive crises and by confrontations which run the risk of an even higher political and social cost for their peoples and for themselves;
— in order to avoid critical confrontations and their negative conse-

quences for those in conflict, they must act jointly with other industrialised countries and with the governments of the third world countries in which the deprived populations live in order to solve the problems of extreme poverty. If action is not taken in this way, the increasing refusal of the poorest peoples in a world becoming ever richer to accept the conditions of destitution in which they live will provide a fertile soil for conflicts in the near future, which are liable to put in danger the developed countries' own security and well-being.

The Myth that the New International Economic Order Can Avoid Making the Essential Internal Social Reforms

A fourth myth, which this time concerns the behaviour of a large number of third world governments, is the belief that a new international economic order more favourable to the economic problems confronting them can enable them to avoid undertaking social reforms which today seem essential.

We have already indicated that the pursuit of growth by itself will not resolve the problems of destitute peoples and even less so when this growth is the result of imitating western models in countries whose socio-economic, cultural and demographic context is very different from that of the west. These policies even serve to increase the internal gap between the advantaged and the marginalised.

This situation becomes even more serious when the leaders of these countries come to power by force and seek only to benefit the privileged and powerful minorities which support them. It is often the case that this occurs with the economic and financial if not political support of the international community, which is more concerned with doing profitable business or with the financial orthodoxy of these governments than with resolving the essential human problems.

As long as these governments, little representative of their peoples, are not convinced that they will cease to enjoy the support of the international community unless they introduce effective internal policies to resolve the problems of poverty among their people — which often implies essential social reforms (for example, agrarian reform) — the problem of poverty in the third world cannot be resolved.

In this matter, it must be repeatedly stressed that, by reason of their activities in the third world, the IMF and the big private banks have a very heavy responsibility for the aggravation of the situation of the poorest populations.

Conclusions

It is essential to react forcibly against these four myths, which have been very cursorily examined, if one wants to reduce as speedily as possible the gap between the declarations on social and economic rights of peoples and the reality of the implementation of these rights. This implies a basic action programme for the right to development.

Before concluding, we would like to add two additional considerations.

The first is that one of the essential conditions of the struggle against extreme poverty is to ensure that the projects for development concerning the poorest populations, which are often undertaken with the support of international organisations, in fact favour the most deprived.

This is not easy for a number of reasons, partly owing to the lack of organisation and of structured relations with the state apparatus of the poorest sectors and partly by their weakness as a political pressure group. This is particularly true in relation to the rural populations among whom are to be found the majority of the poorest in the third world countries.

Moreover, even in countries where the poorest communities are predominant, we find important social cleavages and it is generally the richest or the most powerful who become the normal spokesmen in these communities of the external agencies trying to realise development projects. As a result, these richer or less poor groups (farmers, merchants, local officials) are those who profit more than others from the benefits of the projects.

It must be added that the very poor communities, living in a most precarious state of subsistence, cannot easily accept large-scale external changes owing to the very insecurity in which they find themselves, and cannot rapidly absorb large quantities of resources without destroying themselves. All this goes against the behaviour of governments and international organisations which prefer big projects capable of being presented as models and absorbing important resources.

Finally, it must be noted that poverty is a state in which several situations combine and reinforce each other: lack of education, undernourishment, poor conditions of health and of work, insecurity, passivity, etc. To break this chain implies an integrated action on several complementary fronts and not actions focussed on isolated technical or economic aspects.

It is therefore necessary, if one wants to combat extreme poverty effectively, to modify most of the approaches to the problems of development which are followed today as much by governments of the third world as by international organisations, as these approaches, by favouring above all large scale projects and particular technical and economic aspects, have predominantly benefitted the middle sectors and the local bureaucracies in these countries rather than the truly poor.

The second consideration which seems to us important is that, contrary to what takes place today in the attitude of the developed countries, the political and social struggles in third world countries against governments which are little representative of the interests of the majority of their population, must not be regarded as threats to internal or world stability and security.

This is one of the consequences of the famous theory of 'national security' developed by leaders of the armed forces who see behind every political or social struggle against oppression and economic exploitation a menace to the security of the state and international political stability.

This attitude is particularly strong in the West which sees behind every social struggle in the third world the hand of international communism seeking to de-stabilise pro-western governments and to bring about a revolution. There is a very strong tendency in these countries to look upon the existing order, even if it is based on the worst social and economic injustices, as good in itself, and to regard everything which threatens this order as an evil which must be fought. In the world in which we live, full of inequalities and injustices, the psychological attitude of rich and well-fed people runs contrary to the policy of the most elementary human rights. This is a very important factor which must be considered when analysing contemporary events, and it helps to explain the brutal cleavage between what people say they want to do about human rights and what they do in fact.

Not being a lawyer, I cannot say how these considerations can be incorporated in the spirit of the laws. But it seems to me that it is fundamental to study them in any analysis, like that which this Conference seeks to make, of the relationship between development and the rule of law.

Paris, February 1981

WHAT KIND OF DEVELOPMENT AND
WHAT KIND OF LAW

Johan Galtung

Geneva University Institute of Development Studies,
Process and Indicators of Development Project (GPID)

Introduction

When two extremely rich, complex and above all evolving concepts, such as "development" and "the rule of law" are to be related to each other the agenda of inquiry is in a sense given in advance: first, have a quick look at each of them, second, try to relate them to each other. A special warning against this kind of intellectual exercise should be issued. Both concepts are evolving in a historical context and will continue to do so. Consequently, there is a limit to how much can be obtained from a conceptual, logically oriented analysis. A typology of "development" concepts and "rule of law" concepts may be constructed and they may all be related to each other in the search for compatibilities and contradictions. This is useful, but the fact that both of them are parts of a concrete historical process must not be lost sight of. There may be some kind of overriding compatibility due to belonging to the same historical process; there may be some kind of built-in contradiction stemming from exactly that process.

As an example take the three sets of human rights: civil and political rights (CPR); economic, social and cultural rights (ESCR) and the recent solidarity rights (SR). No doubt the first set is related to the interests of a bourgeoisie fighting its way out of feudal constraints, the second set is related to the interests of the working class and other groups marginalized and exploited, hurt and hit, by the emergence of that class as a dominant class, and the third set is related to the same kind of problems at the international level, an effort to overcome the contradictions created by international capitalism, private and state. And the development concepts may be made to read like chapters in any book on recent history: the first set of concepts is "blue" development, economic growth spearheaded by an entrepreneurial class unfettered by state control or initiative; the second set of concepts is a reaction to this, "red" development, economic growth controlled and initiated by a state bureaucracy, codified in a plan; and the third set of concepts is a reaction to both of the former, "green" development, based more on the autonomy of the local level and the virtues of the smaller economic cycles. Much of the current development debate is concerned with whether one has to suffer the contradictions of the blue to become red and the contradictions of each and both, stemming from the circumstance that they both lead to big systems, in order to become green. As many poor, "third" world countries still are to a large extent green, could they possibly be better off strengthening that aspect, building on top of it only a relatively weak blue and red sector? And could the rich, "first" and "second" — blue and red — countries do better reducing their entrepreneurial and bureaucratic giants, at the same time strengthening old and new types of local communities? The sympathies of the author are in this general direction.

Some Words on "Development"

The brief excursion just made into the history of development/development of history brings out the two key dimensions in development theory and practice, viz.,

level: is it predominantly *macro-oriented*, towards building strong countries (with strong entrepreneurial and/or bureaucratic classes) and a new international order accommodating the changes in power and privileges among countries?
or
is it predominantly *micro-oriented*, towards building strong human beings and strong local communities (or basic autonomous units in general) in which human beings can unfold themselves *à la hauteur de l'homme*?

aspect: is it predominantly *one-dimensional*, and in that case particularly focussing on economic dimensions, on social structure, institution-building, ecological dimensions, cultural aspects, and so on?
or
is there an attempt to be *multi-dimensional*, even "holistic", taking the "totality" as the focus of development, encompassing all dimensions?

This gives us four styles of development; and there can be little doubt that so far we have seen most of the macro-oriented, one-dimensional combinations. There are two basic models, the liberal/capitalist and the marxist/socialist, both focussing on the economic dimension in the blue and red varieties, respectively — one often leading to growth without control, the other to control without growth. The crisis of these two models is what is known today as the "development crisis". Exacerbating the situation is the fact that the superpowers, the US and the SU, demand from their client states that they by and large adhere to the blue and red development models respectively. If not, they are branded as security risks.

At the other extreme, then, is the multi-dimensional, micro-oriented approach, often called community development. It is characterized in most thinking and practice by a high level of local self-reliance, short economic cycles, informal/green economies, direct democracy, much participation, and much emphasis on human growth, personal development. Many such communities, however, tend to focus on only one such aspect and hence become very imbalanced; and many countries, of course, focus not only on the economy but also on very much else (often called social development) and then become more balanced — giving us the last two combinations.

Which is the "correct" style of development? One possible answer to this would be to say "all of them", the answer preferred by the present author, but as the current processes are so overwhelmingly of the macro-oriented, one-dimensional type in the current historical situation a strong emphasis on the opposite type is needed — not a green, but a *greener* approach. Real quality of life can probably best be experienced and obtained at the micro level, but the macro level is a rather strong reality and can both facilitate and impede this quality of life. And however much we may praise holism, total thinking and total practice tend either to lead to inaction (it all becomes too complicated to make any first move) or to totalitarianism (it all has to be changed at once according to total schemes). The latter may not be so dangerous if only one small community is involved, but as a blueprint for a whole country or for *all* communities it becomes very dangerous. Hence starting in one corner, with one aspect, even introducing contradictions between the "old" and the "new" to get a dialectic going, with much richer totalities in mind, may not be the worst approach.

The *basic needs* approach is important in all of this: it is a protest movement, do not forget the micro level, in all the efforts to build strong countries do not forget the more basic purpose of building strong human beings! The developmentalists of the blue and red varieties tried to co-opt this protest movement by making it one-dimensional, focussing on the material needs most clearly related to their economic growth and institution-building only, and have so far been partly successful in this. Precisely because of their success, e.g. in UN organizations dominated by the blue and the red, micro level development is seen as even more important, but it has to cater to all kinds of human needs — material and non-material. No doubt, if the green movement with its anarchist overtones of "small is beautiful" (mindless of the extent to which some big may be necessary) were really successful there would be scope for a protest movement in favour of some more macro-oriented approaches. Today that movement is more than sufficiently "successful", and entrenched.

Thus, development is seen as a complex dialectic between the micro and macro levels and between the one-dimensional and the more holistic approaches. Where do the human rights as a particular type of "rule of law" fit into all of this?

Some Words on "Human Rights"

Basic human rights share with basic human needs a concern for everybody, not only for the needs of the strong and the rights of the privileged. Precisely for that reason the focus should be on the most needy and on those whose basic human rights have been most violated. In principle these are approaches from the bottom up — an indispensable corrective to the top-heaviness and self-serving nature of so much of what elites put forward as "development". Human rights, then, differ from human needs in being institutionalized in a particular way. One may perhaps see them as evolving from a much larger sociological category of *mutual rights and obligations*, the normative material weaving together any human group, defining in sets of expectations (often crystallized as roles, or norm-sets, and as statuses or role-sets) what are the rights and duties of everybody. There are *senders* who expect these norms to be complied with, there are *receivers* whose duty it is to comply with the norms, there are the *objects*, those whom the norm is about (and this may be the sender and/or the receiver, not necessarily third parties), and there is the *content* of the norm. A norm is an S,R,O,C quadruple — what form does that take for the case of a human right? Briefly stated:

In a *human right*

— the *norm-sender* is the UN General Assembly
— the *norm-receiver (débiteur)* who is duty bound to implement the norm, is the government
— the *norm-object (créancier)* is the holder of the right, "everybody", the citizen, the human being
— the *norm-content (objet précis)* is the substantive content of the norm.

Thus, in the particular type of institutionalization of norms characteristic of human rights the object is separated from the sender and the receiver. It is not "I expect you to do this to me and in return I shall do that to you" but "I expect you to do this (positively or negatively defined) to a third party".

It is easily seen that such a concept suffers from two immediate weaknesses. First, it is not really based on mutuality, or at least not explicitly. The citizen has only rights, the government has only duties, and the UN General Assembly is only a source of norm production. That should make one suspicious: what are the duties of the citizens in return for these rights? What are the rights of the governments in return for these duties? And what does the General Assembly (of governments) expect to get in return from the right *and* duty to be a source of norm production? Obviously the citizen should see the government as a major source of righting wrongs, and the government will see itself as one that has the right to be the *état providence*. And the General Assembly becomes some kind of super providence, as a bare minimum.

Both this leads to the same problem as is known from criminal law: the victim recedes into the background, the crime becomes a relation between the state and the defendant, alienating what started as a direct relationship. Similarly a human rights infraction becomes a relation between the defendant government and the organs of the General Assembly, particularly the Human Rights Commission, maybe also, in a sense, the International Commission of Jurists, when it evolves further. In the tradition of criminal law a major function of this alienation is to protect the defendant against the "arbitrary" wrath of the offended, the victim — particularly when/if the victim rallies together his/her friends and starts exercising justice more directly. Could it be that the human rights tradition has a similar function, not only of protecting the victim, against the governments, but also of protecting governments against the accumulated, collective wrath of victims in open mutiny, revolt? Could it be that governments would prefer an arrangement "among gentlemen"; with some expression of moral disapproval on a "today me, tomorrow you" basis, fragmenting to the point of individualization the victims, substituting resolutions for revolutions? As in criminal law, in this kind of intergovernmental criminal law the compensation given to the victims is weak or non-existent, leaving him/her not even with a certificate to the effect that s/he was right, only that the offender was wrong and should be punished, somehow.

Second, there is little doubt that the human rights tradition is more consonant with top-heavy, blue-red development and less with development based on small, basic and autonomous units where the primordial human rights tradition, the mutual rights and obligations, would fit better. Thus, there is an implicit stand taken: the human rights tradition is a macro approach aiming at coming to the rescue at the micro level, and in so doing increasing the legitimacy of an incipient world government/parliament system, with the UN General Assembly as the legislature and a court and a number of executive organs. As rights multiply so would, or should, the machineries to make them really justiciable: detection and reporting processes, adjudication processes, sanction processes, review processes. The more macro the system the more complex the machineries to make the rulers accountable to their subjects; the more complex the machineries, the more macro the system.

None of this should be seen as more than warnings: as long as the basic human rights work in the interests of the most deprived the tradition is invaluable even if it has certain limits to growth of which, at present, we know relatively little. But it raises the question: could something between the codified, top-heavy rule of law and the uncodified, bottom level mutual rights and obligations be more compatible with green development, and hence something *in the present phase of human history* to be encouraged? More explicit, more codified, but also more left to local processes of accountability, breaking the by now age old division of labour that the more terrible the crime, the "higher" the level of the court till one ends up at the intergovernmental level, thereby sanctifying those levels? Of course, there is a very good reason for this: if in the phase of human history where nation-state building and international architecture were the orders of the day most big crimes were committed by big governments and big corporations, then one needed something on top of both for adjudication — particularly important today in the field of solidarity rights. But this leaves the lower levels without a say, they are often sidetracked from the very beginning, and institution-building is not done at that level, at least not so much as at the "higher" levels. What we are looking for is the consistent translation of human rights thinking into municipal law, but then emphasizing the general thrust of the argument, the basic needs entitlement, rather than the universality found, for instance, in the four components of the International Bill of Human Rights. Particular human rights, made specific to local culture and historical context, may be as significant as universal human rights, but one does not exclude the other.

Then, there is another dimension of human rights thinking that is of basic significance for the right to development: is the right *institution-oriented*, or *structure-oriented*? The meaning of this crucial distinction can be seen from a couple of examples:

- in the field of food: is the focus on being fed, or on being able to feed oneself through the appropriate structural arrangements?
- in the field of health: is the focus on access to institutions for somatic and mental health service, or on living in a structure that produces a maximum of somatic and mental health?
- in the field of energy: is the focus on having access to energy conveniently converted, or on being able to obtain conversion, locally?
- in the field of participation: is the focus on access to a ballot box or on life in a participatory structure?

In another document of the GPID project, I have given some indications of what the structural approach in the fields of food, health and energy might mean. The key point would be local self-reliance even to the point of local self-sufficiency where these three fundamentals are concerned, "local" meaning not necessarily the small community, it could also mean bigger units if the economic geography makes self-reliance at the truly local level impossible. With some important technological innovations in recent years, especially in the field of energy conversion, there should be space for some optimism in this field.

In the "structural approach" the basic idea would be that certain goods and services are made available with a certain level of *automaticity*, and certain bads and disservices (eg in the field of pollution) are avoided with a certain automaticity. These factors are built into the structure, as the saying goes — as when a farmer growing food-stuffs for subsistence tries to avoid depletion and pollution because he himself will be the victim of the consequences (the transnational agro-business corporation does not need to take this into account as the consequences will be far away, and when they become too disastrous the TNC will move to other areas on which to prey). In the structural approach certain obstacles are removed by changing the structure — the approach is preventive rather than curative, when the focus is on bads and disservices. All of this can also be done at the macro level, nationally and internationally, by governments and by intergovernmental organizations. But there is one thing that cannot be done at the macro level, and that is direct participation. If one accepts the basic assumption underlying the green approaches, enlightened self-interest, but "self" in the sense of "Self", in the sense of a collectivity small enough to permit not only identification but direct participation so as to trigger off the mechanisms that ensure the automaticity, not as the result of benign action from above but as the accumulated effect of myriads of actions below, then the structural approach has as a condition at least an element of the small. We say an element, for those small communities could, of course, be federated into something bigger, based both on the solidarity within and the solidarity among such communities. The key word is actually *solidarity*, and the key problem is how one builds it so that it increases automatically, making institutionalized attempts to enforce solidarity marginal, residual.

Again, it is obvious where the thrust of the human rights approach has been: *macro-level* rather than *micro-level*; *institutional* rather than *structural*. The first speaks to the interests of the people behind it, probably more attracted by the prospects of work at the macro level — governmental and/or inter-governmental — than at the local level. The latter speaks to their deep ideology, probably more actor-oriented than structure-oriented, more liberal than marxist in another word-pair, and hence more geared towards institution-building than structural transformation. It will probably belong to the picture that these people themselves will either deny the former or deny that it has any significance other than positive, and would be blind to the significance of the latter — seeing, like everybody, better the biases of others than of oneself. But all of this is probably also undergoing change, even right now.

Some Words on the Relation between "Development" and "Rights"

In a sense it has all been said above: it is a question of compatibility and contradiction. But from that it does not follow that the only valid approach is micro-level, holistic development, protected by structure-building mutual rights and obligations. This would first of all presuppose a world where all societies are in the same historical situation (I do not say "stage" or any such term), and secondly presuppose that the good society is the contradiction-free society. Of the two sets of four approaches, one for development and one for human rights, I would be inclined to be in total disfavour of none of them, nor of any of the combinations. The richness and complexity of these schemes bear some testimony to the richness and complexity of the human condition in general. But having said that I think there is little doubt that much more emphasis should be placed on the lower level, local level approaches both for development and for human rights, and on the structural approaches for both of them. The details of this, however, I would prefer to leave for the discussion.

HUMAN RIGHTS, RIGHT TO DEVELOPMENT AND THE NEW INTERNATIONAL ECONOMIC ORDER – PERSPECTIVES AND PROPOSALS

R.N. Trivedi

Director, Human Rights Institute, Lucknow, India

The Concern

History is a mute witness to the most inhuman suffering that man has inflicted on man. He has hoped and allowed himself to be led to the promised land but in the bargain also learnt to obey the command to trample over the hopes and aspirations of others in the fond belief that God is always on the side of the victors. He has thus sought to build a 'Utopia' over the blood, tears and toil of others.

Human rights are to be viewed in the context of human suffering due to oppression. An individual in relation to family, society and the state may be faced with the threat to his rights for which no remedy in the ordinary legal course may be available to him, either on account of his ignorance or helplessness. The two primary factors, reducing a human being to such a state of helplessness, are FEAR and WANT. While fear emanates from the mind, and want from the body, they both contribute to the utter degradation of a human being both mentally and physically and stultify human personality.

In the political chess board both fear and want are used as levers by vested interests for jockeying themselves into power. This struggle for power, although manifest at every stage of human organisation, becomes extremely acute at the political level. Power as a means to control state and power as a means to retain and perpetuate power has often resulted in the worst form of atrocities on human beings.

Man in his vanity has demanded unflinching loyalty from his fellow beings leading them to war in the vain hope that it may be the last, and the humility of defeat as a counter measure giving rise to the basest human passion of hatred and revenge. Highest moral principles have been invoked to torture and subjugate the human body and the human will.

Yet the indomitable spirit of man, phoenix like, has risen from the

ashes of despair to refurbish the bastions of hope, to give new meaning to life and make it worth living. All efforts in this direction, as
history recalls, have been made by demolishing artificial barriers set
up by man against man and glorifying the essential humanism that
unites human beings both in pleasure and pain. Thus through the
ages man has struggled and hoped for a better morrow. *Want* he has
sought to banish by unending toil but the lurking *fear* that the fruits
of his toil and labour may be snatched away from him has to be dis-
pelled by faith. Faith in the form of awareness of his rights as a human being, individually or in a group, to enjoy life together or alone
and to share the bounties of nature beyond the man made barriers —
social, economic, political and geographic.

It is alleged, and not without reason, that there is an elitist approach
to the problem of human rights and that it is the affluent sections of
the society in relation to the State and affluent States in the global
context, which are the major beneficiaries of the cliché of human
rights.

What do human rights mean to the vast majority of illiterate poverty
striken men, women and children in the Third World?

For the toiling peasants, bonded labour, impoverished children and
ill-treated women it remains a platitudinous utopia. In the past 30
years or more a large number of nations have attained political independence from colonial rule. Attainment of political independence
may be the first step towards achieving dignity of man but in order
to ensure that the political independence is not in danger it is necessary that the newly independent countries and economically backward and oppressed nations should get a fair chance of improving the
lot of their citizens.

As rightly observed by the Minister of Foreign Affairs and Minister
for Development and Cooperation of the Netherlands:[1] "The wretch-
ed economic conditions in much of the Third World constitute a serious obstacle to the realization of human rights. In the first instance
this naturally applies to the social rights such as the right to an adequate standard of living, including food, clothing, housing and medical care. The most fundamental human right, the right to life is

---

1) Memorandum presented to the lower house of the States General of the Kingdom of
Netherlands on 3.5.1979 by the Minister of Foreign Affairs and Minister for Development and Cooperation.

threatened by famines and epidemics; the right to work is frustrated by mass unemployment; the right to education remains a dead letter for hundreds of millions of illiterates. At the same time these conditions stand in the way of the realisation of a number of classic freedoms. Illiteracy for example hinders the meaningful exercise of the right to information and the right to take part in politics. Accordingly, it is an undisputed fact that development of the Third World is a necessary precondition for enabling the people who live there – the majority of the world population – to enjoy human rights in a meaningful sense. Views on the connection between development and the promotion of human rights have, however, evolved considerably over the years."

With this end in view the countries of the Third World started pressing for a New International Economic Order (NIEO). Although it took several years for the United Nations' General Assembly to pass its resolution on the NIEO on 1 May, 1974, its adoption was preceded by the first oil crunch in 1973.

When we talk of the New International Economic Order we have to consider the steps that would be necessary to do away with the present division of the world into rich and poor nations and into agricultural and industrial nations. In this connection, W. Arthur Lewis,[2] after a careful examination of the role which geographical, economic, military and other factors could have played in the present division of the world, suggests that "The basic way to create a new international order is to eliminate 50–60 % of low productivity. This would change the factoral terms of tropical trade and raise the price of the traditional agricultural exports.

The most important item on the agenda of development is to transform the food sector, create agricultural surpluses to feed the urban population and thereby create the domestic basis for industry and modern services. If we make this domestic change, we shall automatically have a new international economic order."

Food Security

But the less developed countries are still far from realising the requir-

---

2) W. Arthur Lewis: Evolution of the International Economic Order: Economic Impact, Number Thirty One.

ed improvements in agricultural productivity which according to Lewis seem to be necessary for an "automatic" attainment of the NIEO.

There has been a persistant repetition of drought. It has been observed that there is a drought every six years with chances of its repetition being as high as 75 %. It is also held that optimum buffer stocks of food to tide over calamities should be for about 4 years. There should be a minimum global reserve to respond to short term food crises.

Unfortunately, however, food has been used as a ransom and at times as a weapon in the armoury of foreign policy.

Classic human rights symbolised by liberty and freedom have the right to life as a pre-requisite. The first concern of the Third World has to be to ensure a minimal sustenance for the starving people.

Although food security should be the primary concern in order of priority, it should not be isolated from the total development, in order to realize human rights in its widest concept.

Harry G. Johnson[3] observed that "there is a serious danger to the world economic order of a retreat into mercantilist economic policies as a result of a cumulation of piecemeal decisions the full implication of which are never thought through". The observations of Harry G. Johnson, though made before the resolution of the U.N. General Assembly was adopted in 1974, have proved to be prophetic.

Required Attitudinal Change

Jan Tumlir[4] is of the view that "Given the fact of (i) national sovereignty, (ii) the concentration of international economic transactions and (iii) democratic control of government in the countries among whom these transactions largely take place, we are thus driven to the conclusion that a necessary condition of a change in the effective

---

3) Harry G. Johnson — Address to the British Association for the Advancement of Science, Canterbury, 20 August, 1973 — as quoted by Jan Tumlir: Can the International Economic Order be saved? The World Economy, Volume 1, Number 1, October, 1977.

4) Jan Tumlir: Op.cit.

rules is an agreement among the core countries of the world economy.

We are now in the position to identify the main causes of the difficulty in which the negotiations for the reform of the international economic order have arrived. It lies in the attempt to make the order bear functions which only an organisation can discharge.

But in general an international order which necessarily lacks an enforcement mechanism must be based on reciprocity as a guarantee of good faith. Rules which would not be fair would have no chance of being obeyed.

A reasonably frictionless co-existence of sovereign nations can be maintained only within an international order based on liberal principles."

According to Jan Tumlir the demand for a New International Economic Order is the standard argument of the late comers. It is submitted that this argument based on the plea of fairness and equality cannot itself be deemed unethical. It is not as if the Third World by volition chose to remain backward in matters of economic development. The enquiry into the reasons of such backwardness does not lie within the scope of this paper but it cannot be disputed that those who had already "arrived" had a vested interest in ensuring that the Third World countries do not claim a share in their existing state of affluence. The changing political and economic concepts of the present day world clearly indicate that we have come a long way from the theory of partisan application of laissez-faire combined with "protectionism" in the sphere of international trade.

Philip Alston[5] has observed that "The linking of human rights and NIEO objectives has much to recommend it. In general terms it is clear that the real bargaining power of the developing countries is primarily political rather than economic. By framing their economic demands in terms of human rights issues their political power assumes an added ethical dimension, which, as the Brandt report has pointed out, is an indispensable element in the mobilization of widespread support for a NIEO programme. Thus, extension of the NIEO debate to the UN's human rights fora serves to highlight its ethical content".

---

5) Philip Alston: Development and the Rule of Law: Prevention versus Cure as a Human Rights Strategy, *supra.*

In the world of today, however, where there is professed equality in terms of political independence (although it has unsolvable problems like South Africa, Namibia and the genetically inherent colour discrimination) the "ethical argument" seems to be a philanthropic argument. The Third World countries in the above context ought not to be branded as nations undeserving of equality and fairness in the matter of economic trade.

Attitudinal aberrations of those who violate human rights are elevated to a superior status and the plight of the down trodden is viewed as one which is deserved by them. Unless this is removed the talk about human rights in the field of a new order would be meaningless.

The question, therefore, is one of change of attitude. It is inherent in the realisation of a duty as a human being to uplift the down trodden. The international politics of territorial hegemony, expansion of areas of economic interest, an inbuilt insulation of those who are better off and looking down upon those who are not, however, stand in the way of such a realisation.

Right to Develop

The right to life and liberty is the most basic right. The requirement is not for the recognition of the right to live being a basic right but effective implementation of it which ultimately depends upon economic development.

It is, therefore, necessary to consider development in terms of human rights. As pointed out by the Foreign Minister of the Kingdom of the Netherlands, the "Rights of man, human rights, or fundamental rights are names given to those elementary rights which are considered to be indispensable for the development of the individual." In this context rise in GNP is not to be considered a sufficient basis for ensuring human development unless it is also accompanied by improvement in the lot of the poorest of the poor. What has to be ensured is pervasive distributive justice.

It has, however, to be borne in mind that no level of economic development can be sustained unless there is a check on the growth of the population, nor can the developed nations remain indifferent on the plea that effective measures to check the population explosion have to be taken exclusively by the Third World, for an unchecked growth of population would also affect the developed nations socially, economically and politically. This, however, is to be achieved by means which do not violate human rights.

It is queer that in the 60's the need for economic cooperation and interdependence was being voiced by the developing countries. Since the 70's, however, it is being shared by the developed countries as well. Whether this transformation is due to the oil crunch or to combat the widely shared belief among the developing nations that a totalitarian set up is necessary for rapid economic development has to be analysed.

The argument raised at the national as well as international level is that the right to life in its widest connotation and liberty in its minimal are incompatible in the present socio-economic and political scenario in the Third World. It is urged that in order to bring about economic development, it is necessary to subordinate the classic freedoms. This is a dangerous generalisation. Examples are many to demonstrate that a totalitarian regime does not automatically remove economic backwardness.

Rightly the Manila Conference of the International Law Association[6] rejected the general proposition that the supposed imperatives of economic development require 'trading off' of civil and political rights for the realisation of economic, social and cultural rights and emphasized the need to achieve the two sets of rights through an integrated approach.

International Cooperation in Economic Development: Norms

The concept of interdependence having been increasingly shared by the developed nations in the recent past has resulted in not only an enquiry but an effort to work out the modalities for restructuring economic relations on a global scale. Such restructuring, however, is beset with many inter-related problems — legal, political and economic. If a new order has to be achieved new rules are to be set. The existing regulatory framework has to be altered to meet the new challenges and obligations. Incidental arrangements and decision making procedures have also to be established, e.g. an international code of conduct for transfer of technology, which is under negotia-

6) Manila Recommendations of the International Law Association, 1978.

tion in UNCTAD; a Code of Conduct on Trans-national Corporations (TNCs), which is being formulated by the UN Commission on Trans-national Corporations; a proposal currently being debated for amendment of the GATT and the Paris Convention on Patents.

Establishment of the NIEO and the source of legal obligation towards it was spelled out by the International Law Association Subcommittee in the following terms in its Manila Report, 1978:

"It seems clear, however, that any strategy for the implementation of human rights in regions made up of countries in which mass poverty exists must necessarily concern itself with transforming the material conditions and the environments in which the majority of people in such societies find themselves. Whether this process is characterised as "economic development" or "the realisation of economic and social rights", it must involve a substantial measure of international cooperation".

The norms emerging from the resolution of the Manila Conference in regard to International Cooperation are:

(i)   respect for the sovereign equality of the States;
(ii)   recognition of the principle of interdependence irrespective of the variations of socio-economic and political systems; and
(iii)   acceptance as a *duty* on the part of the developed nations — (a) to remove diverse restraints which continue to obstruct the attainment of development objectives; and (b) to provide positive assistance to promote the universal achievement of the human right to development.

Economic Aid and Regional Security

It is apparent from the non-working of the NIEO in the past seven years that there is something inherently lacking in the institutionalisation of fairness and equality in the charter of economic growth and development of nations. It appears that in order to combat the attitudinal indifference of the rich nations it would be imperative to have regional and subregional groups of the Third World nations in order that they may effectively combat unfairness and unreasonableness. There has been a global tendency to articulate aid with security. The whole question is whose security? Is it political or economic security of the strong and economically affluent nations? If so, it seems to be illogical because it would work against the interests of the militarily weak and economically impoverished nations. If, however, the security is in terms of East-West or North-South it demonstrates the desire to perpetuate the present state of political hegemony which some of the developed countries enjoy over the less developed countries, with a view to keeping the latter in a state of dependence.

Is the Cooperation of the West Optional?

It cannot be over emphasized that with greater realisation of interdependence it is no longer open to the Western countries to treat cooperation with the Third World as a matter totally discretionary and not obligatory. If the basic premise that such cooperation is not a matter of charity is accepted, it would logically follow that cooperation has to be on equal terms. The cooperation of the Western countries with the developing countries would be in its own interest. It should also be realized that economic forces are not immutable. What, for instance, would happen if the alternative sources of energy are found located only in the Third World. The unfortunate position at present, however, is that political considerations are outweighing the economic compulsions for cooperation and hindering the emergence of NIEO.

Human Rights Are Relative/Comparative

The proponents of human rights while evolving an ethical and moral code of conduct should also realize that such conduct has priorities. The demand for human rights in the East and West is based on different concepts. In a country which has a well-fed literate population with developed social security any encroachment on the right to privacy and freedom of the press is elevated to the level of violation of human rights, while food still is the basic right for those who are starving in the Third World. It is this reason which sometimes makes the concern of the Western nations about protection of human rights in the Third World unreal. Human rights make progressive and continuous demands on the economic system. The story of human rights is the story of human aspirations linked with the stages of economic progress. So long as human beings aspire, human rights will be a limitless concept. Liberty-freedom is a necessary prerequisite for human aspirations without which there can be no economic development. Development, which itself is a result of human aspirations at a given level, is further reinforced by rising aspiration levels resulting from the liberty and freedom that it generates.

Unfortunately, however, freedom and liberty are words conceived in political terms and with political constraints. Ideological approaches to liberty and freedom may be at variance, yet their role in facilitating economic development would be indisputable.

It would thus be apparent that the concern of the Western-Northern nations for improving the lot of the Eastern-Southern nations has to be shifted from mere resolutions and platitudinous recommendations, to a positive attitudinal change in terms of cooperative effort to implement the NIEO objectives in conformity with Human Rights.

Conclusions

With this objective in view the following suggestions are put forward for consideration:

(i)   There should be a vigorous attempt to depoliticize the implementation of the NIEO and an effort to rouse the conscience and obligations of those who are in a position at present to extend a helping hand, keeping in mind the fact that economic forces do not always remain constant.

(ii) Since the NIEO has run into implementational difficulties there is a greater need for regional and subregional organisations and institutions in the Third World to resist unfair und unequal treatment by the affluent nations.

(iii) A scheme of development with short term and long term priorities clearly spelt out should be formulated so that the Third World nations should not be continuously in a stage of crisis management but should be in a position to orient their policies to resolve problems in long term perspectives. With this in view there is an urgent need to create an independent international agency to ensure depoliticized minimal food security. The Brandt Commission has set out an emergency programme for 1980—1985 and the tasks for the 80's and 90's for ensuring economic development. There should be a parallel objective set out by human rights organisations to ensure that while implementing the new order human rights do not become a casualty.

(iv) Evolution of a suitable institutional framework for implementing the resolution for the NIEO should be given primary importance.

(v) There has to be monitoring of the grievances of the Third World countries about violation of human rights inthe process of implementation of the NIEO, and with this objective in view a forum at the international level should be created for evaluation, on a periodic basis, of the state of human rights qua the NIEO.

THE RIGHT TO DEVELOPMENT: FROM EVOLVING PRINCIPLE TO "LEGAL" RIGHT: IN SEARCH OF ITS SUBSTANCE

Karel de Vey Mestdagh

Lecturer on International Law, University of Utrecht

CONTENTS

Note: This working paper is a preparatory study for an article published in 28 Netherlands International Law Review (1981), pp. 30–53.

Introduction

On 17 May 1980 Mr J. de Koning, the Minister for Development Co-operation, addressed a public meeting of the Independent Commission on International Development Issues in The Hague. The Brandt Commission, as it is otherwise known, had recently published a report which made various proposals for structural reforms in the economic relations between the developed countries and the Third World — also with the aim of breaking the almost hopeless deadlock the North-South dialogue had reached.[1]

In his address, entitled "The Right to Existence and to Development", the Minister called for legal creativity. The development problem, he said, concerns people who are helpless. "The misery of these people is the real driving force behind development cooperation. They have a *right* to live, and it is our *obligation* to help them... Declaring physical existence to be a right lifts aid in this context out of the realms of charity and accords it the status of a right." Mr De Koning went on to say that at the national level we had been acting on this principle for many years. "In our own countries the weak are no longer dependent on charity; they have gained the right to a secure existence, the right to receive assistance." The Minister considered it of the utmost importance that the "right to development" and the "right to international assistance" be formulated in international law. He concluded by calling for contributions to the discussion on these new rights.[2]

I should like to respond to his appeal by attempting to give a legal definition of the "right to development". My paper is in three parts: in the first I shall outline what has happened so far in international

---

1) *North-South: A programme for survival*, London, 1980.

2) J. de Koning, "Recht op bestaan en ontwikkeling" (The Right to Existence and Development), in *Aspecten van Internationale Samenwerking*, 1980, No. 6, pp. 226 ff.

practice and doctrine in relation to the right to development; in the second I shall set out my own views on the present legal status of this right; and in the third and last part I shall try to interpret the right to development in more detail so that its status, and also its function, in international law can be optimalized.

PART I

History

1. Development

A jurist who deals with the concept of development is skating on thin ice. After all, since Adam Smith wrote his *Wealth of Nations* have not innumerable economists already considered the phenomenon of development without arriving at a unanimous definition?[3] And here I am thinking only of the full-blooded economists who thought and still think in terms of economic growth. After World War II, and particularly in the sixties, a new branch of economics came more and more to the force, known as development economics. The economists in this field include not only the purely economic factors in their approach to the concept of development but also social and cultural considerations.[4] Notwithstanding this lack of agreement in the literature, in practice many international organizations active in the field of international economic development have gradually reached a consensus of opinion on the various components of the concept of development.

In the sixties it was mainly the economic growth of GNP which was

---

3) See for example Lord Robbins, *The Theory of Economic Development in the History of Economic Thought*, London, 1968; and E.E. Hagen, *The Economics of Development*, Illinois, 1968.

4) For a more comprehensive approach of this kind see for example W.A. Lewis, *Development Planning*, London, 1966; G. Myrdal, *The Challenge of World Poverty*, New York, 1970; L.B. Pearson, *The Crisis of Development*, London, 1970; and M. Ulhaq, *The Poverty Curtain*, New York, 1976.

equated with development. The Strategy for the First UN Development Decade, which ran from 1961 to 1970, was based on the idea that an increase in GNP would automatically result in an increase in individual living standards.[5] However, experience showed that this was not the case, and even if there was an improvement in physical living standards, this improvement did not necessarily guarantee a greater appreciation of the non-material facets of human development.

In the seventies a lesson was learnt from the depressing results of the First UN Development Decade: the human aspect became more central, at least in theory, to the development process, and the Strategy for the Second UN Development Decade made this clear in as many words: "the ultimate objective of development must be to bring about sustained improvement in the well-being of the individual and bestow benefits on all."[6] The same phenomenon is found in the strategic reorientation of the World Bank in the early seventies: under the progressive leadership of the then president of the Bank, McNamara, the majority of loans were linked to an improvement in the position of the poorest sections of the population. In the ILO the theory of "basic needs", i.e. the minimum people need in order to survive, was propagated for the first time. And more and more often respect for human rights — irrespective of whether it was a question of the right to food, housing and medical treatment or the right to develop as an individual, with freedom of conscience and the right to physical integrity — was linked to development.

The consensus which has gradually been achieved in the form of many resolutions by the UN and its specialised agencies is essentially to the effect that development may not be regarded as an end in itself. Development is a means of achieving progress in the widest sense of the word. With particular reference to the development problems of the Third World this broad concept of progress is used to mean not only improving the macro-economic position of developing countries — through a strong trading position or a larger GNP, for example, — but, first and foremost, improving the material and non-material living standards of individuals.[7] This latter amounts to

---

5) A/RES/1710 (XVI).

6) A/RES/2626 (XXV), para. 7.

7) *Declaration on Social Progress and Development*, A/RES/2542 (XXIV), Part II, "Objectives"; also A/RES/32/117 (1977), which reaffirms the Declaration on Social Progress and Development.

the implementation of a number of the most elementary human rights, and it has been asked whether development itself should not be formulated as a human right.

As a jurist I shall rely for the time being on the consensus which has grown in the international community concerning the definition of development, since it contains sufficient elements on which to work from a legal basis.

2. A First Definition

An attempt was first made to define the right to development in 1972 in an address given to the Institut International des Droits de l'Homme in Strasbourg by the President of the Senegal Supreme Court, Kéba Mbaye, in which he came to the conclusion that the right to development is a human right. All fundamental rights and freedoms, he argued, are necessarily linked to the right to existence, to an increasingly higher living standard, and therefore to development. The right to development is a human right because man cannot exist without development.[8]

This point of view is a somewhat philosophical one, but Mbaye also argued, more from the legal point of view, that there would be little point in drafting a new proclamation with the aim of creating a new right; the right to development was already contained in international law. In this connection he referred first to Articles 55 and 56 of the UN Charter, in which the joint responsibility of the member states for social progress, development and respect for human rights is a central feature. He then mentioned the Universal Declaration of Human Rights of 1948, Articles 22 to 27 of which in particular are concerned with social and economic rights. The final source Mbaye mentioned for the right to development are the statutes of a large number of specialised agencies of the UN in which international cooperation on the basis of a universal principle of solidarity is of primary importance.[9]

---

8) Kéba Mbaye, "Le droit au développement comme un droit de l'homme" (The Right to Development as a human right), *Revue des droits de l'homme*, Vol. V, 1972, pp. 528 and 530.

9) *Idem*, pp. 526–7.

3. The Third Generation: "Solidarity Rights"

Some years later the right to development became more topical when the jurist Karel Vasak, then director of the Human Rights and Peace Division of Unesco, classified it in a new category of human rights, known as the 'third generation'. In his theory the first generation of human rights are broadly the political and civil rights on the basis of which the state should refrain from interfering with certain individual freedoms. The second generation of rights consists of the social, economic and cultural rights whose implementation requires active involvement by the state. Lastly, the third generation of human rights, in Vasak's view, encompass solidarity rights, among which he includes not only the right to development but also, for example, the right to peace, the right to a clean environment and the right to own the communal heritage.[10] A third category of this kind, which is often regarded as a necessary precondition for the meaningful implementation of the first two categories, finds a great deal of support in the East European doctrine, in which the right to peace is a central concept.[11]

Thus there were two opposing conceptions of the right to development. Kéba Mbaye came to the conclusion that the right to development was already laid down in various instruments of international law; Karel Vasak, on the other hand, adds to the two existing categories of human rights a third category, which may be regarded as including the right to development. I shall return to this difference of opinion later.[12] First, however, I should like to complete my historical account of the right to development by an account of certain attempts to achieve agreement in the UN and a brief report on the doctrinal state of affairs.

4. Establishment of Norms

Partly as a result of the debate initiated in Unesco, the question of the right to development was raised in the Human Rights Commission of the UN. In 1977 the Commission asked the Secretary-General

---

10) Karel Vasak, "A 30-year Struggle", Unesco Courier, November 1977, p. 29.

11) See for example H. Klenner, *Freiheit, Gleichheit und so weiter* (Freedom, Equality etc.), Berlin, 1978, p. 103; and A. Tichonov, *Le droit à la paix* (The Right to Peace), Unesco Doc. SS-78/CONF.630/10, quoted in E/CN.4/1334, p. 80.

12) Infra, p. 26.

of the UN in a resolution to study the international dimensions of the right to development as a human right.[13] This resolution was in fact the first recognition of the right to development as a human right and the starting signal for a series of UN activities.

Within less than a month of the completion of the Secretary-General's study, in January 1979,[14] the Human Rights Commission adopted a resolution stating again that the right to development was a human right and — it was added this time — that equal opportunities for development are as much a prerogative of states as of individuals.[15] As the substance of the right was however still vague, the Commission was unable to agree unanimously on the resolution: the US voted against and there were seven abstentions, all by Western Countries.

It is important to note that in the same year, 1979, the UN General Assembly adopted a resolution reflecting the view of the Commission that the right to development is a human right and that development should be enjoyed by states and individuals.[16] Of the over 150 countries with the right to vote in the General Assembly only the US voted against and seven abstained (Belgium, France, West Germany, Israel, Luxembourg, Malawi and the United Kingdom). Many of the Western countries which voted in favour tabled a declaration emphasizing the need to define the substance of the right to development.[17]

There has been little subsequent progress so far as regards standardization of the right to development. In 1980 the Human Rights Commission again adopted a resolution repeating the view referred to above.[18] The voting did not differ essentially from that of the previous year: the US voted against and four abstained, still including a hard core of France, Germany and Britain, plus Portugal. In view of the fact that it was mainly a question of abstentions rather than votes against, it may be concluded that there is not so much basic opposition from the West to the right to development as a concept, but that a definition of it is badly needed.

13) CHR/Res/4 (XXXIII), para. 4.
14) See E/CN.4/1334.
15) CHR/Res/5 (XXXV).
16) A/Res/34/46.
17) Internal memorandum of the Ministry of Foreign Affairs, No. 66/80.
18) CHR/Res/6 (XXVI).

5. Doctrine in Development

As long ago as the early sixties elements were introduced into the doctrine of international law which are still reflected today in discussion on the right to development. Particularly authoritative at that time were Friedmann and Röling, who were among the first to realize that traditional international law, which essentially lays down rules for co-existence — in other words, for a *modus vivendi* with the aim of interfering with one another as little as possible — provided a framework which was too narrow for the establishment of standards for the conduct of international affairs. In traditional international law the emphasis is on obligations to abstain, based on an abstract formal equality of states, giving rise to rules on non-intervention, diplomatic immunity, etc.

Röling, in his "International Law in an Expanded World" and Friedmann, in his "Changing Structure of International Law", recognized that, owing to growing interdependence, the actual relations between states were becoming more and more a matter of active cooperation instead of passive co-existence.[19] Friedmann was the originator of the concept of an "international law of cooperation", which he placed alongside the traditional "international law of co-existence"; an important place was set aside in it for the general interest of the whole international community as well as the individual interests of states.[20] International cooperation and the general interest, as we shall see, have come to play an increasingly important role in the international community.

Cooperation with developing countries (as part of international cooperation) manifested itself as a phenomenon of international law particularly strongly in the seventies. At first little interest was shown, but interest has grown rapidly since the UN Human Rights Commission has been active in this area.

The first more comprehensive attempt to delineate the contours of the right to development was made in the Secretary-General's report, mentioned earlier, on the international dimensions of this right.[21]

---

19) B.V.A. Röling, *International Law in an Expanded World*, Amsterdam, 1960; and W. Friedmann, *The Changing Structure of International Law*, London, 1964.

20) W. Friedmann, *op.cit.*, pp. 60 ff.

21) E/CN.4/1334.

This is not the appropriate place to comment on the study as a whole; instead, I shall confine myself to the conclusion in the report that there are a large number of principles (of law) based on the UN Charter and the international texts on human rights laid down in covenants, declarations and recommendations which demonstrate the existence of the right to development in international law.[22] Unfortunately this conclusion is based on a wide variety of texts, not all of which are equally relevant, and the need for a right to development, the existence of such a right and its substance are confused with one another.

Also in 1979 the Academy of International Law in The Hague organized a workshop on the right to development. In one of the papers presented on that occasion, Philip Alston placed the emphasis, as regards the recognition of the right to development, on the ethical aspect, and in particular on the notion of "justice". Justice contains a strong element of reciprocity (do unto others...) and is consequently contained in concepts such as interdependence and solidarity. According to Alston these concepts are at the root of the right to development, and he adds that in many respects the notion of justice is as relevant to the legal as to the ethical basis.[23]

The last event concerning the right to development I would mention is a UN seminar held at the request of the Human Rights Commission in summer 1980. Although in theory the seminar was attended by experts who were not acting under the instructions of their governments, it turned out to be a politically loaded meeting. Consequently a straight-forward factual discussion of the ins and outs of the right to development did not take place, and an evaluation of the results would not be particularly interesting.

The paper presented to the seminar by Verwey should, however, be mentioned here. His approach is highly detailed and well documented. Ultimately, however, he is striving largely for recognition of the developing countries as a special category of subjects in international law. Clarification of the concept of the right to development tends to

---

22) *Idem*, para. 305.
23) P. Alston, "The Right to Development at the International Level", in *The Right to Development at the International Level*, Workshop, The Hague, 16—18 October 1979, Alphen aan den Rijn, 1980, p. 103.

be blurred by the large quantity of material he puts forward to support his thesis.[24]

Verwey concludes that states and individuals have the right to economic and social development. Whether the right to development may be restricted solely to economic and social development is a question I shall return to later, but in my view he poses the right key question, which is whether states have a duty to implement (economic and social) human rights not only within their own territory but also outside it.[25] Verwey answers both questions in the affirmative and draws the conclusion that there is a right to development and an obligation to cooperate.[26]

Verwey's argument that developing countries should be recognized as a special category of subjects in international law calls for comment. The writer notes a tendency which in his view implies such recognition: this he distils from the work of and in the UN, the IMF, the World Bank, GATT and the EEC.[27]

In my opinion there are considerable objections to recognizing developing countries as special subjects of international law — even if such recognition, as in Verwey's view, applies only for a transitional period; it involves creating not only two kinds of subjects of the law but also two kinds of law. In my view it would be infinitely preferable to further underpin and extend international law as a unity so that legitimacy and legality cover each other in a coherent system of international cooperation. If not, new creations will look very much like

---

24) W.D. Verwey, *The Establishment of a New International Economic Order and the Realization of the Right to Development and Welfare: A Legal Survey*, HR/Geneva, 1980/ BP.3. In the epilogue to his study the writer returns to the right to development and rightly emphasizes that it is related not only to the achievement of a new international economic order but also that there is a close connection between the right to development and the national economic order. In this connection the governments of developing countries also bear a large measure of responsibility; pp. 74–75.

25) Verwey, *op.cit.*, p. 23.

26) *Idem*, p. 35; it should be noted that Verwey's phraseology is not always equally incisive, varying from "one can probably successfully try to establish the existence of a duty of states to cooperate" (p. 25) to "one can now put forward convincing arguments to sustain the thesis that such an obligation exists" (p. 35).

27) *Idem*, pp. 35–50; see also the same writer's *The Recognition of the Developing Countries as Special Subjects of International Law Beyond the Sphere of United Nations Resolutions*, Workshop, The Hague, 1979, *loc.cit.* (footnote 23), p. 372.

legal escapism, and refuge will be sought in solutions which are illusory.[28]

It is questionable, in fact, whether recognizing developing countries as special subjects of international law — which would serve as the basis for the right to development — would be more effective than recognizing underdevelopment or lesser development as a basis for differential treatment of and between states. As I shall demonstrate, present international law is flexible enough to allow the development of new legal concepts.[29]

PART II

International Law Aspects

6. The Right to Development as an Evolving General Principle of Law

Most writers who have dealt with the right to development so far have produced a profusion of arguments to prove that this right exists, with all the rights and obligations it entails. This has been done, however, without precisely indicating either the substance of the right to development or the identity of its subjects.[30] The conclusion they reach consequently seems to have been arrived at too

---

28) On the same lines see P.J.I.M. de Waart, *Volkenrecht in Samenwerking* (International Law in Cooperation) Deventer, 1978, p. 9. This writer raises the same objection to the introduction by Friedmann of the "international law of cooperation" alongside the "international law of co-existence"; the French writer Flory also distinguishes a separate right of development and accordingly arrives at a right to development which is the special prerogative of developing countries: see M. Flory, *Droit International du Développement*, Paris, 1977, pp. 47–8.

29) See in particular the development of the principle of solidarity and the principle of substantive equality, *infra*, pp. 22 ff.

30) See also Verwey, who recognizes this problem: *op.cit.*, p. 4.

blindly, in a grey area of the law. This grey area is characterized by a dialectic between the phenomena of legitimacy and legality. In simple terms, it could be said that today's legitimacy is followed by tomorrow's legality.[31]

A right, in the sense of the rights and obligations of a subject of the law, is arrived at as a rule in international law only with the consent of the states involved. Their consent may be embodied in a treaty or in international custom. The Statute of the International Court of Justice lists treaties and customs among the recognized manifestations of international law.[32]

A state may be bound by international law not only through a treaty or custom but also on the basis of general principles of law.[33] These general principles may be divided into two categories. The first category contains those principles which are so fundamental to law in general or to international law that they must be regarded as forming a self-evident part of it, irrespective of whether they are specified therein or not. The second category covers those principles which, as a component of most national legal systems or forming part, by virtue of treaties or custom, of international law (in another field) lend themselves to corresponding application for the purpose of filling gaps in international law.[34]

The first category, the "basic principles of law", essentially comprises principles of the law of treaties, such as *pacta sunt servanda* and *nemo plus iuris transferre potest quam ipse habet*, and substantive principles of law, such as the right to self-determination and a

---

31) For an interesting account of this matter see R.J. Dupuy, "Declaratory Law and Programmatory Law: From Revolutionary Custom to 'Soft Law' ", in R.J. Akkerman (ed.), *Declarations on Principles*, Leyden, 1977, pp. 247 ff (p. 252); also O. Schlachter, "Towards a Theory of International Obligation", *7th Virginia Journal of International Law*, 1967, pp. 300 ff; Abi Saab refers to the "threshold of law" in G. Abi-Saab, *The Legal Formulation of a Right to Development*, Workshop, The Hague, 1979, *loc.cit.* (footnote 23), p. 160.

32) Article 38, para. 1(a) and (b); for the definition of 'recognized manifestations' see M. Bos, "The Recognized Manifestations of International Law", *20 German Yearbook of International Law*, 1977, p. 9, where he introduces the term 'manifestations of international law' to replace the customary 'sources of international law'.

33) Article 38, para. 1(c).

34) P. van Dijk, "Het Internationale Recht inzake de Rechten van de Mens" (International Law on Human Rights), in *Rechten van de Mens in Mundiaal en Europees Perspectief*, 2nd. ed., Utrecht, 1980, p. 16; and F.A. von der Heydte, "Glossen zu einer Theorie der Allgemeinen Rechtsgrundsätze" (Notes on a Theory of General Principles of Law), 33 *Friedens-Warte*, 1933, pp. 189–300.

large number of non-derogatory human rights (the right to life, the prohibition of torture and slavery, freedom of trade unions, etc.). Most of the former, the basic principles, are essential principles without which there could be no law. They are, as it were, the definition of international law and there is a lot to be said for not classifying them among the general principles of law as referred to in Article 38(c) of the Statute of the International Court of Justice, but regarding them as elements of the "general concept of law".[35]

The substantive principles of law, on the other hand, are in general "evolved" principles, i.e. principles which regularly occur in the practice of states and in decisions of international organizations; consequently they have already passed the stage of repeated application in the international community. Most of them are abstractions from a large number of rules and have been accepted for such a long time and so universally that they are no longer directly associated with the practice of states.[36] As such these are general principles of law recognized by the international community. The — no doubt broad — interpretation of Article 38(c) adopted here derives from the need felt from time to time in the international community to recognize certain rights in principle as a kind of "code of conduct", although the time is not yet ripe for a precise definition of such rights. However, the fact that they have found recognition as principles (the many rights in the Universal Declaration, for example) may provide a powerful incentive for the elaboration of their substance, for instance in treaties. The evolved substantive principle may therefore play an important part in the "progressive development of law".

Evolved principles of this kind display close similarities with international customary law. They differ from customary law, however, as they do from treaties, in that custom and treaties are both formulated (or established, in the case of custom) in what are usually fairly clear rights and obligations with specific subjects bearing these rights and obligations. This is not, as a rule, the case with general material principles of law, which, as we have just seen, are formulated (necessarily) as broad unspecific principles, for example the right to self-determination.

Their elaboration in more concrete form again requires the consent of states in the form of treaties or customs. The prohibition of tor-

---

35) M. Bos, *loc.cit.*, in GYIL, 1977, pp. 38—42.

36) I. Brownlie, *Principles of Public International Law*, 2nd ed., 1973, p. 19.

ture and slavery and the freedom of trade unions, however, show that some principles are *in essence* capable of being specified as rights, obligations and subjects, but even then, as a rule, in the form of treaties or the practice of states.

Returning to the right to development, we find that under current international law it would be going too far to interpret this right — as has been customary hitherto — as already being the source of the concrete rights and obligations of clearly specified subjects. This would need agreement between the states embodied in a treaty or a rule of customary law, necessarily based on the practice of states, which already recognized those rights and obligations quite distinctly. This is not the case, either in the bilateral or the multilateral practice of states. International practice — at least the consensus on the right to development — dies, however, indicate the clear beginnings of recognition of the right to development as a general principle of substantive law in the sense mentioned above.

A large and still growing number of treaties, declarations and recommendations, many of which are rightly mentioned in the Secretary-General's report,[37] can be cited as an indication, or even proof, of a consensus on the need for development and cooperation with developing countries. All these texts contribute to the substance of the right to development as a general principle of law. Taken together, however, they do not automatically add up to a right to development with the rights and obligations which that entails for individual states.

This is not to say that the right to development is not binding as a general principle of law. On the contrary, if it can be said to be a general principle this means that all states have the duty to recognize it and promote it. The international community not only has a legal duty to refrain from opposing and impeding the exercise of the right to development, but is also under a positive obligation to help in securing its realization by promoting its exercise.[37a] As we have seen, a general principle of law takes on a life of its own as an abstraction of an evolved consensus. As a principle it becomes part of the foundations of international law. Although the international community is therefore co-responsible for the implementation of the right to development, it would be going too far to adduce state liability.

---

37) E/CN.4/1334, p. 29 ff.

37a) See also H. Gros Espiell, *The Right to Self-Determination: Implementation of United Nations Resolutions*, United Nations, New York, 1980, p. 10.

Schachter comments on the acceptance of co-responsibility as follows: "we can find preferences based on need expressed or implicit
throughout the entire range of international decision-making pertaining to development... What is striking about this conception is not so
much its espousal by the large majority of poor and handicapped
countries but the fact that it has been accepted — by and large — by
the more affluent countries to whom the demands are addressed. The
evidence for this can be found not only in the international resolutions with which the rich countries have concurred but also, and
more convincingly, in the series of actions by them to grant assistance and preferences to those in the less-developed world... the scale
and duration... have been substantial enough to demonstrate the
practical acceptance of a responsibility based on the entitlement of
those in need."[38]

To support the interpretation of the right to development as an
evolving general principle of law I shall now consider some of its
foundations or origins.

6.1. Practice in the General Assembly

I indicated earlier that the right to development as an evolving principle of law can be derived from a long series of treaties, declarations
and recommendations. If, to support the consensus on this principle,
we take the UN Charter as a source, we find that international cooperation in finding solutions to economic, social, cultural and humanitarian problems (including the promotion and encouragement of respect for human rights) is one of the objectives of the Charter.

Articles 55 and 56 of the Charter specify this objective more precisely. Article 55 states that the UN is required to promote:

a. higher standards of living, full employment and conditions of
   economic and social progress and development;
b. solutions of international economic, social health, and related
   problems; and international cultural and educational cooperation; and
c. universal respect for and observance of human rights and funda-

---

38) O. Schachter, "The Evolving International Law of Development", *Columbia Journal of
Transnational Law*, 1976, pp. 9—10.

mental freedoms for all without distinction as to race, sex, language or religion.

Article 56 adds that all members pledge themselves to take joint and separate action (in cooperation with the UN) for the achievement of the purposes set forth in Article 55.

In this connection reference should also be made to the "Declaration on Principles of International Law concerning Friendly Relations and Cooperation among States" of 1970. This authoritative declaration, in which the General Assembly again laid down a number of principles of international law and formulated various new principles, also sets out the obligation of states to work together for the purpose of achieving peace, human rights and economic progress.[39]

At the beginning of my paper I mentioned the close link between development and human rights: a large number of texts on the subject of human rights in fact incorporate the element of development, either implicitly or explicitly. Article 22 of the Universal Declaration of Human Rights, for instance, states that everyone has the right to social security and is entitled to realization, through national effort and international cooperation, of the economic, social and cultural rights indispensable for his personal development. Article 28 adds that everyone is entitled to a social and international order in which the rights and freedoms set forth in the Universal Declaration can be fully realized.

The two 1966 International Covenants on Human Rights contain articles which are unequivocal with regard to the existence of a right to development, or an obligation to cooperate. Article 2 of the International Covenant on Economic, Social and Cultural Rights explicitly states that each state is obliged to take steps, both independently and in the context of international aid and cooperation, to move ever further towards universal realization of the rights recognized in the Covenant. Article 11 of the same Covenant recognizes the right of every person to a reasonable living standard, including adequate food, clothing and housing. To this is added that parties to the Covenant shall take suitable measures to ensure the realization of this right, recognizing the essential importance of voluntary international cooperation. As regards implementation of the right to be safeguarded

---

39) A/Res/2625 (XXV).

from hunger, the Covenant explicitly states that states shall take measures both independently and in the context of international co-operation.[40]

It would be going too far in the present context to consider *in extenso* the wide variety of declarations and recommendations formulating the principle of development and development-related international cooperation, whether controversially or not. I would refer to the Secretary-General's report for a more complete account.[41] It should be borne in mind, however, that all the important documents produced in the seventies on the problems of development — for example, the Strategy for the Second UN Development Decade (1970),[42] the Declaration on the Establishment of a New International Economic Order (1974),[43] and the Charter of Economic Rights and Duties of States (1974)[44] — refer in one way or another to the importance of international cooperation for the purpose of development.

I shall confine myself for the moment to one of Goodrich's conclusions. In his view, without underestimating the work of the UN and its specialised agencies in other fields, it can justifiably be said that aid to the Third World for its economic, social and political development is the activity which has produced the organization's most important results.[45]

It is not only in the UN General Assembly, in fact, that the right to development has a long history as an evolving principle. Numerous other international organizations in the last thirty years have been active in the field of development and international economic cooperation.

As a standard measure of the work of the UN and other international organizations as regards the right to development, two increasingly sharply delineated principles of international economic law may be mentioned, namely the principle of solidarity and the principle of substantive equality.

---

40) Covenant on Economic, Social and Cultural Rights (1966), Article 11, para. 2.

41) E/CN.4/1334, para. 64 ff.

42) A/Res/2626 (XXV).

43) A/Res/3201 and 3202 (S-VI).

44) A/Res/3281 (XXIX).

45) L.M. Goodrich, *The United Nations in a Changing World*, New York, 1974, p. 228.

6.2. The Principle of Solidarity

A systematic account of the origin and substance of the principle of solidarity was given by VerLoren van Themaat, in his recently published study of international economic law.[46] VerLoren van Themaat outlines the development of this principle against the background of the increasing interdependence in international economic life. In his view a principle of solidarity did not enter international economic law until the advent of international economic organizations, which in turn did not emerge until economic interdependence had reached a certain level. As economic dependence on the behaviour of other countries grows, the organization of economic cooperation with those countries becomes more sophisticated. The same phenomenon of increasing interdependence explains the development of an active legal principle of solidarity in international economic organization.[47]

In his opinion, three main forms of the principle of solidarity obtain in the present stage of the evolution of law:

1. obligations on all states separately to take account in their actions of the interests of other states (or their subjects);
2. mutual (bilateral or multilateral) financial or other assistance to overcome economic difficulties (including technical assistance to developing countries and trading preferences for those countries to compensate for deficits); and
3. organized coordination of economic policies.[48]

The principle of solidarity, interpreted in this way, is expressed in international economic organizations such as the IMF, GATT, the World Bank, the OECD, COMECON and the European Communities. All the existing, purely or predominantly Western international economic organizations (except GATT), VerLoren van Themaat continues, at present apply the most far-reaching third form, organized coordination of economic policies. Examples can also be cited of one of the other two forms of solidarity (this is also true of GATT). Many international organizations, including not only numerous specialised agencies of the UN itself but also the OECD, the World Bank group and COMECON, are now active almost exclusively in the field

---

46) P. VerLoren van Themaat, *Rechtsgrondslagen van een Nieuwe Internationale Economische Orde* (Legal Bases for a New International Economic Order), The Hague, 1979.
47) *Idem*, pp. 245–6.
48) *Idem*, p. 199.

of positive integration, i.e. coordination and cooperation in economic policies.[49]

I should like to record one distinct reservation on VerLoren van Themaat's interpretation of the principle of solidarity. A true principle of solidarity presupposes a community of interests — a unity in the group which enables it to show its mutual dependence — and can only exist if the general interest and therefore the interests of others, are taken into account in considering one's own interests. In other words, there can be no principle of solidarity if — and this is the impression given by VerLoren van Themaat — only one of the three forms he gives is present. All three of them at least must be present as elements, component parts, of the principle of solidarity; the word "forms" used by VerLoren van Themaat is not a very felicitous choice of term. The great importance that he attributes to self-interest in the will or intention of the individual state may be regarded as a realistic point of departure for evaluation of the practice of states in the international community of today.

VerLoren van Themaat's principle of solidarity displays obvious similarities with the "international law of cooperation", as defined by Friedmann in the early sixties. In Friedmann's words "[the] move of the international society, from an essentially negative code of rules of abstention [the traditional international law of co-existence] to positive rules of cooperation, however fragmentary in the present state of world politics, is an evolution of immense significance for the principles and structure of international law".[50] Now, almost twenty years later, VerLoren van Themaat can fill in the fragmentary basis referred to by Friedmann with a large number of examples from the practice of the international economic organizations.

The idea behind the three main forms of VerLoren van Themaat's principle of solidarity is to be found in Friedmann's conception, which includes the statement that "unlike the traditional law of nations, which is predicated on the assumption of conflicts of national interests, cooperative international law requires a *community* of interests. The challenge posed by the changes in the structure of contemporary international society does not eliminate the pivotal importance of self-interest. The emerging international organizations are tentative expressions of new world-wide interests in security, survival

---

49) *Idem*, p. 200.
50) W. Friedmann, *The Changing Structure of International Law*, London, 1964, p. 62.

and cooperation for the preservation and development of vital needs and resources of mankind".[51]

6.3. The Principle of Substantive Equality

Another principle underlying a large number of international documents, one on which the co-responsibility of the international community for development is based, is the principle of substantive equality. Originally inter-state commerce was subject at most to the principle of formal equality, which was expressed in international economic relations in such things as full reciprocity, negotiations based on the *quid pro quo* (nothing for nothing) principle and the "most favoured nation" clause. In brief, formal equality amounts to an absolute prohibition of discrimination.

With the increasing intensification of economic relations and the resultant interdependence, however, it was found that formal equality of this kind made sense between states of more or less the same economic strength and in colonial relationships where, for the purposes of decision-making, a large number of weaker economies formed part of relatively strong economies, but in economically asymmetrical relationships this type of equality was not a very healthy principle. Nowadays this is particularly true of relations between the industrialized countries and the Third World. For example, if the developing countries are regarded as an important market for products from developed countries then it certainly makes sense to increase the purchasing power of the poor countries. This means, among other things, that young industries in those countries must be protected for the time being against fierce competition, that products manufactured by those industries may be exported to the West and elsewhere, and that in general these countries should be given financial assistance. In this way the Third World obtains currency and resources with which to buy products in the West.

Apart from this element of self-interest based on interdependence, which can be translated into purely financial-economic terms, the constant political pressure of the developing countries for a better economic position has also been a decisive factor in the breakdown of the principle of formal equality. As we have seen, development has been the main area of the UN's work in the last 35 years, which

---

51) *Idem*, p. 367.

received an added impulse from the flood of new nations entering in the sixties. The establishment of the UN Conference on Trade and Development (UNCTAD) and the insertion of a special chapter on development in the General Agreement on Tariffs and Trade (GATT) were important milestones during that decade. In the seventies the political pressure from the Third World acquired a structural character when the abolition of economic inequality was placed in the context of the search for a new international economic order.

This constant political pressure, which gradually increased awareness in the international community, and the economic necessity, already mentioned, of changing asymmetrical relationships are important elements underlying the principle of solidarity and especially the second form (second element) distinguished by VerLoren van Themaat, namely mutual financial or other aid to overcome economic difficulties. Consequently the principle of solidarity has made increasing inroads on the principle of formal equality; the latter has been superseded in relations with developing countries by the principle of substantive equality, which states that unequal cases shall be treated unequally in proportion to the degree of inequality.[52]

This principle of substantive equality is expressed, for example, by the granting of greater protection to the industries of less developed countries (extended also to weaker regions and sectors in the EEC). The principle can also be found in the preferential access to markets in the rich countries accorded to developing countries (e.g. the Generalized System of Preferences), measures to compensate for loss of revenue or deficits (e.g. the Lomé Convention's Stabex and Minex mechanism), and the transfer of financial resources to support the development process.[53] The principle of substantive equality also underlies the desire of the developing countries for more equal representation in various financial and economic organizations. The votes in these organizations are "weighted" according to financial power, which means that developing countries have a minimal number of votes despite the fact that these organizations take decisions relating to development in the Third World.

---

52) In this connection see for example A.A. Fatouros, "Participation of the 'New' States in the International Legal Order of the Future", in *The Future of the International Legal Order*, Vol I (C.E. Black and R.A. Falk, eds.), Princeton, 1969, p. 365; and A.A. Yusuf, *Differential Treatment as a Dimension of the Right to Development*, Workshop, The Hague, 1979, *loc.cit.* (footnote 23), p. 233.

53) See also P. VerLoren van Themaat, *op.cit.*, p. 243.

For a detailed discussion of these examples of the principle of substantive equality in practice I would refer to the studies by VerLoren van Themaat and Verwey already mentioned.[54]

These, then, are the basic facts concerning the right to development as an evolving general principle of law. As a provisional conclusion to the recognition of this principle I would recall the resolutions of the UN Human Rights Commission and the General Assembly, which stated in so many words that the right to development is a human right and that development is the prerogative of states and individuals.[55]

If these resolutions now form a conclusion, they also represent the beginnings of the next step, which is towards a right formulated in concrete terms, i.e., a "legal right" with specified entitlements, obligations and subjects.

Although these resolutions by the Commission and the General Assembly must be interpreted as recognizing a broadly formulated principle of law, they also refer to the substance and subjects of the right to development in that — to summarize the texts of the last thirty years — they state that it is a human right and stipulate that development is the prerogative of both States and individuals.

On the basis of these UN indications for the further elaboration of the right to development I shall attempt to arrive at a serviceable formulation of this right.

---

54) See footnotes 46 and 25 respectively.
55) CHR/Res 4 (XXXV) and CHR/Res/6 (XXXVI); and A/Res/34/46.

PART III

Nature and Substance

7. The Nature of the Right to Development

The UN's definition of the right to development raises certain questions. For instance, it is stated first and foremost that it is a human right. Must it be assumed, then, that this is a new right to be added to the existing list of human rights? This idea was put forward in the Human Rights Commission,[56] and is supported by, among other things, Karel Vasak's theory on the 'third generation' of human rights.[57]

Verwey, in his paper for the UN seminar on the right to development, rightly asks whether it is worthwhile or even advisable to further complicate the debate on human rights by introducing a 'third generation'.[58] Even among jurists trained in international law the discussion is already confusing enough when it comes to linking the two existing categories of economic, social and cultural rights, and political and civil rights. But apart from the more theoretical problems, a great deal is still lacking in the implementation of these internationally recognized rights in practice. Although the 1966 Covenants on human rights entered into force in 1976, the most fundamental rights in both of them are still being violated — even now, five years later. It is difficult to monitor their observance really effectively.[59] This being the case, I fully share the view of Verwey that at the moment it would be more effective to concentrate on the means available of exerting pressure on the international community to implement those rights whose existence is recognized universally and whose substance is not disputed.[60] The difficulty is, however, that these means

---

56) E/CN.4/SR.1504 (1978), p. 32.

57) *Supra*, p. 5.

58) W.D. Verwey, *op.cit.*, p. 5.

59) See for example P. Alston, "The United Nations Specialized Agencies and Implementation of the International Covenant on Economic, Social and Cultural Rights", *18 Columbia Journal of Transnational Law*, 1979, p. 79; and in particular T.C. van Boven, "Internationale instrumenten en procedures ter bevordering en bescherming van de rechten van de mens" (International Instruments and Procedures for the Promotion and Protection of Human Rights), in *Rechten van de Mens in Mundiaal en Europees Perspectief* (2e ed), Utrecht, 1980, pp. 44—54.

60) Verwey, *op.cit.*, p. 5.

exist only in very primitive form, if at all, and consequently cannot have much effect. Special attention should be devoted to this point.

It should be made absolutely clear that the international community has no need for new human rights, especially in the context of development,[61] which is in general a question of the most elementary right to a dignified existence, a right which is laid down for instance in the Universal Declaration of Human Rights, the two 1966 Covenants and a large number of ILO Conventions. What it amounts to is the achievement of these truly fundamental rights. The urgent need to achieve them, even though it is based to some extent — as we have seen — on increasing interdependence and thus to a considerable degree on self-interest, underlies the right to development. This need also determines the nature of the right; the right to development assists the more effective implementation of existing rights. Only in this way does it make sense to interpret the right to development as a human right, as it is described by the UN. Just as development is not an aim in itself but a means to an end,[62] the right to development is not a new material right. It should be understood as an instrumental right (or, rather, a right of an instrumental nature).[63] In this sense the right to development may well be a means, as indicated by Verwey, of exerting pressure on the international community to implement those rights whose existence and substance are not in dispute.

8. The Substance of the Right to Development

In contrast to the right to development as a broadly formulated general principle of law as recognized by the international community,

---

61) It is noteworthy that even the Russian writer Kartashkin rejects the third category fairly categorically: "What is required at the present time is no third covenant or another set of rights, but the fullest possible realization of the fundamental human rights and freedoms already anchored in the Universal Declaration and other relevant documents". V. Kartashkin "Human Rights and the Modern World", *International Affairs*, 1979, p. 54; cf. my comment, *supra*, at pp. 5/6.

62) Kéba Mbaye, *loc.cit.* (footnote 8), p. 510.

63) A right with a similar instrumental nature is the right to self-determination, which is concerned with the realization of a large number of other rights. As regards the external effect in relation to nations the right to self-determination is concerned for example with the implementation of the principle of sovereign equality and the freedom to dispose of natural wealth and resources; as regards its internal aspect it is concerned with the provision of opportunities for individuals to participate in the administration of the state.

for the next step it is of the utmost importance to specify the rights and obligations and thus to define them as precisely as possible. First, however, something needs to be said about the subjects, i.e. the bearers, of these rights and obligations.

Recent UN resolutions on the right to development state — having emphasized that it is a human right — that equal opportunities for development are as much a right (prerogative) of states as of individuals.[64] From this phraseology it is plain that we are dealing with a human right owing to individuals, while equal opportunities to develop are also a right of states. Notwithstanding the somewhat ambiguous UN texts on this matter, the latter cannot be said to be a human right in the proper sense.

Hitherto a distinction has been made in human rights jargon between individual and collective rights; in my view the second category can comprise only those rights exercised by individuals in groups, i.e. the right to association and assembly, trade union rights, etc. The right to self-determination is also classed as a human right, but this is a right of peoples and not of states.[65] In this connection the wording used by the Human Rights Commission and the General Assembly could give rise to confusion.

At this point it is important to note that the UN has recognized the two aspects of the right to development — i.e. an individual and an (inter-)state aspect — and that these aspects have been brought together in a resolution. The coupling of the individual right with the right of states is the most innovatory element of the right to development. I shall base my detailed consideration of rights and obligations on this combination.

8.1. The Individual Right to Development

The individual aspect of the right to development has been described by the UN as a human right, but as I have already maintained it cannot be interpreted as other than a right of an instrumental nature. In

---

64) CHR/Res/6 (XXXVI) and A/Res/34/46.

65) See Article 1 of both Covenants (1966). In fact more and more writers can be found convincingly defending the argument that the right to self-determination also extends to individuals; see, inter alia, H. Gros Espiell, The Right to Self-Determination, New York, 1980, p. 10.

order to determine the substance of this individual aspect of the right to development — or, rather, to determine what the right to development is meant to achieve — the existing Bill of Rights needs to be consulted. It includes the Universal Declaration and the two 1966 Covenants.

In this connection it should be remembered that the UN has repeatedly stated explicitly that development comprises facets of physical, spiritual, and social and economic welfare. This view is in turn closely related to recognition of the fact that political and civil rights are indissolubly linked to economic, social and cultural rights. The preambles to both of the 1966 Covenants leave no doubt on this score. The 1968 Proclamation of Tehran[66] again explicitly emphasized their inseparability. Reference may also be made here to the Declaration on Social Progress and Development adopted by the General Assembly in 1969, which states that social progress and development should be aimed at the continual improvement of the material and non-material living conditions of all individuals.[67] A more recent General Assembly Resolution of 1977 likewise emphasizes the fact that all human rights are indivisible and interdependent.[68]

If we consider these documents we can draw no other conclusions than that the right to development as an individual right must be aimed at the realisation of both categories of human rights, i.e. economic, social and cultural rights and political and civil rights. Van Boven, Head of the Human Rights Division of the UN, says: "The right to development is a holistic concept which seeks to create a synthesis of a whole range of existing human rights which are informed and given an extra dimension by the emergence of a growing international consensus on a variety of development objectives".[69] The substance of the right to development, as far as its individual aspect is concerned, could therefore be described as a synthesis, or rather aggregate, of existing rights.[70]

The discussion on the substance of the right to development must be seen against the background of large-scale underdevelopment in the

---

66) This Proclamation was adopted by the International Conference on Human Rights in 1968 and was confirmed by the General Assembly in A/Res/2442 (XXIII).

67) A/Res/2542 (XXIV), Part II, Objectives.

68) A/Res/32/130, para. 1(a).

69) ST/HR/SER.A/8, p. 41.

70) See also P. Alston, loc.cit. (footnote 23), p. 102; and ST/HR/SER.A/8, para. 72.

Third World and, in particular, the over 780 million people who according to estimates by the World Bank, live in absolute poverty. Absolute poverty means more than just an extremely low income; it also means malnutrition, poor health, inadequate housing and illiteracy.[71] In essence this situation, which is summarized rather euphemistically, and less forcefully, in the term "underdevelopment", amounts to the fact that a whole host of elementary human rights are not being implemented. In view of the facts the right to development cannot be concerned with anything other than the realisation of the most fundamental human rights.[72] For the greatest possible effectiveness (for which the right to development should be treated as an instrumental right) a number of well-defined minimum levels must be sought in the two spheres of economic, social and cultural rights, and political and civil rights.

All this does not mean, of course, that the right to development is not a general, universally applicable right. On the contrary, it should provide a firm foundation for everyone who feels that the most basic rights of either category are being violated.

On the assumption that the right to development is an aggregate of the two existing categories of human rights, minimum levels of *basic rights* will have to be sought in the existing Bill of Rights. By basic rights I mean, with Van Dijk, all rights relating to man's most basic material and non-material needs, without whose realisation a dignified existence is not possible.[73]

The following basic rights will convey some ideas of what I mean: the right to life and the closely associated right to adequate food, clothing, housing and medical care.[74] In addition, a minimum level of personal security should be guaranteed, as should freedom of thought, conscience and religion.[75] Most of these rights are in fact

---

71) *World Development Report 1980*, p. 33; G. Adler-Karlsson, "Eliminating Absolute Poverty: An Approach to the Problem", in *Reducing Global Inequities* (Wriggins and Adler-Karlsson, eds.), New York, 1980, p. 125.

72) Also W.D. Verwey, *op.cit.*, p. 11.

73) P. van Dijk, "De Rechten van de Mens en Ontwikkelingssamenwerking; enige beginselen" (Human Rights and Development Cooperation: some principles), 5 *NJCM Bulletin*, 1980, p. 12.

74) Covenant on Civil and Political Rights, Article 6, in conjunction with Covenant on Economic, Social and Cultural Rights, Article 11.

75) Covenant of Civil and Political Rights, Articles 7, 8, 9, 10 and 18.

already recognized in the 1966 Covenant on Civil and Political Rights as rights from which no derogation is permissible even in time of public emergency.[76]

In addition to these basic rights a minimum level of opportunities for individuals to participate in the development process must be guaranteed through the right to development (thus the right to development is closely linked with the internal aspect of the right to self-determination).[77] Declarations and action programmes to which I have already alluded have emphasized the importance of such participation, for example the 1968 Proclamation of Tehran,[78] the Declaration on Social Progress and Development adopted by the General Assembly in 1969 and reaffirmed in 1977,[79] and the action programme adopted by the World Employment Conference held in 1976.[80] A recent political document which may be cited in this context is the report of the Brandt Commission, which states for example that "in achieving the main objectives of development, no system lacking in genuine and full participation of the people will be fully satisfactory or truly effective".[81]

Of essential importance to effective participation are the right to education and the right to take part in cultural and scientific life,[82] freedom of expression and the right of association and assembly,[83]

---

76) Article 4, para. 2.
77) Verwey, in his paper for the 1980 UN seminar, does not agree with this 'holistic' approach. He prefers in the first instance to apply what he calls a 'narrow concept' which gives priority to several basic economic and social rights. He believes that 'Erst kommt das Fressen, dann die Moral' (food first, morals later) applies to all hungry and despairing people wherever they live. In the immediate future — Verwey regards the 'narrow concept' as a preliminary measure which he sees in a dynamic context — 'the concept of development, in the perception of those segments of the world's population who need it most, is a simple and narrow one' (see pp. 9—13). I wonder whether this view of the situation is not oversimplified. Surely in many cases, if not all, the promotion of social and economic development is of fundamental importance to such development. And in many countries is it not the trade union movement which is the first victim of the violation of political and civil freedoms? For some other arguments see also Kéba Mbaye, "Le Développement et les droits de l'homme" (Development and Human Rights), *Revue Sénégalaise de Droit*, 1977, pp. 31—2 and 36.
78) Paragraph 3 (see also footnote 66).
79) A/Res/2542 (XXIV) and A/Res/32/117, Art. 5.
80) For example P. Alston, "Human Rights and Basic Needs: A Critical Assessment", *Revue des Droits de l'homme* 1979, Vol. XII, pp. 24 ff.
81) See *North-South: A programme for survival*, London, 1980, p. 133.
82) Covenant on Economic, Social and Cultural Rights, Articles 13 and 15.
83) Covenant on Civil and Political Rights, Articles 19, 21 and 22.

including the right to form free trade unions, which may be invoked internationally against a state through the legal order established by the ILO, even if that state has not ratified the conventions relating to this right.[84] These *rights of participation* are essential, in one form or another, to the realisation of the basic rights already mentioned; they are more closely related, however, to the economic, social, political and cultural traditions of the various communities than are those basic rights.[85]

"Ways in which the poor can be helped to participate in the development effort must be determined by each country in the light of its problems and possibilities".[86] This means at the administrative level, for instance, that in a situation of social and economic deprivation forms of government and participation may be chosen which are different from the parliamentary democracies in Western countries. It should also be borne in mind that a highly stable government is generally needed to carry through the often painful process of development, and that in many Third World countries the problems are so great that there has been no chance — certainly not in the short time since becoming independent — for "Her Majesty's loyal opposition" to develop as in Western democracies.[87]

Responsibility for the realisation of the individual's right to development as described above is primarily that of the state. In fact, this is true of the whole development process. This was recognized as early as 1950 by the General Assembly,[88] and was reaffirmed by the Strategy for the Second UN Development Decade (1970).[89] In order to implement the right to development it should be the policy of the

---

84) P. van Dijk, "Het Internationale Recht inzake de Rechten van de Mens" (International Law on Human Rights), in *Rechten van de Mens in Mundiaal en Europees Perspectief*, 2nd ed., Utrecht, 1980, pp. 16—17; and N. Valticos, "Les méthodes de la protection internationale de la liberté syndicale" (International Methods of Protecting Trade Union Freedom), *Recueil des Cours de l'Académie de Droit International*, 1975, Vol. I, pp. 85—135.

85) P. van Dijk, *op.cit.*, in 5 *NJCM Bulletin*, 1980, p. 13.

86) *North-South: A programme for survival*, London, 1980, p. 133.

87) K. de Vey Mestdagh, "De rechten van de mens en het ontwikkelingsbeleid" (Human Rights and Development Policy), Intermediair, 1979, No. 44, p. 3; see also *Human Rights in a One Party State*, International Seminar convened by the International Commission of Jurists, London, 1978.

88) A/Res/400 (V).

89) See A/Res/2542 (XXIV), Article 8, and A/Res/2626 (XXV), para. 11 respectively; also P.J.G. Kapteyn, *De Verenigde Naties en de Internationale Economische Orde*, (The United Nations and the International Economic Order), The Hague, 1977, p. 56.

state to safeguard the various basic rights and rights of participation of every individual irrespective of race, colour, sex, age, language, religion, and political or other belief. Both the Proclamation of Teheran[90] and a more recent resolution of the General Assembly[91] make this quite clear.

This is not to say that the substance of the right to development is thus fully established. All the documents which place the main responsibility for development with the developing countries themselves have added, since the early fifties, that the international community has co-responsibility: it is a matter not only of 'sound and effective national' but also of 'sound and effective international policies of economic and social development'.[92] The right to development therefore applies not only between individuals and the state but also between states.

8.2. The Right of States to Development

Until now we have been concentrating on the individual, which is the logical consequence of the fact that the bearers of human rights are ultimately individuals or groups of individuals. We have seen that people should also be pivotal to the question of development. The state bears primary responsibility for the development of the community and thus for the realisation of the most elementary rights of individuals. However, the right to development is also, as the Human Rights Commission and the General Assembly have explicitly stated, a right which states themselves should also be able to claim.[93]

This conclusion is a necessary consequence of previous texts adopted by the UN in this connection. At the end of the previous section I mentioned a number of resolutions which referred to the international context as well as to national policy. The Declaration on Social Progress and Development states in clear terms that social progress and development are in the common interests of the international community, which should take joint and individual action to supplement national efforts to improve the standard of living.[94] I would

---

90) Paragraph 13 (see also footnote 66).
91) A/Res/32/130, para. 1(b).
92) See footnotes 88—91.
93) CHR/Res/5/ (XXXV) in conjunction with A/Res/34/46.
94) A/Res/2542 (XXIV), Article 9; also A/Res/32/117 (1977).

also refer to the relevant articles in the UN Charter, the Universal Declaration of Human Rights and the two 1966 Covenants, and to the outline of the principle of solidarity and the principle of substantive equality which I put forward as an argument to support the consensus on the right to development as a general principle of law.[95]

Van Dijk rightly states that it is one of the essential characteristics of international law on human rights that it not only imposes an obligation on states to implement those rights within their own boundaries but also renders states co-responsible for implementation in other countries.[96] This co-responsibility involves not only supervision and correction; where a state falls short of the international standard because it lacks the necessary resources, or where the government does not possess the means and power needed to mobilize in sufficient measure the resources available in the country to that end, other states have the duty to help it to reach that standard with the aid of their more extensive resources.[97] This duty to assume co-responsibility consequently constitutes the basis for the inter-state component of the right to development. The bearer of the right is the impoverished state, the bearer of the obligation the state which is in a position to provide assistance.[98]

Tentative Conclusion

It has been submitted that the right to development is an evolving principle of international law. At present, the basic factors of the protracted process of consensus-building with regard to the recognition of this principle (e.g. the practice in the United Nations and the principles of solidarity and substantive equality) imply already certain obligations incumbent upon the international community as a whole. Nevertheless, the precise substance and subjects have not yet been specified in any international legal instrument, except for a first indication given by the UN Commission on Human Rights.

If the substance of the right to development, which I have attempted

---

95) *Supra*, pp. 17 ff.

96) P. van Dijk, *op.cit.*, in 5 *NJCM Bulletin*, 1980, p. 18.

97) *Idem*, p. 19.

98) In this connection see also T.C. van Boven, "Some Remarks on Special Problems Relating to Human Rights in Developing Countries", *Revue des droits de l'homme*, Vol. III, 1970, pp. 383 ff.

to define in terms of the rights and obligations of developing and developed countries, is to have the necessary legal basis and specificity, it must be laid down in treaty form. The fact that a number of obligations have already been incorporated in treaties is of lesser importance. The order of responsibility for realisation of the right to development indicated will have to be clearly reflected: in brief, this means that the state has primary responsibility for the realisation of basic rights and rights of participation, and if the state is unable to guarantee the realisation of the individual's right to development because it lacks the resources, the international community becomes jointly responsible individually and collectively. This interlocking of the individual with the state and the state with the international community is the innovatory element in the right to development.

It should perhaps be pointed out that the obligation to assume co-responsibility cannot be restricted to development cooperation in the strict sense; the achievement of more equitable international economic structures and efforts to establish a new international economic order to replace relations which form an obstacle to development are part of this responsibility, which is exercised in many different forums and negotiations. This of itself means that the inter-state aspect of the right to development can only be defined in fairly general terms as yet. It also follows from this that the right to development cannot readily be expressed in one single legal instrument, in this case a treaty, incorporating all its aspects and providing for the necessary sanctions.[99]

In fact the present UN definition of the right to development, as a human right, should be abandoned. Where the right to development relates to individuals, it is an aggregate and therefore a multiplicity of human rights; apart from this the individual aspect is only one component of the right to development. As we have seen, the right of states to development cannot be described as a human right.[100] The fact that human rights are violated if the right to development is not realised is a different matter. In a more general definition it would be better to refer to a *right of individuals and states to development.*

---

99) G. Abi-Saab, *The Legal Formulation of a Right to Development*, Workshop, The Hague, 1979, *loc.cit.* (footnote 23), p. 168.

100) *Supra*, pp. 166/167.

KEEPING HUMAN LIFE HUMAN:
ALTERING STRUCTURES OF POWER ECONOMIC BENEFITS AND OF INSTITUTIONS

A. Caesar Espiritu

Professor of Law and Director, Graduate Studies Program, University of the Philippines

The notion that the world community should so arrange its international affairs so that every man, woman and child at least has life, and perhaps even a chance at liberty and happiness, is consonant with the declared values of our twentieth-century world community. But despite all our platitudes about an abundant life for all in this planet, equality of access to the necessities of life had never been operational for the world community as a whole. It quite suddenly is possible today. The present global negotiations in the halls of the United Nations probe deeply into the distribution of wealth and income both inside and between the "developing" and "developed" societies.

It has become increasingly apparent that the principal limits to sustained economic growth and accelerated development are political, social and institutional, more than just physical. To ensure accelerated development, two general conditions are necessary — first, far-reaching internal changes of a social, political and institutional character in the developing countries and, second, significant changes in the world economic order.

Thus, the struggle for development and human rights should be waged at all levels in both the international and national fronts. The nationalists of the Third World, whose primary concern is the restructuring of political and economic institutions in their societies, would be wrong if they forget that no matter how egalitarian and just their societies might hopefully become, their people will never attain a high quality of life unless they are able to change the inequitable structures of commodity trade, finance, tariff and non-tariff barriers to exports of industrial goods, technology transfer, the exploitation of the world commons, and other aspects of international economic and social relations. On the other hand, they would be extremely naive if they were to champion the cause of a new international economic order in international fora without realizing that unless they are able to work for new national economic orders at home, they would be fighting only for the political and economic elites at home, rather than for the broad masses of their people.

A case study would be instructive. Let us look at the Philippine situation.

Our economy is stable, it is true. It has grown at an appreciable rate, it is true. Yet withal, we cannot run away from the existence of the harsh fact that the development efforts in the country have not been primarily directed at meeting the basic needs of the population, much less to remove the underlying structural obstacles at the root of injustices in human relations. Because the majority of people have not really been afforded the opportunity to effectively participate in the economic and political decision-making processes that affect their lives, the exploitative social, political and economic structures have been perpetuated, dooming them to economic degradation.

It does not require any searching examination to come to this conclusion. Our economic dualism is so patent. Side by side with, say, 1,000 or so plush homes in Makati, one would easily be able to see 10,000 shacks of the very poor — the epitome of inequality in the Philippines. Then, within a stone's throw of all these are the magnificent Philippine International Convention Center, built at a tremendous cost, which can be the pride of any country in the world — even the richest of them — and the really imposing Cultural Center of Manila, as well as the prestigious Heart Center in Quezon City.

Beyond doubt, the majority of people are overwhelmingly poor, but this poverty is camouflaged by the number of visible gadgets of affluence, such as the cars and other private vehicles choking the streets of Metropolitan Manila.

How does one explain this? The explanation is simple. No matter how poor the country is, in aggregate terms, there is a 10 % of the population which enjoys 38.8 % of the total income of the country — i.e., 4.8 million of our people, out of 48 million, are affluent. That is quite a big number.

On the other hand, 50 % of our population — i.e., 24 million — are poor, enjoying only 24.5 % of total national income. Of this number, according to government estimates, at least 42 %, or 20 million, have incomes below the absolute poverty level. And way down the base of our social pyramid, some 14.4 million, comprising 30 % of the total population, are wretchedly poor, receiving only 9 % of the national income.

According to a national survey conducted by the Department of Social Services in 1975, 95 % of our people eat three meals a day, but for 66 % of them, the food is completely inadequate for good health.

Three out of every five pre-school children are undernourished, according to our Department of Health in 1976, with extremely low protein and calorie intakes. An integrated health service program in one province — Capiz — found the malnutrition there worse than has been depicted by the Department of Health. There, of the 49,948 children aged six in the province, 42,017 are malnourished. And potable water supply benefits only 42 % of our population; 58 % of drinking water is of questionable quality.

Finally, 32 % of our families have sanitary toilet facilities. Another way of putting it is that 68 % of the families, with some 30 million members, incredible as it may seem, are, in this modern age, doomed to the use of insanitary toilets. Imagine that!

Yet there are 13 de luxe hotels — set up to meet the basic needs of our people? But the majority of our people would not have the nerve to enter the ground of that Manila Hotel!

But of course, our country is not unique in this respect.

The development process that has so far been observed in many countries of the Third World has been termed by some writers as "maldevelopment". This is understandable; the current international discussions reflect a new concern for the liberation of all men and women from exploitation and alienation. This concern is combined with an anxious question on the future of human society.

There is a real danger, however, in concentrating only on the international approaches to the establishment of a new international economic order — and forgetting that without reforms at home, international reforms, no matter how fundamental, will ultimately be meaningless to the majority of our people.

In a new national economic order, the satisfaction of basic human needs should be enjoyed by all the people — food, clothing, housing, health, education, transportation, and communication. In other words, a new international order must be complemented by a new national development model which must give the first priority to the improvement of the quality of life for the most deprived strata of the population. This satisfaction of needs should, however, not be dissociated from the appropriate structural transformation at all levels, from the village or neighborhood to the planet, to enable those concerned finally to manage their own lives, their own affairs, and, therefore, their total needs.

But surely, this cannot come about without destroying the conditions which have given rise to relations of domination and dependence among our people. Surely, unless opportunities were opened for active participation by the people in the shaping of the structures which govern the production, processing and distribution of their basic needs for material survival, these same repressive structures will doom them to abject poverty and degradation. For the harsh fact remains that in our society, as in the other poor societies of the world, it is really our own elites who, together with the powerful forces in the West, have become, wittingly or unwittingly, the main agents of domination.

A new development strategy for the Third World should, thus, above all seek to alter the structures of power, of economic benefits and of institutions which deprive people of their human rights. This new strategy calls for the organization and mobilization of the poor in these countries for self-reliant development, for mobilization and organization provide the most effective means whereby the poor are enabled to marshal resources to protect their rights and assert their interests in their dealings with people in power — e.g., landlords, creditors, employers, government officials. Such strategy also calls for the return of civil rights of which they have been deprived in many countries. The obstacles to political and economic organization, including the prohibition on strikes, should be eliminated. Beyond this, of course, popular control of government and accountability of officials through systems of checks and balances and periodically conducted free elections by secret ballot are among the important manifestations of people's participation in development.

Parenthetically, in many countries of the Third World emergency rule or martial rule exists, or where it does not, internal security laws substantially repress the civil rights of the people. It can be conceded that in many developing societies a strong leader may be necessary to hold the country together and lead it to paths of social peace and progress and secure justice and the common good. But it is also a fundamental principle of democratic politics that all great decisions of government must be shared decisions. Development under the rule of law requires the eager maintenance of a polity that strikes a constitutional balance to achieve the two fundamental correlative elements of constitutionalism, namely the legal limits to arbitrary power and complete political responsibility of the government to the governed.

Altering power structures is important yet for another reason. The growing militarization of many governments in developing societies creates political environments in which the sharing of decisions in political processes is precluded. As guardians of the ruling class, men in uniform decree what is right or wrong. Force is used to arbitrate disputes or conflicts of opinion, and organized violence becomes an essential ingredient of the apparatus of power in the name of national security.

This is important, because to our sorrow, we Asians have experienced the militarization of the politics of our societies. And militarization puts a back-breaking burden on the poor societies of Asia, among whom it is most prevalent. To maintain their armed forces, Asian nations spent $35 billions, 5.2 % of their combined gross national product in 1977, which is more than NATO's 4.4 %. In contrast, however, during that same year, Asian nations spent $23 billion, 3.45 % of their combined GNP, for education, and $8 billion, 1.2 % of their combined GNP, for health. But in nations where the majority of the people are desperately poor as we are in most of Asia, simple justice and common sense would seem to demand that these expenditures be pared to the bone, and every available cent be used to eradicate poverty.

As a former senator in the Philippines has pointed out, some 15,000 people died violently in 1974 in that country, perhaps half of them because of clashes between the military and rebel and dissident forces. But in that same year, some 46,000 people died of pneumonia; 31,000 of tuberculosis; 15,000 of avitaminosis and other forms of nutritional deficiency; and 12,500 of malignant neoplasms — all 76,500 deaths caused by diseases that could have been prevented or cured. Yet that year, the Philippine government spent only $3 per capita for health, compared to $8 per capita for the military. Quoting David K. Whynes, the Filipino senator points out that what makes the situation even more alarming is that in 11 of 15 Asian countries for which he has compiled data, he has shown that military expenditures grew from 1972 to 1977 at higher annual rates than the annual population growth rates.[1]

By way of conclusion, it should be stated again that the UN and its agencies belong to one arena in which the struggle for development and human rights should be carried out, but such struggles should be inextricably linked to the struggle for justice in human relations in the first arena — the national level.

Indeed, development should be given a wider perspective. It should meet both the material and non-material needs of the people. The central issue — i.e., development by whom and for whom, should be faced squarely. Only if this is done can development be seen as a liberating process, as the creation of the conditions for peoples, particularly those at present oppressed and marginal, to identify their own needs, mobilize their own resources and shape their future in their own terms.

---

1) *The Economics of Third World Military Expenditures*, London: Macmillan, 1979.

HUMAN RIGHTS AND DEVELOPMENT:
A DIFFICULT RELATIONSHIP

Luis Pásara

Director, Centre de Estudios de Derecho y Sociedad
(Centre for Studies of Law and Society), Lima, Peru

Human rights and development structural problems have to be analysed as a whole. The shift to a "fourth phase" by the United Nations, mentioned by Philip Alston, is in this respect a very encouraging step. Of course, it is impossible to understand what the causes of the human rights cases are without careful and close consideration of the social environment in which those violations take place.

However, the main purpose of this paper is to point out some difficulties to be faced when the "structural approach" to human rights is substituted for the traditional, "non-political" case-by-case approach. At least three aspects should be noted:

(i)   the problems arising from the lack of a consensus definition of development;
(ii) the difficulties of having a politicised version of human rights; and
(iii) the particular role of lawyers in the less developed countries.

Defining Development

Two decades ago, when the word began to be widely used, it was possible to work with two or three different theories of development. But these theories have only obstructed strong and important discussions. Moreover, the frustrating experiences in pursuing development goals in our countries have led to the realisation that the goals themselves needed to be redefined.

To mention only a few aspects of the problem: the role to be played by the state vis-à-vis private groups, the strength and constraints of international support, the alignment in the world fight for power, the technology to be used in the real development process... are some of the crucial issues that are still far from reaching clear and obvious solutions. Ideologies and political prejudices make more obscure and confusing the way to find out what are the correct answers for a given society.

As a result we are not capable of articulating a proposal, or a set of prescriptions, meaning what development is for a non-developed country. In the process we have learned that there are no "technical" solutions; that technicians are able to offer us different alternatives when a political option has been reached, because development is unavoidably a political issue.

As a consequence it is not surprising that some liberal proposals — as for open political participation, for example — are now considered subversive by an important number of governments ruling the non-developed countries. Even the neutral language that some technicians prefer is considered not value-free by those rulers, contributing in this way to making the issue even more political.

Politicising Development

Each time the subject of development arises, different highly political versions about it emerge. To this sort of politicisation two different elements have contributed.

On the one hand, a variety of efforts looking for a radical transformation have taken place in the third world since 1959, when the Cuban revolution gained power. Under different inspirations and with different purposes, civilian and military leaders, guerrilla forces and regular armies, marxist parties and social-democratic or even religious forces have developed a very important and rich experience trying to alter some non-developed societies in a radical way.

As a consequence of these experiences, some of the original assumptions underlying development theories began to be discussed. Let us take the problem already mentioned of the state's role. In most of the non-developed countries there is a lack of tradition for political participation — and of stable institutions for that purpose. More concretely we have not gained the experience of having a government and an organised opposition: both strong. Each time a reform oriented government has come to power in the non-developed countries, a not exactly loyal opposition, representing vested interests groups, has arisen trying to make a *coup d'état*.

In that concrete context it is possible to explain why the notion of a "strong government" has been presented as a requisite by most of the change oriented thinkers in our countries. Of course, in that notion we do have an important step for the justification of an authoritarian regime.

This particular example shows that the way to organise political life in our countries — precluding basic freedoms — is not necessarily the perverse expression of personal will. We are not suggesting that regimes of this kind are justified by the nature of our societies. Instead we are trying to explain why it is in the case in our countries that authoritarianism flourishes so easily... frequently in the name of development.

On the other hand, politicisation of human rights also comes from the ideological discussion between rightist and leftist sectors of our societies. A truly reactionary view of life and politics has tried — and tries now — to ignore the global political meaning of social life. This perspective is largely responsible for the "technical" approach to human rights and for denouncing as "politics" the efforts to take into systematic consideration the social and economic conditions of a given country.

While conservative sectors try to isolate politics, revolutionary forces have played the same game but by using human rights as a tool just for their political goals. Those groups' claim to respect for human rights has been limited to the extent that such claims could be useful to their sectorial objectives and strategies. For instance, the right to personal freedom, the right to speech and others are recognised — in this leftist behaviour — only when these rights are to be exerted by popular sectors, not the bourgeoisie or other capitalistic oriented sectors.

Manipulation of human rights for political reasons has made it more difficult to present the real, universal and non-party meaning of them. To some extent this sort of politicisation weakens the capacity of human rights to be persuasive to those of good faith in our societies.

The consequences of a certain human rights weakness should be noted. In our countries there is no chance to emphasise the civil and political rights against the social, economic and cultural human rights. We do have two types of regimes: those respecting neither rights and those not respecting the political rights area in the name of development.

Lawyers on Their Own

For a long period of time we have been expecting too much from the lawyers. While different ideologies insisted on ethics as the main content of law, the real facts of life taught differently. We tried to convince ourselves that the lawyer was the advocate of justice. Certainly, people perceived more clearly what the lawyers' task in fact is and depicted it through jokes and stories. When the International Commission of Jurists in 1966 defined what the lawyers' approach to human rights *should be* (extensively quoted by Alston, pp. 000—000), it may have under-estimated the real conditions for practitioners' work.

Our problem must be presented from the non-developed countries' perspectives. Some of the characteristics of our countries make it more difficult for lawyers to play the game of justice administration as persons who can be free on the professional labour market we are talking about. This market is particularly small in our countries: a very narrow sector of all society can afford a lawyer. Even unionised workers are a minority among the workers. In these conditions the professional labour market tends to be a closed rather than an open one.

Vested interest groups are few. Persons of families in power are easily identified by name. Then, lawyers soon identify themselves with their clients and their interests. The question, again, cannot be only a moral one.

Of course, a very distinguished minority of lawyers make the decision to fight in legal terms against the prevailing interests in society. But under the conditions of these "oligarchical" societies their decision is a subversive one. There is no room for a liberal practice of the legal profession.

It is true that during his academic formation at law school the legal student receives an orientation to justice as defining his career. But the contradiction with life is so deep that he learns cynicism very soon.

This situation is the basis of the relationship between the legal profession and the accomplishment of human rights in our countries. "Be realistic" for our lawyers means "get stable, safe work among the wealthiest portions of the dominant class". Unavoidably this type of professional practice — in a direct or indirect way — results in a position against the majority of the population. When his clients abuse the human rights of poor people he can have an uncomfortable feeling, but cannot forget that his success in professional life depends on clients of this sort: the powerful whose control in our societies does not respect human rights.

On the other hand, to maintain ethical standards in legal practice means to protest systematically, and resist rich and powerful groups whose action prevents real implementation of human rights. In this respect it is necessary to take into account the small differences between civil and military regimes in Latin America. Both have used — and are ready to use — repression to the extent needed to hide the largely non achieved popular demands.

Obviously we do not intend to justify the conduct of most of our lawyers. But we have tried to present facts that allow us to be consistent with the right purpose to analyse our problem — law and lawyers as well as human rights — in a rather structural comprehensive perspective.

REALIZING THE RIGHT TO DEVELOPMENT:
THE IMPORTANCE OF LEGAL RESOURCES

Clarence J. Dias

President, International Center for Law in Development, New York

The Right to Development

A recent United Nations document,[1] reviewing the evolution and scope of the right to development indicates that based on major United Nations' instruments and debates there exists "a general consensus as to the need for the following elements to be part of the concept of development":

— the realization of the potentialities of the human person in harmony with the community should be seen as the central purpose of development;
— the human person should be regarded as the subject and not the object of the development process;
— development requires the satisfaction of both material and non-material basic needs;
— respect for human rights is fundamental to the development process;
— the human person must be able to participate fully in shaping his own reality;
— respect for the principles of equality and non-discrimination is essential; and
— the achievement of a degree of individual and collective self-reliance must be an integral part of the process.

If "the right to development" is indeed intended to be taken seriously as more than slogan and rhetoric, it might offer unique opportuni-

1) Report of the Secretary General, Commission on Human Rights, *Question of the Realization in all Countries of the Economic, Social and Cultural Rights Contained in the Universal Declaration of Human Rights and in the International Covenant on Economic, Social and Cultural Rights and Study of Special Problems Which the Developing Countries Face in Their Efforts to Achive These Human Rights. The International Dimensions of the Right to Development As a Human Right in Relation With Other Rights Based on International Cooperation, Including the Right to Peace, Taking into Account the Requirements of the New International Economic Order and the Fundamental Human Needs,* para 27. (E/CN.4/1334, 2 January 1979).

ties for revitalizing what to the world's impoverished millions appear to be the jaded and anaemic concepts of "human rights" and "rule of law". From the perspectives of the victims of lack of development or maldevelopment (the intended beneficiaries of the newly-fashioned right to development), for too long the "rule of law" has meant little more than "the law of the ruler" and "human rights" no more than the rights of ruling elites to perpetuate dependency, exclusion and exploitation.

But the scale and degree of human misery and impoverishment in the world today resulting from the denial of human rights is such that concerned lawyers and jurists must indeed go beyond debunking the myths surrounding such concepts as "rule of law" and "human rights". Exposing what goes on in practice in the name of those concepts may indeed be a necessary and important first step but revitalizing those concepts and striving to make them meaningful in reality is perhaps the even more necessary and important next step. It is to this latter task that perhaps the right to development offers opportunities.

This paper seeks to undertake a preliminary and tentative exploration of the roles of lawyers and jurists in assisting efforts to realize the right to development. It may well be (as Philip Alston's basic working paper asserts) that "a human right to development is now firmly entrenched in United Nations human rights doctrine" and that "in terms of international human rights law, the existence of the right to development is a *fait accompli.*" Moreover, the concept of the right to development may indeed be "the single most important element in the launching of a structural approach to human rights." But in most developing countries it remains a concept whose potential has yet to be realized. For developing country jurists the challenge lies in contributing to such realization through activities geared to standard-setting, promotion, protection and, perhaps most importantly, redesign of the structures of law.

Standard-Setting

As at present articulated, the right to development represents an aggregation of concepts. For lawyers and jurists, part of the challenge lies in translating those concepts into enforceable legal norms which can influence law at various levels: the international, national and local. The concept of the right to development necessitates the development of legal norms embodying the following concepts:

— *Human Development.* If the central purpose of development is the realization of the potentialities of the human being, what legal norms are needed to support that purpose? *Rights* in people to demand their human development? *Duties* of government to undertake programmes of human development? *Evaluative criteria* for assessing state activity (human impact statements analogous to environmental impact statements)? *Rules* establishing (or balancing competing) development priorities?

— *Meeting Basic Human Needs.* If development requires the satisfaction of both material and non-material basic needs, how can those whose basic needs are not being met compel the reorientation of development priorities? Can norms be fashioned out of this principle to channel the exercise of discretion in the direction of meeting basic human needs? State control over resources to meet basic human needs is both pervasive and growing in developing countries. Can the above principle be invoked to fashion new obligations/fiduciary relationships for state agencies involved in the production or distribution of basic resources?

— *Participation.* What is needed to ensure that the human person be able to participate fully in shaping his own reality? Education to enable genuine, meaningful and full participation? People's organizations as vehicles for participation? State institutions and processes that permit participation? Rights against exclusion?

— *Self-Reliance.* If the achievement of a degree of individual and collective self-reliance must be an integral part of the development process, how can self-reliance be fostered? Through new kinds of cooperation among those commonly felt to be disadvantaged by poverty? Through a major shift away from reliance on existing state institutions towards reliance on the collective efforts of the impoverished to redress the conditions of their impoverishment?

Each of the above four concepts (which constitute the building blocks of a human right to development) creates the need for new standards. The challenge to jurists is not only to elucidate these standards but to fashion instrumentalities through which those standards will be rendered effective at the various levels of the structures of law: international, national and local.

Promotion and Protection

Lawyers involved in the promotion of human rights during 1955—65 found themselves ill-at-ease, ill-equipped and ineffective. Their efforts were accordingly "weak and poorly defined and directed" and most of the promotional measures taken were not of an essentially preventive nature (see Alston above). Learning from that experience, jurists attempting to promote the right to development must concentrate their efforts towards enhancing the ability of the impoverished to assert for themselves their right to development. Similarly, learning from the earlier experience during the phase of protection of human rights during 1965—75, jurists must appreciate the scope for protection that lies in preventive action, e.g., by securing real and meaningful participation as a means for conflict avoidance; by creating structural conditions which are less amenable to human rights violations.

Some ongoing activities are sketched below as illustrative of the approach to promotion and protection suggested above. A group of third world lawyers, sharing concern about growing impoverishment in their own countries, have been working to develop legal resources needed for the mobilization of the rural poor for self-reliant development (Paul and Dias: 1980). Out of these efforts to mobilize the oppressed to resist their oppressors has come the realization of the importance of collective action and therefore of the right to organize. Accordingly, while work continues at grass-roots level, some of the lawyers involved are also turning to an examination of the status of the right to organize under international law.

Convention 141 of the ILO, adopted by the International Labour Conference of 1975, calls for legal recognition of a universal right of "rural workers" to form "non-state" rural organizations "of their own choice". The term "rural workers" includes small holders, tenants, labourers, share-croppers and self-employed home workers. The convention declares:

Article 3:

1. All categories of rural workers, whether they are wage earners or self-employed, shall have the *right to establish and to join organizations of their own choosing without previous authorization.*
2. The principles of freedom of association shall be fully respected; rural workers' *organizations* shall be independent and voluntary

in character and *shall remain free from all interference, coercion or repression.*

3. The *acquisition of legal personality* by organizations of rural workers shall not be made subject to conditions of such a character as to restrict the application of the provisions of the preceding paragraphs of this Article.

4. In exercising the rights provided for in this Article *rural workers* and their respective organizations, *like other* persons *or organized collectivities, shall respect the law of the land.*

5. The *law of the land shall not be such as to impair*, nor shall it be so applied as to impair, *the guarantees* provided for *in this Article.*

Article 4:

It shall be an *objective* of national policy concerning rural development to *facilitate* the establishment and *growth*, on *a voluntary basis*, of strong and independent *organizations of rural workers*.

Convention 141 of the ILO suggests the purposes of these rights with some explicitness: freedom to form organizations; freedom to determine the law governing the structures; freedom to use it as a vehicle for participation in legal administrative and political forums; freedom to develop it as a vehicle for economic activity; freedom to give it legal capacities.

A "recommendation" enacted by the same conference, in effect, sets out some assumptions underlying these guarantees: rural organizations are envisioned as vehicles of "defence" of the "interests of rural workers," and as vehicles to enable more effective "participation" in state structures — not only participation in "the formulation" and "implementation" of "programmes of rural development" (at "all stages"), but also in the "evaluation" and determination of accountability of those who manage them. Further, rural worker organizations are to be vehicles for direct access to goods and services controlled by the state; they are to be vehicles for initiating local public works — and they are to be vehicles for organizing new kinds of co-operatives and other forms of groups-managed economic activities.

Concerned lawyers in developing countries can play important roles in promoting Convention 141, for example, by:

(i)   bringing the rights under the Convention before rural workers who might then work to assert those rights. Thus, for example, the Convention was brought to the attention of a group of land-less, low-income rural workers in the Philippines at a tripartite workshop which brought them together with landowners and administrators from the Rural Workers Office of the Ministry of Labour. As a result, the workers expressly endorsed the Convention and referred to it as a source of support for some of their demands which they presented to the government in a communique at the end of the workshop.

(ii)   helping create public opinion within their country to ensure that their government not only ratifies the Convention but also follows up with implementing legislation where necessary.

(iii) examining and evaluating existing national laws in terms of their consultancy or infringement of the provision of the Convention. Existing laws and modes of administration in many countries often stand in sharp contradiction to the rights enumerated by the Convention. Laws which require registration and official approval of voluntary associations can be used to frustrate formation of "legal" groups. State laws which prescribe a fixed structural form for voluntary organizations, which seek to enjoy legal capacities to make contracts or own property, contradict (or may be used to contradict) the "right of rural workers to form organizations of their own choice;" and they may, in any event, deny values of endogeneity in group formation which are basic to self-reliant approaches to rural development. Penal laws which proscribe vaguely defined activities such as prohibitions against threats of disorder, often are construed to create opportunities to legitimize suppression of group activities which cause no demonstrable harm. Similarly, licensing laws which regulate group activities — such as holding meetings, or engaging in ordinary economic pursuits — are inconsistent with essential premises of the right to development, at least to the extent that licensors are vested with discretion uncircumscribed by law.

Lawyers and jurists in third world countries can thus help replace laws which are hostile to collective self-reliance activities with those which are more supportive of such activities. Despite neglect or repression, in much of the third world groups — varying in size, function, form and relationship with the state — have continued to be part of the rural scene. Some are small and rooted in tradition; some provide organizational forms for mutual self-help, savings or construction of desired community facilities; some have grown as vehicles of protest; some are in overt opposition to governments of the day. In view of this resurgence of endogenous, community rural organizations in many countries of the third world, it seems all the more imperative that jurists address some of the issues relating to the right to organize.

The approach to promotion and protection of human rights illustrated above may differ from that conventionally adopted by human rights jurists but over the long term such an approach (where feasible) may well prove more effective than the approaches which charactized the 1960's. Lawyers must see their roles as going beyond providing access to remedial institutions. Existing structures rooted in law remain obstacles to the realization of the right to development and lawyers will need to play their part in the redesign of such structures.

Lawyers, Legal Professions and the Right to Development

In most third world countries, "present legal systems are structured in favour of the powerful and wealthy" and a major obstacle to improving the responsiveness of legal systems to problems of the poor is that "legal systems tend to presume that wealth and access should be correlated" (ESCAP: 1981).

"It is common knowledge", writes a Nairobi law teacher, "that the majority of Kenyan citizens want nothing to do with official law." The observation seems widely true in rural settings throughout the world. Several factors contribute to this aversion. The processes of official law generate delays and expenses which often inflict inordinate hardship on litigants, and they are premised on values which are often hard for rural people to understand, much less share. The institutions which produce or reproduce and interpret state law are often distant, both socially and geographically, from rural communities. Ordinary people who seek out lawyers and courts are handicapped by language barriers and processual complexities. Their contacts with law reinforce their negative perceptions. Criminal law generates a large part of the work of rural courts and it is often effectively used (or abused) by local rural elite groups — public and private — to intimidate and subjugate rural communities. Infrequent attempts by the poor, or their leaders, to assert claims against oppression often

produce unsatisfactory outcomes. Litigants go deep into debt to secure professional assistance and even with that assistance they incur
risks (sometimes increased by lawyers) of endless rounds of litiga-
tion. The rights, certainty and formal equality promised by jurists
who extol the rule of (official) law may seem illusory to those who
view it from this kind of experience.

Ignorance and avoidance of law, and incapacity to use it, contribute
to the impotence of the rural poor, and their needs for legal resources
are rarely perceived and seldom made manifest by those who would
help them. Conversely, dominant groups and official bodies are able
to institutionalize transactions and relationships which produce impoverishment by maintaining the impression that these practices are
sanctioned by law.

Lawyers and legal professions today tend to be very much a part of
the problem. In some respects, the view that the legal profession "has
a tendency to be blind to the structures which support or even cause
the problems with which they are dealing" may err on the side of un-
derstatement (Galtung: 1977). Lawyers, by trade are manipulators:
of language; of process; of facts and the interpretations given to
them. The professionalization of the delivery of legal services has led,
inevitably, to lawyers developing their manipulative skills on behalf
of the highest bidder for such services.

Realizing the right to development will inevitably require "legal resources" — i.e., the development of collective community knowledge
and capacity to use law. To the extent possible, community paraprofessionals, legal self-reliance, and the development of community dispute processing institutions as alternatives to courts, may help provide legal resources without reliance on professional lawyers. However, there will be a continuing need for lawyers in a variety of roles,
for example:

— *Advocate* of collective demands and group interests in both courts
 and in administrative, legislative and other institutions of policy
 articulation and implementation.

— *Educator* helping develop community awareness and knowledge
 of relevant laws and helping train community paraprofessionals.

— *Critic* of proposed or existing legislation and administrative actions
 which impinge on the rights and interests of disadvantaged self-
 help groups.

— *Law Reformer* asserting carefully studied, documented claims for changes in legislation and state structures.[2]

— *Jurist* developing new jurisprudential concepts needed to realize the right to development. For example, if the right to participation is to be taken seriously, perhaps existing concepts of law are inappropriate since remedies against exclusion are usually available only when the complainant can show that there was a specific right to participate which was denied. Perhaps a new concept of *lawless exclusion* needs to be fashioned which would place the onus on the state authority to prove that exclusion was justified by law, all other kinds of exclusion being deemed lawless (i.e., unsupported by law) and therefore illegitimate. Similarly, if state control over resources needed to meet basic human needs is to be directed towards meeting such needs, perhaps new concepts structuring discretion are necessary. A concept of *lawless discretion* (i.e., unsupported by law) would again place the onus on the authority concerned to establish that his exercise of discretion was in fact justified by law, all other kinds of general exercise of discretion being needed to be guided by the principles contained in the right to development.

Legal specialists working to articulate and realize the right to development may indeed need to adopt new roles, new strategies, new skills and a new jurisprudence.

New Roles

Lawyers working for impoverished *groups* may not have "clients" in the traditional sense, and relationships with those they seek to help must be quite different if the lawyer is to be identified as a resource by the group. In a sense these lawyers must be more "proactive" in relation to the cause they serve, more directly engaged in working

---

2) The approach being suggested here calls for ad hoc "law reform commissions of and for the poor". For example, such a "commission" might be created to address problems of rural credit and indebtedness or prices of particular commodities or problems of rural tenants. This "commission" would be a non-state, participatory body, representative of those groups whose concerns provided the reasons and impetus for the law reform effort. In terms of "operating style", the commission might do what conventional "law reformers" often fail to do — it would go to the problem: it would hear the grievances of the poor in places and settings which encourage full and candid discussion. It would seek principles and proposals for reform from the people affected — and thus seek to impart new, endogenous concepts into state law. It would then seek to publicize the needs and demands of communities and lobby for reform (Paul and Dias: 1980).

with group "clients" in helping them define the problems to be addressed, and choices among strategies to be used. At the same time, the lawyer's precise role at any given time — whether counsellor, catalyst, scribe, advocate or simply provider of information — must be determined by the group in order to assure their self-reliance and avert their continued dependency upon professionals.

New Strategies

Legal strategies for changing structures, for example, of rural development, or creating new ones, may entail both traditional methods of legal recourse (e.g., defensive or offensive action in court), but also strategies of political recourse (e.g., the use of deputations, demonstrations of protest, use of media — to set out a group's grievances and to establish the essential legitimacy of its position through appeals to legal principles, official ideologies or policies). Strategies to change structures may begin by focusing on particular claims and demands for specific remedies: thus, the teaching urged by many community organizers is to begin by thinking in terms of specific victories which can be won and which, if won, may provide the demonstration effect to give a group strength and experience to move to new objectives. Organization seems to grow out of successful experience, and wither when perceptions of uncertainty, ineptitude or failure gain sway.

New Skills

Lawyers working with groups will need to know what other organizers must learn, and be capable of integrating that knowledge with perceptions of legal roles. All of this — plus the very character of the setting and the problems to be faced — call for an awareness of the need for new skills and new knowledge (including knowledge of laws and customs often unfamiliar to urban-centered practitioners). It also calls for a new literature (e.g., legal analyses of the histories of experiences of rural organizations) and a new jurisprudence.

A New Jurisprudence

The right to development entails a rethinking of the values and concepts underlying law, for example, governing public administration,

voluntary associations, cooperative activities, modes of dispute resolution. At a more basic level perhaps one must develop new perspectives on the requisites for legitimacy of state structures, the value of
endogenous ones, or new perspectives on the nature of valued human
rights. Conventional discourse on human rights draws a dichotomy
between "economic and social" rights — which are often depicted
as "affirmative" obligations to be assumed by the state and "political
and civil" rights which are often depicted as "negative" rights of individuals. The right to development seems to emphasize the collective value and sharing aspects of "political" rights of association and
the symbiotic relation of these rights to economic and social rights.

References

Philip Alston, *Development and the Rule of Law: Prevention versus Cure as a Human Rights
Strategy*. Basic working paper, *supra*.

ESCAP, *Working Paper on Law and Participation, Economic and Social Commission for
Asia and the Pacific*, 1981.

Johan Galtung, *Is the Legal Perspective Structure Blind?* Oslo, 1977.

James C.N. Paul and Clarence J. Dias, *Law and Legal Resources in the Mobilization of the
Rural Poor for Self-Reliant Development*, International Center for Law in Development,
1980.

The paper also draws on materials from related publications of the International Center for
Law in Development:

Clarence J. Dias, Robin Luckham, Dennis O. Lynch, James C.N. Paul, *Lawyers in the Third
World: Comparative and Developmental Perspectives* (ICLD: 1981).

John B. Howard, *The Social Accountability of Public Enterprises: Law and Community
Controls in the New Development Strategies* (ICLD: 1980).

ICLD, "Research Priorities for Another Development in Law", *Development Dialogue*
(1978:2).

James C.N. Paul and Clarence J. Dias, *Law and Administration in Alternative Development:
Some Issues, Choices and Strategies* (ICLD: 1981).

THE LEGAL NEEDS OF THE POOR TOWARDS AN ALTERNATIVE MODEL OF GROUP ADVOCACY

Neelan Tiruchelvam

Associate Director, Marga Institute, Sri Lanka; Executive Director, Asian Council for Law in Development; Board Member, Sri Lanka Foundation and Human Rights Centre, Sri Lanka

The Search for 'Another Development'

Asian scholars concerned with alternative paradigms of development have shown increasing interest in human rights issues which arise in the process of development. A few have called for the reexamination of the 'prevailing international tradition of human rights' in the context of the indigenous legal process and the developmental experiences of specific Asian societies. Others have pointed to the need to move away from a legalistic concern with civil and political rights towards a focus on ethical issues implicit in the choice of specific developmental goals, strategies and instruments. Groups have been formed to examine a central ethical dilemma faced by specific societies and how such dilemmas were perceived and managed by elite groups in such societies. These case studies have further contributed towards the elaboration of an ethical frame of reference for the appraisal of the developmental processes and experiences of specific Asian societies. Such an ethical frame of reference has drawn its elements from the spiritual and cultural traditions of Asian societies and the serach for 'another development'. While there has been growing interest in the conceptual aspects of human rights and development, the problems of enforcement and the satisfaction of basic needs has received little attention.

The purpose of this paper is to examine the differential legal needs of the poor in the content of a specific society's commitment to human rights and social justice. The paper examines the prevailing system for the delivery of legal assistance, and develops an alternative model of group advocacy. This paper draws on an ongoing programme of 'dialogic research' on the needs of the rural and urban poor and of workers and villagers in the plantation sector in Sri Lanka. The data generated by this project has yet to be fully processed, but has nonetheless provided valuable insights into unmet legal needs of socially and economically disadvantaged groups. The failure to devise procedures and institutions with the capacity to respond meaningfully to such needs has thwarted social legislation, social welfare programmes and distributive policies. We will draw attention to some of the perception of different legal needs in each of these sectors with a view to illustrating the need for an alternative approach to legal assistance.

Legal Needs in a Village Community

The first category examined was a village in the central highlands where land ownership based on caste supremacy was an essential feature of the social structure. The Buddhist temple in the village was a unifying force, exercising a powerful influence over the cultural, social and economic life of the community. This authority flowed partly from the ownership of more than half the land within the village. An elaborate service tenure system attached to the land, through which high caste land owning families were periodically called upon to perform ritualistic services to the temple in satisfaction of their tenurial obligations. Land owners further consolidated their social position by holding appointments as village administrators and as officials who allocated irrigation resources. Demographic processes, land fragmentation, the expansion of the plantation economy contributed towards dispossession of small land owning peasantry and accentuated their dependence on the powerful and influential land owning families. The lower caste groups, however, were able to align themselves with a major political party and through patronage networks gain access to employment and trade opportunities. They also benefitted from the distribution of the 'surplus' under the land reform law. But this again appeared to have been temporary and with political reversals there was a continuing impoverishment and landlessness amongst these groups.

Although laws have been directed towards the abolition of service tenures, the regulation of rentals, modes of payment and prohibitions against evictions, the benefits of this legislation were not adequately understood by tenant cultivators and landless labourers. The legal relations between tenants and owners formed part of a wider network of economic, social, familial and cultural ties. Share croppers who were conscious of some of their rights were reluctant to assert them in the belief that they would forfeit other benefits for which they were dependent upon the land owner. There were many irregularities and malpractices in the registration of cultivators, which 'affected cultivators' were unable to prevent. Powerful landowners also employed various devices to evade these statutory obligations with regard to rentals and protection of tenants. Small land owners and poor cultivators felt that they were discriminated against with regard to access to agricultural credit, fertilizers, and other agricultural inputs. There were similar complaints of indifference and arbitrariness by officials administering crop insurance schemes.

Legal Needs in an Urban Squatter Settlement

The other sector looked at related to an urban squatter settlement in the city of Colombo. In 1977 it was estimated that out of a city population of 562,160, the estimated slum and shanty population was about 350,953. The basic needs of squatter and shanty dwellers, as they relate to sewage facilities and water services are inadequately met by Municipal authorities. It has been estimated that almost fifty families utilise a single water tap at the road side. The need to employ legal processes to compel authorities to take more meaningful measures to satisfy these needs was recognised. There was concern with the uncertain legal status of slum dwellers who work within the informal sector. The protective arm of the State (as it relates to labour regulations, minimum wage laws) did not extend to persons who are employed in this sector. On the other hand itinerant vendors were subjected to harassment for non-compliance with health laws and consumer protection laws which embody middle-class values inappropriate to this sector.

Legal Needs in the Plantation Sector

The next category relates to the legal needs of the poor in the plantation sector. The low income of the workers in this sector is often compounded by their insecurity of employment and their indebtedness to the estate staff and local moneylenders. Their uncertain legal status further locked them into the estate economy with very little hope of subsidiary income from livestock or the cultivation of small agricultural plots. The condition of children in this sector was found to be particularly depressing. They are often malnourished, unclothed and have no access to even elementary education. Some of the children of the poorer families are compelled to seek domestic service to escape the deprivation of absolute poverty. The legal needs of the community were identified as follows. Firstly, the need to give legal shape to contractual relationships between workers and management as they relate to the rates of remuneration, regularity of employment, etc. There is the further need to enforce management responsibility towards resident labour as regards medical facilities and education. Secondly, the need more specifically to assert the right of children as articulated in the proposed Children's Charter and related legislation, and thirdly, to ensure more equitable access to State-aided social welfare and health care programmes. Fourthly, workers need a great deal of assistance in securing their citizenship and enforcing the civic and other rights associated with this status. Constitutional provisions relating to non-discrimination and equality before the law were found to be ineffective, since the workers were poorly informed of these rights and provided with no legal weapons to assert them. We next examined the extent to which the existing scheme for the provision of state aided legal assistance is responsive to these needs.

Shortcomings of the State Legal Aid Scheme

The Legal Aid Scheme in Sri Lanka has a history of diverse management. The scheme was initiated by the legal profession and subsequently came under direct control of the Law Society. However, during the early seventies Legal Aid was taken over by the State and operated under the political direction of Justice Ministry officials. Lack of resources and the non-involvement of the profession eroded the effectiveness of the scheme. The legal profession responded by launching a parallel scheme. However, today a Legal Aid Law has been enacted to provide the institutional framework for the delivery of legal assistance. The law instituted a Legal Aid Commission consisting of representatives of government and the legal profession. A Legal Aid Advisory Council consisting of 30 Members was also established. The objectives of the Legal Aid Commission included the provision of legal action to deserving persons, and the conduct of legal and other proceedings for and on behalf of such persons. The law has, however, been criticised for creating a legal aid bureaucracy which would consume most of the pittance that has been extended to it for financing its activities.

Our analysis reveals that the Government Legal Aid scheme is constrained by several structural factors. Firstly, it is primarily directed towards legal representations of claims by individuals in disputes which are inter-personal in nature. The scheme does not have the capacity to direct itself towards the representation of group or class interests.

Secondly, even within the sphere of interpersonal disputes it is limited to the formal judicial arena. It is not integrated into the process of nonformal conflict resolution at the grass-root level, and accordingly does not adequately draw on processes which have the force of social control in indigenous society. Neither does the scheme extend to the provision of assistance to indigent cultivators who may seek to challenge illegal evictions by land owners before Agricultural Tribunals.

The scheme similarly has not sought to aggregate individual claims into collective demands for normative and institutional change in social welfare programmes.

Thirdly, the modes of advocacy were normally limited to the preparation of legal pleadings and oral representation in the courts of original and appellate jurisdiction. Rarely have professional services taken the form of structuring small scale business transactions, or of counselling on the legal prerequisites for the establishment of a credit co-operative organisation or a tenant's association. Similarly, group advocacy could take the form of drafting model legislation and/or administrative regulations which could enhance access of the underprivileged to social and economic benefits. There are multiple arenas in which the advocacy of group interests can find creative and effective expression. This potential has not been fully realised.

Fourthly, the existing scheme has proved to be reactive i.e. it responds passively to the problems of those who may accidentally stumble upon its office. The legal aid survey revealed that 87 % of the respondents were unaware of the existence of the scheme and several of those who sought assistance could not get past the screening procedures. The scheme needs to reach out to those who are ignorant and those who lack the means or the courage to seek out legal assistance. The scheme should be proactive in that it would be decentralized and physically located in urban slums, fishing villages, and agricultural communities. The volunteers should acquire familiarity with the basic needs and grievances of the poor and seek to translate them into legal demands.

Fifthly, the quality of the legal services is often uneven. The personnel engaged in the performance of professional tasks are often inexperienced or poorly motivated in view of the low remuneration and lack of professional kudos. There are some instances where professional negligence may have contributed to the dismissal of claims by accident victims. Besides, the formal interactions between legal-aid lawyers and clients tend to reinforce the dependence of beneficiaries on the paternalistic delivery systems. It is a framework which discourages frank and open discussion of problems and the identification of underlying grievances. The social and cultural barriers to the access of the under-privileged to legal administrative processes are internalised within the government legal aid office.

A New Model of Legal Assistance

Our proposal is, therefore, directed towards the elaboration of a new model of legal assistance to the poor. The elements of this model include,

(a) emphasis on collective demands and group interests;
(b) establishment of clinics which are proactive in that they actively seek out the grievance of poverty groups and advocate their interests;
(c) expansion of the arenas of group advocacy to include administrative, legislative and other spheres of policy articulation and implementation;
(d) multiplication of the types of assistance to include counselling, the structuring of transactions, and the formation of associations; and
(e) the structure of the delivery system to include participatory involvement of potential beneficiaries. Such participation to take the form of management of legal aid schemes, dissemination of information about social welfare schemes and redistributive legislation and an encouragement of self-help.

The implementation of the model would need to be preceded by the following steps:

(a) a careful examination of the differential legal needs of the urban and rural poor, the plantation workers and other socially and economically disadvantaged groups;
(b) the identification of informal social processes of para-professionals who are responsive to these needs;
(c) operation of social welfare programmes directed towards the satisfaction of the basic needs of the poor;
(d) an examination of the implementation of the more important distributive legislation, social welfare policies and programmes; and

(e) a study of the existing market for the provision of legal services.

The location of clinics would also need to be carefully determined. At such location we would need a socio-economic data base and a pool of voluntary workers who could be drawn into the management of the scheme. The physical characteristics of the legal aid offices would also be an important consideration. Their physical location and furniture arrangements must be such as to make the poor comfortable within its environment. The identification of the personnel who as professional attorneys or legal assistants would service the legal aid schemes would also require careful consideration. It is extremely important that these personnel should be technically competent and strongly motivated to work with poverty groups. The personnel should be able to overcome cultural barriers and achieve a measure of social acceptability within the community. Pleasant, kind and courteous personnel would add to the attractiveness of the scheme to indigent clientele. Some systematic efforts should be made to involve law students and legal apprentices in the community clinics. The means by which the clinics could be linked to a programme of clinical legal education could also be considered. Specific proposals would need to be formulated with regard to community participation in the management of the scheme. The criteria of eligibility for assistance would need to be defined. Should legal assistance be provided to all members of a poverty community without distinction or should a line be drawn between applicants on the basis of income or family size? One of the first tasks of the managers of such a clinic would be to define the range of activities that may appropriately be undertaken by community clinics. Some guidelines in the form of a code of conduct should enable the legal aid attorney to work outside the confines of the lawyering role without compromising the ethical standards of the profession. The problems of financing and raising resources for the continuation of the clinic would need to be addressed.

A National Poverty Law Centre

An important component of the model would be the establishment of a National Poverty Law Centre. Such a Centre could co-ordinate the work of community clinics and advocate the interests of diverse communities at the National level. This could take the form of legal challenge to legislation and administrative action which infringe fundamental rights; the filing of complaints against maladministration before the Parliamentary Commissioner for Administration (Ombudsman); and the institution of class actions to defend the public interest on environmental, consumer protection and human rights issues. The more localised efforts of the community clinics could be aggregated at this level into demands for more basic changes.

If the potential law and legal system as a resource for victims of inequity and injustice is to be realized, a transformation of the existing approach to legal assistance would be required. It is through such an approach to group advocacy that the grievances of the socially deprived and economically disadvantaged can be converted into enforceable claims, and a system pushed to its ultimate equities.

PROJECT SARILAKAS: A PHILIPPINE EXPERIMENT IN ATTEMPTING TO REALIZE THE RIGHT TO DEVELOPMENT

A. Caesar Espiritu and Clarence J. Dias

This interim report was prepared by drawing heavily upon materials generated under the project by the Rural Workers' Office of the Department of Labor.

Development and Development Strategy

Development as a concept has assumed many changing meanings during the last two decades and even the term "basic human needs strategy" (BNS) of development has been given different meanings by different interest groups: bilateral and multilateral donor agencies, first world governments, third world governments and communities of the impoverished.

Since the right to development can also assume very different contours depending on what concept of development is envisaged, it might be helpful at the outset to distinguish between two different interpretations of BNS which are commonly used to give content to the concept of development (Blaikie, Cameron and Seddon: 1979).

A conservative BNS strategy is concerned with problems of coping with poverty. A radical BNS strategy sees the redistribution of power as its central issue. Given the very wide differences between the two approaches, it may help clarify objectives and strategies if the salient features of each of the BNS approaches are identified.

The *conservative* BNS starts by identifying the poor and quantifying poverty. The tendency is to see the "poor" divorced from social reality and relationships as a stratum (e.g., the bottom 40 %) and a target group whose poverty is a quantifiable deficiency. Problems of measurement of poverty immediately become a major issue. Measurable variables (e.g., undernourishment or illiteracy) which may often be symptoms of the problem, tend to become the problem itself. Measurable aspects of poverty tend to get overemphasized while qualitative aspects are either omitted or "tacked inconsequentially onto the end of a list of quantifiable consumption criteria" (Blaidie et al: 1979). The implementation agencies for a poverty eradication programme tend to become institutions of the state itself — a tendency which is attractive to consultants and donor agencies alike. In the definition and implementation of BNS, participation in decisions tends to be additional and optional. In sum, this version of BNS degenerates into a welfare system delivered by the institutions of state.

The *radical* BNS strategy, on the other hand, starts by attempting to tackle the structural causes of poverty. The major relationship in which virtually all the poverty stricken are involved is that of working for, or under the control of someone else. The initial problem, therefore, is to shift the balance of power in favour of labourers and all those who are in contractually weak positions with regard to owners of the means of production. The strategy therefore involves reorganizing production. This may involve, certainly initially, a movement away from commodity production for distant markets or state trading corporations towards producing goods for local consumption. Loss of state and export revenues may well mean that such moves will be opposed by forces far wider than the local employers faced with a loss of power. But the *vital* point is that the poor must increasingly participate not only at the moment of distribution where they are often in a position of disadvantage through indebtedness, but also in the production decisions. It might be argued that in this respect BNS is simply utopian, but the struggles of the poor to achieve for themselves their basic needs have tended to be "unseen", either underrated or in some cases conveniently forgotten. The existing struggles by the deprived to secure their own basic needs through direct action and local organization (local self-help groups, trade unions, etc.) are themselves an important part of a BNS which needs no official opening ceremony, and which already has a long history (Blaikie et al: 1979). The *radical* BNS strategy, therefore, seeks to alter relations of production and property rights. It seeks to address the root causes of the crisis: entrenched economic and political interests at the international and national level. It stresses participation in the definition and implementation of BNS as an essential prerequisite and emphasizes the need to formally enlist the involvement of the groups at present excluded from decision-making at all levels and all stages of a project with the right of veto. Not surprisingly, the *radical* BNS runs the risk of being finally unacceptable in practice to those who are presently conceived of as the agencies for its adoption and implementation, e.g., the international and national aid agencies and the nation states.

The SARILAKAS Project

Project SARILAKAS is an attempt, within a micro setting, to realize the right to development through adopting a radical BNS strategy. SARILAKAS comes from the Tagalog word *"sariling lakas"* which literally translated means "own strength." Project SARILAKAS is being undertaken by the Rural Workers' Office (RWO) of the Department of Labor. RWO is itself rather unique in that although it was created to perform traditional bureaucratic functions (such as formulation of policies and labour standards for protection of rural workers), part of its mandate is "organization of rural workers."

Due to the inadequacy of information and data on landless rural workers, RWO decided that it would undertake a pilot project for rural workers involved in sugar production, since they were one of the most exploited and impoverished groups in the country. RWO began by undertaking a participatory action-research project in which the landless rural workers actively participated in problem identification, analysis and formulation of solutions in four pilot sites representing typical sugar-production communities. One 'facilitator' was fielded per project site for three months, starting in December 1980, to assist the people in the different research processes involved.

The research study culminated with the holding of a National Tripartite Conference in July 1980, attended by representatives of the landless rural workers, employers, businessmen and heads of different government agencies. At the start of the conference, case reports on the living and working conditions of the landless rural workers from the four sites were presented for deliberation and immediate action. This tripartite group came up with recommendations outlined in a communique which is annexed to this report as an example of the outcome of a participatory approach to problem identification. This phase of the project had been code-named Project AID (Action Identification for the Development of Landless Rural Workers) and it is perhaps indicative of the impact of the project process that RWO soon abandoned the nomenclature of Project AID because it overemphasized dependency and adopted the code name of SARILAKAS which emphasized self-reliance. What occurred at this stage, however, was more than a mere name change. Project AID had stressed the availability of governmental resources external to the community (e.g., loans under the Land Bank of the Philippines Loan Guarantee Program). Project SARILAKAS stressed building up the strength of the community so as to avoid perpetual dependence on government resources.

The goal, objectives, role of SARILAKAS workers, and schedule of activities of SARILAKAS were articulated as follows:

Goal

To change the unjust exploitative social, economic and political structure into a free and just society through collective action and formation of self-reliant organizations.

Objectives

1. Rural workers will develop some forms of participatory, self-reliant organizations of their own, through which they will engage in mutual help and cooperate in economic and social activities, and develop solidarity and bargaining power to promote their common interests.
2. SARILAKAS cadres will gain skills and experience in sensitizing work to promote participatory organizations of rural workers around group-based economic and social cooperation.
3. The role of the SARILAKAS cadres will be to sensitize the poor people to make them conscious of and understand present unjust and exploitative social, economic, political structures and their capacity to change these structures through self-reliant organizations and collective action.

Activities

1. Two teams, of two SARILAKAS cadres each, to be assigned full time to two pilot sites to stimulate rural workers in group discussions and collective action.
2. The cadres to share their interests and experiences on an ongoing basis with other SARILAKAS cadres in different stages of work and with representatives of Proshika, PIDA and PIDIT (projects in Bangladesh, Sri Lanka and India which share project SARILAKAS' concerns and approach).
3. Ongoing training of SARILAKAS cadres in the village through self-learning, village investigation, interaction group learning, group investigation, collective discussions, deeper investigations, collective action, for the analysis and deeper discussions and continuing action, etc.

4. Regular local and national participatory evaluation and reflection sessions of SARILAKAS experience.

The SARILAKAS Project Sites

The Rural Workers' Office conducted situation-specific studies (employing both survey and participatory research methodologies) at four sites, randomly selected in Binalbagan (Negros Occ.), Balayan (Batangas), Tibiao (Antique) and Barotac Nuevo (Iloilo). The surveys and their analysis were carried out by community facilitators who resided in and identified themselves with the respective communities of the rural workers.

Each of the surveys in the four provinces have brought out the fact that landless rural workers suffer from poverty and deprivation. The income levels are not enough to provide for their basic needs. However, employment, poverty and deprivation among the rural workers do not follow a uniform pattern. Relatively speaking, the sugarcane mill workers have an assured employment and are better off than the self-employed. Sugarcane plantation workers also indulge in other economic activities subsidiary to their main occupation, like fishing, poultry, livestock and rice and corn cultivation. The earnings of workers' households differ from milling to off-milling seasons. A typical worker may earn pesos 2,465 a year and live in a nipa bamboo house (leased from the planter). His basic furniture may consist of only a few items which may include a radio, kerosene lamp and a couple of cans. Often no toilet facilities are available. A community open well is generally used for drinking and washing. Mostly, he stands indebted and is underemployed. A stable job means six to seven hours work a day, five to six days a week, three to four weeks a month and seven to eight months a year. The majority of rural workers' households have large families, ranging from seven to ten members. Literacy rate is quite low, child mortality high, medical facilities scarce and costly. Investment and loan capital is hard to come by. The tenancy sharing was reported to be on a 50-50 basis for inputs as well as the yield. Particularly in Antique tenancy and fishing are common part-time activities.

Brief descriptions follow highlighting the specific problems encountered in three of the four sites.

Balayan (Batangas)

The site here comprises 624 people (living in 113 households) of whom approximately 80 % are agricultural laborers. There are nine major landowners (one of whom is a cousin of the Mayor) who have what are in effect tenancy-at-will arrangements with the labourers under what is called a *kartilya* system. The *kartilya* is a small notebook given to each tenant which bears the name of the tenant and contains a statement of accounts as between tenant and landlord. The *kartilya* represents the only record the tenant has of his tenancy. On the death of the tenant the book goes to the male heir along with the debts of the deceased! The tenants are supposed to be sharing both the inputs and the produce with the landowner on a 50-50 basis. In fact the landowner either makes the tenant bear all the costs of the inputs or else makes the tenant pay half of an artificially jacked-up price for fertilizers provided by the landowner. The landowner keeps the entire profits of sales of molasses and undervalues the price at which the produce is sold. Since the tenants have no legal standing to deal directly with the *Central* (the State Sugar Purchasing Enterprise) they have to take on faith what the landowner states the crop yield to have been. Although the landowner collects the sale price as a lump sum from the *Central*, he disburses it to the tenants only in instalments and often insists on paying in kind with products (such as rice) whose price he overvalues. Such benefits as the workers are entitled to under law (e.g., a Social Amelioration Bonus under Presidential Decree 621) remain unpaid by the landowner. Through a stranglehold over credit for subsistence needs, the landowner is able to both intimidate and subjugate the tenants.

The response of the tenants was to form an organization which initially had 80 members who filed complaints for the non-payment by the landowner of Social Amelioration Benefits (which the landowner had in fact collected from the government but failed to disburse to the tenants). Prompt action was not taken by the authorities on the complaint and under pressure all but eight members withdrew their complaints. At the end only four complainants remained and they were bought off. This unsuccessful confrontation left the tenants' organization considerably weakened. While the tenants remain most vulnerable, the landowners remain dominant. They are well organized and meet weekly in their own organization. They have easy access to alternative labour and have greater staying power and capacity to bear losses. One landowner (having other lands too) threatened to deliberately let the crop rot rather than settle grievances with his tenants.

Tibiao (Antique)

This site comprises three villages. Amar is a rice farming village comprising 98 households where the tenants have a crop-sharing scheme similar to the one described in Balayan. Malabor is primarily a fishing village nearly half of whose 264 households rely on fishing to earn their living. This village privides the migrant workers for the Hacienda San Jose sugar plantation (which is another site selected by the SARILAKAS project). The fishermen in Malabor have formed an organization through which they have successfully approached the Philippine Land Bank for loans. Their livelihood has been recently threatened by the decision of the local municipality to divide the fishing area into zones and lease out fishing rights to concessionaires. In order to make a bid for such a concession, a sizeable deposit must be put up which the fishermen are not in a position to provide. The largest concessionaire in the area is the Mayor. The villagers of Malabor have also undertaken labour for the National Immigration Authority (NIA) who have initiated an irrigation project. The villagers claim that over ₱ 72,000 in unpaid wages are owed to them by NIA.

The village of Importante is a rice farming village comprising some 338 households. One of the main problems in this village is that a large number of families have cultivated and improved a wide portion of upland areas for many years only to find out that these are within the forest reserve area.

All three villages have a population of migrant labour working under a *contratista* system. The *contratista* (a recruiting agent) is given money by the landowner who fixes a price for the migrant labourers' work. The *contratista* exploits the migrant workers in a variety of ways despite there now being in existence a law (Department Order #7 of the Ministry of Labour) governing all *contratista* arrangements.

Binalbagan (Negros Occidental)

This site, Hacienda San Juan, comprises an island privately owned and run as a *hacienda* (plantation). The owner also owns four other haciendas in different areas. The island comprises 300 hectares of land of which some 100 hectares are planted to sugar cane. Coconuts are grown on part of the remaining land and fishing provides a secondary occupation for the residents of the island. The plantation hosts a thousand people organized into 109 households. The plantation is run by an administrator (because the owner is absent) who is a cousin of the wife of the owner and who, not surprisingly, is also the *barangay* captain. The Mayor of Binalbagan is the uncle of the hacienda owner. The workers on the hacienda fall into three categories — resident workers (some 100 in number), seasonal workers (some 30 in number, mostly women and children), and migrant workers (called *sacadas* and numbering some 40 odd coming from the neighbouring provice of Antique).

The resident workers are supposedly paid a daily wage and a living allowance but in fact are rarely paid for more than five days a month and the hacienda administrator justifies this on the ground that the hacienda, being mechanized, cannot really support so large a number of resident workers. The resident workers suffer from "padded" payrolls, and from arbitrary job assignments controlled by the *cabo*. They have minimal social security benefits. The landlord sells the residents a "rice ration" at a price higher than the market price and this gets cut off if the resident's indebtedness exceeds ₱500. The administrator is also a usurer. The resident workers are aware of their exploitation most of which results from abuses by the administrator or the *cabo*.

The *sacadas* (migrant workers) were first brought into the plantation in 1967 because of disputes with the resident workers. Since then the administrastor continues to bring in the same *sacadas* from year to year partly to reward loyalty but mostly because the *sacadas* are indebted or have inherited the debts of their father. The *contratista* (a hacienda employee) serves as an agent dealing with the administrator and the *sacadas* as an intermediary. He controls payrolls, rations and subsistence credit.

There are some 50 fishermen on the island and the administrator has permitted them to be organized (while bluntly prohibiting such efforts regarding the resident workers). This organization has been successful in securing credit from the Philippine Land Bank.

The SARILAKAS project workers have decided on a strategy of withdrawing from this project site and working instead with the *sacadas* in their own province of Antique in an attempt to enhance the capabilities of the *sacadas* to act as change-agents on the hacienda. Support to the fishermen's organization will continue but will be provided outside the hacienda from Antique.

Strengthening Legal Resource Capabilities of Rural Workers

Representatives from all of the SARILAKAS project sites came together at a workshop to review the problems identified by the studies
described above. Although the solutions to the problems differed
from place to place, a number of areas were identified common to all
the provinces such as identification of specific project proposals for
employment generation, ensuring availability of credit for production and consumption uses, enforcement of labour laws, conscientization of rural workers, promotion of action groups and rural workers' associations, security of tenancy, solution to the *contratista, an-
ticipo* and *pakiao* systems, medicare and recreation facilities for the
rural workers and their families. (Special attention was paid to the
problems of the *sacadas*. The majority of *sacadas* are often recruited
through *"contratista"* (labour contractors) who finance their transportation and family consumption needs through advances or *(antici-
po)* during the lean months of the year.)

As a result of discussions during the workshop, the Rural Workers'
Office (RWO) was asked to do four things:

— encourage the conscientization of rural workers and promote
  group action and group resources to develop a basis for the sound
  growth of rural workers' association;
— assist rural workers' groups in all educational matters which may
  enable the rural workers to participate in the process of development;
— identify concrete projects for income generation; and
— adopt the necessary measures to implement the projects mentioned above.

However, it may not be enough for a workers' organization to be fully aware of its situation and responsibilities. It must also possess the
competence necessary both to defend its interests and undertake self-
help projects. Since social and political processes are deeply intertwin-
ed with law, it becomes necessary for project SARILAKAS to examine whether rural workers' organizations must be prepared to deal
with legal issues. Moreover, if there was such a requirement for legal
expertise among rural workers and rural workers' organizations there
would be formidable obstacles to having such requirements met. Legal expertise must be internalized if it is to be an effective weapon.
To the extent possible, legal expertise must reside among the workers
themselves to avoid an excessive dependence on outside legal re-

sources. External service is often very expensive and often results in a stereotyped approach to workers' problems, preventing the development of avenues that might have been suggested and explored by the workers themselves. In a word, dependence on outside legal resources denies workers the chance to examine circumstances and effect changes through their own efforts.

In order to have a systematic examination of the relevance of law and legal resources to the SARILAKAS project, a small workshop was convened in February 1981. Participating in the workshop were the SARILAKAS cadres, the SARILAKAS project staff and director from the Rural Workers' Office, a few sympathetic Philippine legal experts and a couple of legal researchers from India who were experienced in working on problems relating to legal resources needs of specific grass-roots organizations and who had worked with organizations like PIDIT and PIDA (organizations that the SARILAKAS project staff finds value in maintaining contact with).

At this meeting there was consensus that legal resources were essential to rural organizations in creating an awareness of rights, assisting mobilization, defending against suppression, formulating tactics and strategies to press claims and advance demands, resolving conflicts inevitable in the process of self-assertion and self-help, and in the organization and management of collective economic activities. However, it was essential to guard against creating dependence on external legal experts. It was also necessary to guard against an overemphasis of legal issues or too traditionally legalistic an approach to the solution of problems. What was needed was not so much a lawyer providing legal aid to rural organizations as a legal resource person capable of identifying with the community and playing essentially an information providing role: one which would facilitate the community in the formulation of its own tactics and strategies.

It was thus decided to augment project SARILAKAS by initiating *within* that project a pilot effort at strengthening legal resource capabilities of rural workers' organizations.

The Legal Resources Project Within SARILAKAS

True to the spirit of SARILAKAS, the legal resources sub-project would not be designed from above but would be allowed to emerge out of a process of continuing interaction with the communities concerned. In order to achieve this the first step would be to introduce into each of two selected SARILAKAS project sites (Balayan and Tibiao were selected as the most appropriate sites) a *legal facilitator* to work closely alongside the existing SARILAKAS *community facilitators*.

The legal facilitator would be recruited from newly graduated law students who were fully qualified to practice as lawyers. The legal facilitator would undergo an orientation and training period during which emphasis would be placed on developing knowledge and skills rele--vant to the legal resource needs at the project site. The legal facilitator would then be immersed in the community at the project site for a period of three months. During this period he would, adopting a participatory research method, seek to identify the legal resource needs of the community and of the community's rural workers' organization. During this period the flow of information would not be one-sided and it would be expected that, where appropriate, the legal facilitator would also begin to share with the community information about relevant legal rights, procedures and remedies.

At the end of this three-month period, the entire SARILAKAS project staff (including the two legal facilitators) would convene and develop a programme of work (for the next 12 months) which would be geared to strengthening the legal resource capabilities of the communities in the two project sites. During this 12-month period the legal facilitator's role would not be that of a lawyer for the community. Rather he would concentrate on two tasks:

— helping build up legal resource capabilities within the rural organization and the project site; and
— helping the rural organization formulate its own tactics and strategies involving recourse to law.

Once the rural organization had decided upon a strategy of recourse to law, the legal facilitator's task would then be to assist in implementing that strategy by helping the organization gain access to needed legal expertise whether local or in Manila. The emphasis here is on a "delivery system" of legal knowledge and skills which would be founded upon the principle of *participatory involvement of and control* by the client group.

In order to back up the legal facilitators in their educational and other activities at the project site, a small core group of legal experts and legal researchers would be convened, as and when necessary, by the SARILAKAS project director in Manila. This core group would undertake research on legal aspects of problems identified at the project sites, would also develop community-oriented curriculum and materials for the legal facilitators to use at the project sites, and would initiate, at the direction of the community, appropriate legal action (where needed) in Manila.

Additional back-up to the two legal facilitators at the project site would be provided by a *roving legal facilitator* who would coordinate and liaise between the two project sites and the core group in Manila.

Possible Legal Tasks and Strategies

Because the legal resources sub-project has been initiated only recently and because the project activities are not to be designed from above but are to emerge out of a process of continuing interaction with the communities concerned, it is premature at this juncture to do more than indicate very tentatively, on the basis of existing interaction with the communities, some possible lines that activities under the project might take:

1. Rural workers' organizations have been formed at the project sites. These organizations have obtained legal status under a special law which RWO secured (a law which does not force the organizations into the institutional form prescribed by the general law on cooperatives). RWO has also prepared in local languages a draft model constitution which these organizations can adopt. However, the organizations will have to evolve their own organic rules and processes and their own endogenous internal law. Moreover, once sufficient experience is built up with working the RWO model constitution, the latter can be revised and amended to reflect the lessons learned from such experience.

2. The communities will decide upon specific projects for employment generation. In the implementation of these projects a whole variety of needs for legal resources may emerge.

3. As the communities begin to change production patterns and production and property relations, conflicts will inevitably be generated. Legal resources may become necessary to handle these conflicts, resist suppression, retaliation or efforts to frustrate the activities of the communities. It would be important at that stage

to ensure that the communities decide what strategies of recourse or non-recourse to law they adopt since they will have to bear the costs and benefits of whatever course of action is adopted.

4. Law reform activities will emerge from the experiences of the rural workers' organizations. Thus, for example, the entire scheme of administration of the social amelioration bonus will need to be revised; the scope of protection of labour welfare legislation will need to be broadened so as to deal with relationships such as the *pakiao* system prevalent under customary law. Indeed some aspects of customary law might themselves need drastic reform. The existing system of state concessionary awards of fishing rights will need to be modified. A whole agenda for law reform might unfold and the agenda will be all the more impelling because it unfolds from experienced hardships and difficulties.

5. A whole range of educational materials will need to be prepared dealing with laws affecting rural workers. RWO has already made a significant start in this regard by compiling a comprehensive collection of laws and regulations affecting rural workers. But much team work will need to be undertaken by legal experts and community members if the compilations are to be converted into a form of materials easily understandable and usable by the community.

The process of identifying what is needed to assist the realization of the right to development is indeed a continuing one. Satisfaction of one set of needs may well generate a whole new category of needs. Removal of structural obstacles at local level to the realization of the right to development will inevitably involve, sooner or later, action at national and international levels. The sugar industry in the Philippines is heavily influenced by multinationals. Sugar, from the national government's perspective, is a significant export crop and foreign exchange earner. The sugar worker may well appear to be a powerless pawn to be manipulated by national and multinational interests. For this very reason, perhaps, he provides the severest challenge to the effectiveness and creditability of a human right to development.

References

1. Piers Blaikie, John Cameron, and David Seddon, *The Logic of a Basic Needs Strategy: With or Against the Tide* (June 1979).
2. Rural Workers' Office, Ministry of Labor, *Project Action Identification for the Development of the Landless, Near Landless and Other Low-Income Rural Workers in Sugar-Producing Communities* (June 1980).
3. Labor Standards Division, Institute of Labor and Manpower Studies, *Sacada Study* (undated).

ANNEX

Communique

1. We endorse ILO Convention 141 and Recommendation 149 affirming among other things the workers' right to organize and to be protected by government from any forms of harassment in the exercise of this basic right.

2. We affirm the principle that regular access to information regarding the marketing and pricing arrangements for Philippine Sugar is a right that should be honored through periodic communication or publication to all sectors represented in this Tripartite Conference for mutual enlightenment about the problems and challenges facing the industry.

3. We endorse the progressive example of several planters in setting aside a portion of their lands to be cultivated by resident workers for supplementary food needs during the off-season months.

4. We accept the principle of land reform of sugarlands along cooperative lines to be tried on a voluntary or pilot basis as an opportunity for workers to participate fully in the ownership and management of their resources and as an alternative solution to the social problems besetting the industry. Just compensation along with investment and tax incentives for landowners should be considered integral elements of this land reform proposal.

5. We address ourselves to concerned government agencies and appropriate institutions regarding the following points:

   — that all labour laws be strictly enforced, and all labour cases be expeditiously acted upon;
   — that the social amelioration program be reviewed and other welfare benefits decreed for sugar workers be followed;
   — that the social services pertaining to health, education, and general welfare, as well as infrastructure facilities like roads and aquatic resources be directed towards the socio-economic development and advancement of rural workers in general and sugar workers in particular;
   — that the Sugar Act of 1952 be now enforced.

6. We propose a representative for the labour sector, chosen by legitimate labour organizations in the sugar industry, in PHILSUCOM to exemplify the representation principle of this Tripartite Conference in the highest decision-making body of the industry.

7. In the light of the adverse conditions affecting the sugar workers at this time, we recommend that PHILSUCOM take immediate steps to raise the composite price of sugar to allow a proportionate share of welfare benefits to accrue to workers under P.D. 1614, P.D. 1634 and P.D. 1016.

8. In share-tenanted areas of the sugar industry, we propose that the sharing of produce and expenses be more equitably regulated or changed into a leasehold arrangement under P.D. 1425. Furthermore, more binding contracts could be adopted to replace the traditional *"kartilya"* system.

9. We believe that the problems of migrant sugar workers *(sacadas)* can be solved not only in the canefields of Negros and other sugar-producing areas, but also in Antique and other places of the workers' origin by providing the full opportunities for socio-economic development like fisheries, forestry, and lowland and upland development programs in these places.

10. We participants in this Tripartite Conference, wholeheartedly support the principle of tripartism based on mutual trust and respect among the major sectors in the sugar industry. We further subscribe to the ethical principle involved that conferences like these can continue to be constructive forums for discussing vital issues, provided there is complete confidentiality without fear of reprisal against any participant or group. We also recommend that a post-Tripartite committee be established under the RWO to monitor and help carry out the guidelines embodied in this Communique in the same spirit of tripartism.

SUMMARY OF DISCUSSIONS AND CONCLUSIONS
OF THE INTERNATIONAL COMMISSION OF JURISTS
1981 CONFERENCE ON
DEVELOPMENT AND THE RULE OF LAW

1. The Conference first considered the concepts of 'development', 'human rights' and the 'right to development'. It then discussed a number of related topics, including militarisation, participation, agrarian reform, and the role of lawyers and legal assistance.

Development

2. The concept of development was considered in terms of the growth of the gross national product (GNP), the meeting of 'basic needs', and a 'global' concept of development embracing all human rights.

3. The need was recognised for a balance in development policies between investment aimed at increasing long term economic growth and investment aimed at meeting basic needs, particularly by strengthening local communities to make possible development on the basis of 'self-reliance'. However, as the emphasis has hitherto been placed on the first of these aims, priority should now be given to the second. Experience has shown that development strategies based solely on the objective of GNP growth and following the western model of industrial development have often worsened the position of the rural and urban poor, who constitute a large majority of the population. This has resulted in grave violations of their economic and

social rights, and frequently also of their civil, political and cultural rights.

4. In general terms, the concept of development refers to the kind of society one is aiming to build. This should be a society in which everyone has real access to all human rights. Development policies which concentrate on relieving "absolute poverty" or on meeting "basic needs" can properly be adopted as matters of first priority. However, they should not be seen as sufficient goals in themselves; as policy goals they would be inadequate and would tend to relegate the countries concerned to a permanent status of dependency. Moreover, the satisfaction even of basic needs would be permanently achievable only with structural changes at all levels, local, national and international, that would enable those concerned to identify their own needs, mobilise their own resources and shape their future in their own terms.

5. Development should, therefore, be seen as a global concept including with equal emphasis civil and political rights and economic, social and cultural rights.

6. Strict application of the principle of non-discrimination on grounds of race, colour, sex, language, religion, political or other opinion, national or social origin, property, birth or other status was seen as an essential element in development policies and programmes.

Human Rights

7. The traditional approach to human rights has been to consider separately civil and political rights on the one hand and economic, social and cultural rights on the other. True development requires a recognition that the different human rights are inseparable from each other, and development is inseparable from human rights and the Rule of Law. Likewise, justice and equity at the international level are inseparable from justice and equity at the national level. All these, taken together, are essential elements in the realisation of the human potential and the common aspirations of mankind.

8. Human rights organisations have tended to concentrate mainly on violations of civil and political rights. In keeping with the growing demand for a fuller realisation of human freedoms in our times they

should now become involved in the more complex field of social, economic and cultural rights.

9. The enjoyment of the totality of human rights calls for the organisation and mobilisation of the poor in developing countries for self-reliant development. Mobilisation and organisation provide the most effective means whereby the poor are enabled to marshal resources to protect their rights and assert their interests in their dealings with people in power, such as landlords, creditors, employers, government officials and transnational corporations.

The Right to Development

10. There was prolonged discussion about the use of ther term 'right to development', some finding that it was too vague a concept to constitute a legal right, some that its use would distract attention from and weaken the plurality of concepts in the International Bill of Human Rights. Others argued that the right to development embraced all human rights, and that it was a useful instrument for ensuring a true human rights content in development policies. They urged that the implementation of the right to development in this global sense should be considered as a condition of legitimacy of a government, and that there was also an international right to development to be implemented not only by development aid, but by removing the asymmetry in economic relations between North and South as illustrated by ruinous deteriorations in the terms of trade. It was argued that the legal basis for the right at both the international and national level was to be found in Articles 1, 55 and 56 of the UN Charter, in Articles 22—28 of the Universal Declaration of Human Rights and in the two International Covenants.

11. Eventually, agreement was reached upon the following formulations concerning the right to development.

12. Development should be understood as a process designed progressively to create conditions in which every person can enjoy, exercise and utilise under the Rule of Law all his human rights, whether economic, social, cultural, civil or political.

13. Every person has the right to participate in, and benefit from, development in the sense of a progressive improvement in the standard and quality of life.

14.   The concept of the right to development needs to be more fully elaborated as a legal concept. Nevertheless it already serves to express the right of all people all over the world and of every citizen to enjoy all human rights. The duty of governments to promote the development of their people is often a legal obligation which can be derived from the constitution. At the international level it is, as yet, largely based on a moral obligation of solidarity. There are, however, clear beginnings of recognition of the right to development as a general substantive principle of international law.

15.   Implementation of the right to development implies the realisation of a number of conditions at the local and national level as well as at the international level. These include the participation of those concerned in the formulation and application of development policies, the adoption of policies based on the principle of self-reliance, and respect for all human rights under the Rule of Law.

16.   The primary obligation to promote development, in such a way as to satisfy this right, rests upon each state for its own territory and for the persons under its jurisdiction. As the development process is a necessary condition for peace and friendship between nations, it is a matter of international concern, imposing responsibilities upon all states.

17.   In addition to a state's legal obligation to cooperate with other states in the process of development, in accordance with Articles 55 and 56 of the UN Charter and other international and regional instruments, each state has a moral if not a legal obligation to collaborate in rendering the international economic order more just and equitable.

18.   Consequently, a state promoting its own development within its available resources is entitled to the support of other states in the implementation of its policies. The industrialised countries should cooperate with the developing nations to achieve a New International Economic Order with a more just and equitable distribution of the world's resources and wealth.

19.   In recognition of the relevance of all human rights to the development process, governments of all countries which have not yet done so should be urged to sign and ratify the two International Covenants on human rights, and the Optional Protocol to the Covenant on Civil and Political Rights.

20.   In promoting human rights of all kinds, priority should be given by the international community, as well as by states, to positive rather than negative measures. Experience has shown that sanctions against impoverished countries tend to provoke defiance rather than compliance. In cases of the breakdown of the rule of law, or other grave violations of human rights, the response of the international community should aim primarily at the restoration of these rights and the provision of assistance to victims, rather than the mere condemnation of the violations or the punishment of offenders.

Militarisation

21.   During recent decades the traditional role of the military, to safeguard their country against invasion, has in many countries been replaced by the self-appointed task of overthrowing the government, imposing authoritarian regimes, and suppressing the rights of the people. Frequently this is done in the name of "national security" or in the guise of furthering development. Assisted by the world arms race, east-west competition and its client system, and the activities of state and private arms dealers, these seizures of power by force or threats of force have resulted in the direct or indirect control of society by an overweighted military sector.

22.   The first and outstanding consequence is a total disregard and suppression of human rights. Some economic gains in terms of GNP growth have at times been achieved, but in such cases they have been accompanied by torture and other gross violations of individual and group rights. Declaring that the state should protect itself against subversion the military forces in the state become increasingly powerful, economically and politically. In some cases the failure of civilian governments to solve national problems has been used as the justification for introducing systematically repressive regimes, but these in turn have usually proved incapable of finding a solution to the problems.

23.   Military regimes in developing countries tend to divert a disproportionate amount of the country's scarce resources to military purposes.

24.   The militarisation process in both industrialised and developing societies needs to be vigorously exposed and condemned. For example, $500,000 million per year, or 6 % of the total world output, is

devoted to military expenditure. The growth of military expenditure continues in all countries under all systems. In recent years the total growth in military expenditure in third world countries, where the people are desperately poor, has increased $1\frac{1}{2}$ times as fast as their GNP. The combined expenditure on militarisation in all asian countries in which data are available is now higher, as a ratio of GNP, than that of the NATO countries, and much higher than their expenditure for education and health services. Of course, military expenditure in the North far exceeds the expenditure for development.

Participation

25. The adoption by the international community of the principle of the right to development offers a unique opportunity for revitalising what to the world's millions appear to be innocuous or at times even irrelevant concepts of "human rights" and "the rule of law". As seen from the perspective of victims of maldevelopment, "the rule of law" and "human rights" appear as no more than the rights of ruling elites to perpetuate dependency and exploitation. Lawyers attempting to promote the right of development should therefore concentrate their efforts on enhancing the ability of the impoverished to assert for themselves the right to development. Attention should be given to the scope for protection that lies in preventive action, e.g., by securing real and meaningful participation as a means for creating structural conditions which are less amenable to violations of human rights.

26. The vital need for participation by all people in the decision-making processes that affect their lives and fortunes should, however, take such forms as are decided upon by or in agreement with the people themselves. The people should evolve their own basic procedures and processes and decide the particular institutions and procedures suitable for the fuller realisation of this right.

27. Increases in development assistance and resource transfers have not always resulted in increased development or in the promotion of human rights. Sometimes they have generated a growing sense of secured dependence; at other times they have supported repressive policies. Assistance leads to true development only if there is a political will, obtained by consensus, for its proper utilisation, — if there is true participation by the people who should be its beneficiaries. In most cases the people are far removed from policy making and im-

plementation, with the result that aid has often been channelled for personal gain or for repression; its beneficiaries have been mainly an urban élite or the authoritarian regimes themselves. To avoid these consequences, preference should be given to project aid over programme aid. Likewise, care should be taken that development assistance does not increase the arsenal of weapons for the suppression of human rights.

Reasons for the Continuance of Poverty

28. It was argued that the contrast between the enormous growth in production and productivity in the world in the last thirty years and the reality of destitution for so many people was due to certain myths that govern the policies of development and the relations between states and peoples:

— The myth of growth as the solution to the problem of poverty. A considerable increase in the standard of living of the majority of the population can be obtained with a lower rate of growth in the GNP if, instead of focussing the main effort on growth, it is focussed on the way to resolve the problem of poverty.

— The myth of western style modernisation. When the western model is transferred to third world countries, only a minority of the population can be incorporated as modern producers and consumers. It may be added that the western model itself is in crisis today.

— The myth of international solidarity between states. In the relations between states the egoism of national interest predominates.

— The myth that a 'New International Economic Order' can relieve governments of developing countries from the necessity to make essential internal social reforms. The struggle for a New International Economic Order should be inextricably linked to the struggle for justice in human relations internally.

Agrarian Reform

29. The phenomenon of 'maldevelopment' was illustrated by the failure of agrarian reform in many third world countries. Examples were given of a pattern to be found equally in Latin America, in Africa and in Asia.

30. The failure of agrarian reform programmes has been due not only to obstruction by powerful landowners, bureaucrats and, at times, the legal process. It has also been undermined by failure to support the transfer of land ownership with the necessary services to enable the new owners to farm the land effectively. These include appropriate education and technology, agricultural credits and cooperative marketing services, as well as agricultural pricing policies which make it possible for peasants to farm their land economically.

31. The lack of these facilities has often been due to an excessive emphasis in development strategies upon industrialisation and production for export, rather than seeking to satisfy basic needs as far as possible from within the country's own resources under self-reliant strategies. The effort to make third world industrial exports competitive in the international market has required a low wage policy in industry, leading in turn to excessively low pricing of agricultural products. This, together with the use by the larger landowners and by transnational corporations of advanced agriculture machinery to produce cash crops for export, has reduced severely employment opportunities in the rural areas and contributed to the massive exodus from the country to the cities, which then transfers the poverty from the country to urban shanty towns.

32. This process has had disastrous effects upon the economic and social rights of the rural population. When those affected have sought to organise to assert their rights and reverse these trends, they have frequently been subjected to severe repression, denying their basic civil and political rights.

33. These problems are unlikely to be resolved merely by establishing more democratic processes in the election of national parliaments. They also require, as already stated, meaningful participation by the communities concerned in the formulation and implementation of development policies, and freedom to these communities to organise themselves so as to assert their rights and mobilise for self-reliant development. Making a reality of civil and political rights at all levels is an essential element in a programme of agrarian reform, as of other development policies.

Labour and Social Legislation

34. Labour and social legislation in all countries should be in accor-

dance with the basic ILO Conventions and should guarantee the freedom of association and freedom of expression of all workers, rural and urban, to enable them to organise and engage in concerted activities. This will enable them to participate actively in shaping the structures which govern the production, processing and distribution of goods to satisfy basic needs for material survival.

35. It was suggested that human rights organisations should manifest their concern about the violation of human rights by some transnational corporations which exert pressure on the governments of third world countries to prohibit the right of workers to strike, as a means of ensuring competitive production in international trade.

The Role of the Lawyer and Legal Assistance

36. A special responsibility rests upon members of the legal profession to contribute to the development of the Rule of Law in such a way as to promote development.

37. The task of the legal profession, in the context of the impoverishment of peoples in the third world, is not only to provide them with traditional legal aid but to build up their legal resources, i.e., the development of their community strength, knowledge and capacity to make use of the law. Towards this end, a new type of legal professional is required, who will be:

— an advocate of collective demands and group interests both in courts and in administrative, legislative and other institutions,
— an educator helping to develop community awareness and knowledge of relevant laws and helping to train community para-professionals,
— a critic of proposed or existing legislation and administrative actions which impinge on the human rights of impoverished groups,
— a law reformer asserting claims for changes in legislation and state structures, and
— a jurist developing new jurisprudential concepts needed to realise the right to development.

38. Lawyers in the third world, as elsewhere, have traditionally been linked with the ruling élites. The remoteness of successful lawyers from the majority of the population makes it difficult for them to

sense and understand the needs of the people, though there have been some notable exceptions. There is also a serious shortage of lawyers in many developing countries.

39. Third world lawyers face an option between defending the interests of a minority who can afford their services and accepting the moral commitment to give professional support to the demands of the impoverished majority for their human rights. It is usually easier to interest young lawyers in such work than those who are already established and fully occupied in their profession. It is also easier for these young lawyers to win the confidence of the poor and understand their needs. The development of internship programmes for newly qualified lawyers in this role should be considered in cooperation with law faculties in the third world.

Subjects for Study

40. It was agreed that many of the issues discussed call for further study by human rights lawyers aided by experts in other fields. Among those mentioned were:

— the actual relationship between development policies and human rights observance in different countries, circumstances and periods;
— the reasons military take-overs occur in some countries and not in others;
— access to the courts, including constitutional, legislative, procedural and other obstacles;
— the way in which some of the activities of financial institutions, transnational corporations, banks and money-lenders effectively act against the enjoyment of human rights;
— the possibility of drawing up a draft model code for legislation relating to development, for distribution to parliaments and courts;
— recent experience in the field of human rights and development, including the more successful projects and experiments;
— the need for a free and independent judiciary and adequate legal services as an indispensable part of the process of development.

41. It was also suggested that seminars echoing the themes of this Conference should be held in different regions and countries on various aspects of human rights with subjects appropriate to the situations in those countries.

LIST OF PARTICIPANTS

Members of the ICJ

1. Badria Al-Awadhi	Dean, Faculty of Law & Sharia, Univ. Kuwait; Assistant Prof. and former Head of Dept. of International Law; Specialist on Int. Law of the Sea.
2. William J. Butler	Chairman, Executive Committee, ICJ; President of the American Association for the ICJ.
3. Joel Carlson	Professor, Hofstra Univ. Law School; Member, Bar of New York (1975), South Africa (1954), Botswana (1962), Swaziland (1962); former Senior Research Fellow at Center for Int. Studies, New York Univ. (1971–74).
4. Haim H. Cohn	Former Justice of the Supreme Court, Israel; Minister of Justice (1952–53); Attorney-General (1953–60); Chairman of Israeli National Section of ICJ.
5. Roberto Concepcion	President of the Philippines Commission of Jurists; Professor of Law; Chief Justice & Chairman, Presidential Electoral Tribunal (1966–73); former President of the Integrated Bar of the Philippines.
6. Alfredo Etcheberry	Professor of Criminal Law, Univ. of Chile; Director, Inst. of Penal Sciences; Academic Vice-Rector of Catholic Univ. of Santiago.
7. Guillermo Figallo	Member of the Supreme Court of Peru; former President of the Agrarian Tribunal; Member of the Andean Commission of Jurists.
8. Heleno Claudio Fragoso	Professor of Law, Rio de Janeiro Univ.; Deputy Secretary General of the Int. Ass. of Penal Law; Member of Brazilian Federal Bar Association Council.
9. Lord Gardiner	Former Lord Chancellor of England (1964–70).
10. John P. Humphrey	Professor of Law and Political Science, McGill Univ.; former Director, UN Division of Human Rights; former Member of the UN Sub-Commission on the Prevention of Discrimination and Protection of Minorities.

11. **P.J.G. Kapteyn**	Member, Neth. Council of State; Chairman, Committee on the Elimination of Racial Discrimination (UN Convention) (1976—77); former Professor of the Law of Int. Organisations, Utrecht & Leiden Universities.
12. **Kinuko Kubota**	Former Professor of Constitutional Law, Seiki Univ.; former Secretary of the Japanese Section of the ICJ.
13. **Tai-Young Lee**	Director, Korea Legal Aid Center for Family Relations; Professor & Dean, College of Law and Political Science, Ewha Womans Univ. Attorney-at-Law.
14. **Sean MacBride**	Minister for External Affairs, Ireland (1948—51); Sec.-Gen. of ICJ (1963—70); UN Commissioner for Namibia (1974—76); Nobel Peace Prize.
15. **Kéba Mbaye**	President of the Supreme Court, Senegal; President of the ICJ; former President of the UN Commission on Human Rights.
16. **Torkel Opsahl**	Professor of Law, Univ. of Oslo; member, European Commission on Human Rights.
17. **Gustaf Petren**	Judge of the Supreme Administrative Court of Sweden since 1972; former Ombudsman (1968—71); Sec. Gen. Nordic Council (1954—72); Assistant Prof. of Administrative Law, Stockholm Univ. since 1949.
18. **Shridath S. Ramphal**	Secretary-General, Commonwealth Secretariat; former Minister of Foreign Affairs and Attorney General of Guyana.
19. **Tun Mohamed Suffian**	Lord President of the Federal Supreme Court, Malaysia; Chancellor of Univ. of Malaya, 1964.
20. **Amos Wako**	Chairman, Law Society of Kenya; Sec.-Gen. African Bar Association; Sec.-Gen. Inter African Union of Lawyers.
21. **Thiam-Hien Yap**	Attorney-at-Law; Member of Constituent Assembly (1958—59); Officer, Inst. for the Protection of Human Rights.

Honorary Members of the ICJ

22. **Arturo A. Alafriz**	Executive Vice-President, Philippine Commission of Jurists; former Solicitor-General; Council Member, International Bar Association.
23. **A.J.M. van Dal**	Former Supreme Court advocate, Netherlands; former Sec.-Gen. of ICJ.
24. **Eli Whitney Debevoise**	Attorney-at-Law; former Chairman, Executive Committee of ICJ (1962–76); former General Counsel, Office of the US High Commissioner for Germany.
25. **Per Federspiel**	Former Vice-President of the ICJ; President, Danish Section of the ICJ; Minister of Special Affairs (1945–47); Member of Danish Parliament; Delegate to the UN Assembly (1946–49); Member UN Palestine Commission (1947–48); former Member, Consultative Assembly, Council of Europe.
26. **Norman S. Marsh**	Law Commissioner; C.B.E., Q.C.; former Fellow of Univ. College Oxford; former Sec.-Gen. of the ICJ; former Director, British Inst. of International and Comparative Law.

Members of ICJ National Sections

27. **Augusto M. Amores**	Judge, Court of First Instance, Manila.
28. **Alfredo L. Benipayo**	Judge, Court of First Instance, Manila.
29. **Chris de Cooker**	Member, Executive Committee, N.J.C.M. (Netherlands Section of the ICJ); Lecturer on Int. Law, Leiden Univ.; staff member, Europa Institute, Leiden, Univ.
30. **Ross M. Crotty**	Advocate, New Zealand; LLM, Univ. Virginia.
31. **Tage Domela Nieuwenhuis**	Lecturer in Int. Law, Leiden Univ.; staff member of the Europa Inst., Leiden Univ.
32. **George R. Fournier**	Vice-President, Canadian Section of the ICJ; Judge, Superior Court, Quebec.
33. **Henk Grootveld**	Sec.-Gen. N.J.C.M.; Lecturer on Civil Law, Leiden Univ.
34. **Robert Guile**	Vice-President, Canadian Section of the ICJ.

35. **Kamal Hossain**	President, Bangladesh Section of the ICJ; Associate Justice of the High Court Division, Supreme Court; former Law and Foreign Minister of Bangladesh.
36. **David Kennedy**	Lecturer on International Law, Univ. of Kiel.
37. **Lauri Lehtimaja**	Executive Secretary, Finnish Section of the ICJ. Legislative Counsellor, Ministry of Justice.
38. **Clive Mostert**	Professor of Law, Univ. of Saskatchewan; former Secretary-Treasurer, Canadian Section of the ICJ.
39. **Robert Nestdale**	Member of the Executive Committee, Australian Section; Advocate.
40. **Pierre Oliviers**	Secretary, Belgian Section of the ICJ; Advocate.
41. **Tom Sargant**	O.B.E.; J.P.; Secretary of "Justice", British National Section of the ICJ, since formation in 1957.
42. **Madhu P. Sharma**	President, Nepalese Section of the ICJ.
43. **Paul Sieghart**	Chairman, Executive Committee of "Justice"; a Governor, British Institute of Human Rights; Trustee, European Human Rights Foundation.
44. **Manfred Simon**	Président de Chambre Honoraire à la Cour d'Appel de Paris.
45. **André Tremblay**	Professor of Law, Univ. of Montreal; advocate.

Development Experts

46. **Philip Alston**	Consultant on the right to development to UN Division of Human Rights, Geneva.
47. **Jacques Chonchol**	Former Minister of Agriculture, Chile; Professor, Institut des Hautes Etudes pour l'Amérique Latine, Paris.
48. **Clarence J. Dias**	President, International Center for Law in Development, New York.
49. **Augusto C. Espiritu**	Professor of Law and Director Graduate Studies Program, Univ. of the Philippines.

50. Johan Galtung	Coordinator Project on Goals, Processes and Indicators of Development, UN University, Geneva.
51. Luis Pasara	Director, Centro de Estudios de Derecho y Sociedad, Lima.
52. Neelan Tiruchelvam	Director, Division of Law and Development, Marga Institute, Sri Lanka; Executive Secretary, Asian Council for Law in Development.
53. R.N. Trivedi	Practicing lawyer; Director, Human Rights Institute, Lucknow.
54. Karel de Vey Mestdagh	Member of Executive Committee, N.J.C.M.; Lecturer on International Law, Utrecht Univ.

ICJ Secretariat

55. Niall MacDermot	Secretary-General; former Minister of State, United Kingdom.
56. Hans Thoolen	Executive Secretary; former Sec.-Gen., N.J.C.M.; former Lecturer in Comparitive Constitutions Law, Univ. of Leyden.
57. Alejandro Artucio	Legal Officer, Uruguayan Advocate.
58. Daniel O'Donnell	Secretary, Centre for the Independence of Judges and Lawyers.
59. Nana Moeljadi	Secretary.
60. Karin Stasius	Secretary.

Assistants from Netherlands Section of ICJ

61. J. Nuyten	Student, Leiden Univ.
62. T. Zwart	Student, Leiden Univ.

Date Due

OCT 22 1991